Anja Peleikis
Lebanese in Motion

In loving memory of *Hajjeh* Zahra and *Hajj* Nahme
and to Djamil Paul

Anja Peleikis is a postdoctoral research fellow at the Max Planck Institute for Social Anthropology in Halle/Saale, Germany. Having worked on Lebanese transnational migration and mixed Christian/Muslim localities in the context of civil war and displacement, she has recently switched her regional focus from the Middle East to Eastern Europe, concentrating on questions of place, memory and legal pluralism in the Curonian Lagoon Region of Lithuania (www.eth.mpg.de/people/peleikis/index.html).

ANJA PELEIKIS
LEBANESE IN MOTION
Gender and the Making of a Translocal Village

[transcript]

This book was printed with the financial support of the Max Planck Institute for Social Anthropology Halle/Saale.

Gedruckt mit Unterstützung des Max-Planck-Instituts für ethnologische Forschung in Halle/Saale.

Bibliografische Information der Deutschen Bibliothek
Die Deutsche Bibliothek verzeichnet diese Publikation in der Deutschen Nationalbibliografie; detaillierte bibliografische Daten sind im Internet über http://dnb.ddb.de abrufbar.

© 2003 transcript Verlag, Bielefeld
Typeset by: more! than words, Bielefeld
Printed by: Majuskel Medienproduktion, Wetzlar
ISBN 3-933127-45-9

Distributed in North America by:

Transaction Publishers
New Brunswick (U.S.A.) and London (U.K.)

Transaction Publishers   Tel.: (732) 445-2280
Rutgers University   Fax: (732) 445-3138
35 Berrue Circle   for orders (U.S. only):
Piscataway, NJ 08854   toll free 888-999-6778

Contents

Preface and Acknowledgements 9

1. The Local and the Translocal: An Introduction 13
Rethinking Migration 18
Gender in the Translocal Village 23

2. From Experience to Text 25
Mobile Fieldwork 25
    Researcher, Woman, Mother, Daughter-in-law and (Ex-)Wife 30
    Learning to be a Daughter-in-law 35
    Being a (Working) Mother 37
    Changing Locations 38
Telling and Writing Lives: The Politics of Representation 42

3. The Emergence of a Translocal Village 45
Places and Emotional Landscapes 45
    Producing Nostalgic Places of Memory 47
    Producing Traumatic Places of Memory 53
    Producing Gendered and Generational Narratives of Place 59
Moving through Places 72
    The Lebanese in West Africa 75
    The Lebanese in Côte d'Ivoire 79

4. The Translocal Village in Practice 85
Moving People 85
    Moving Families 88
Moving Goods 93
Moving Messages 96
    Female Spaces – Nodal Points of Information 101
Moving Social and Religious Events 103
    Ramadan in the Translocal Village 105
    Commemorating *'ashura* Translocally 107
Moving Organisations: Translocal Political and
Religious Affiliations 110
    Zrariye Youth Club 110
    El-Zahraa 111
    Islamic Centres 113
    Harakat Amal 114

5. **GENDERING THE TRANSLOCAL VILLAGE** 121
   Gendered Mobilities 121
     Renegotiating Marriage Practices in the Translocal Village 125
   Women's Diversity: Deciphering Translocal Female Identities 128
     Translocal "Modern Muslim Women" 129
     Translocal "Westernised Women" 149
     Marriage and Education as Identity Markers 153
     Women's Differences – Women's Shared Struggles 162

6. **BEYOND TRANSLOCALITY** 165
   Cosmopolitans and Translocals 165
     Salwa: Making a Home of her Own 167
   Blurring or Reproducing Transnational Kinship and
   Confessionalist Boundaries? 174

   Notes 179
   Bibliography 187

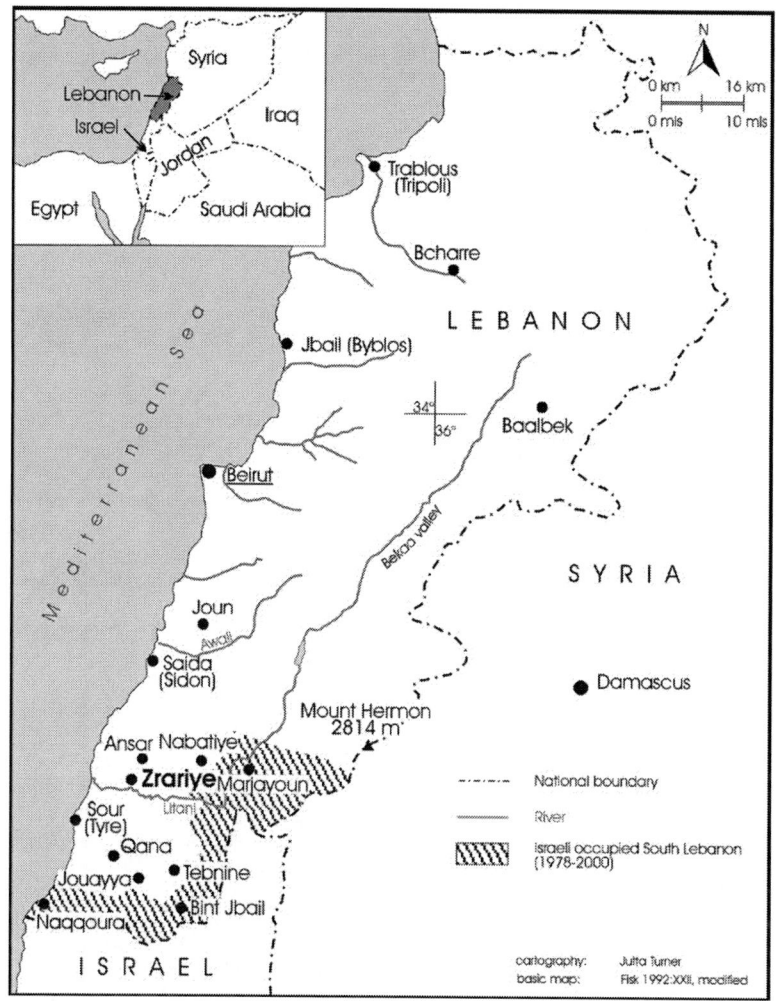

Lebanon and the position of Zrariye

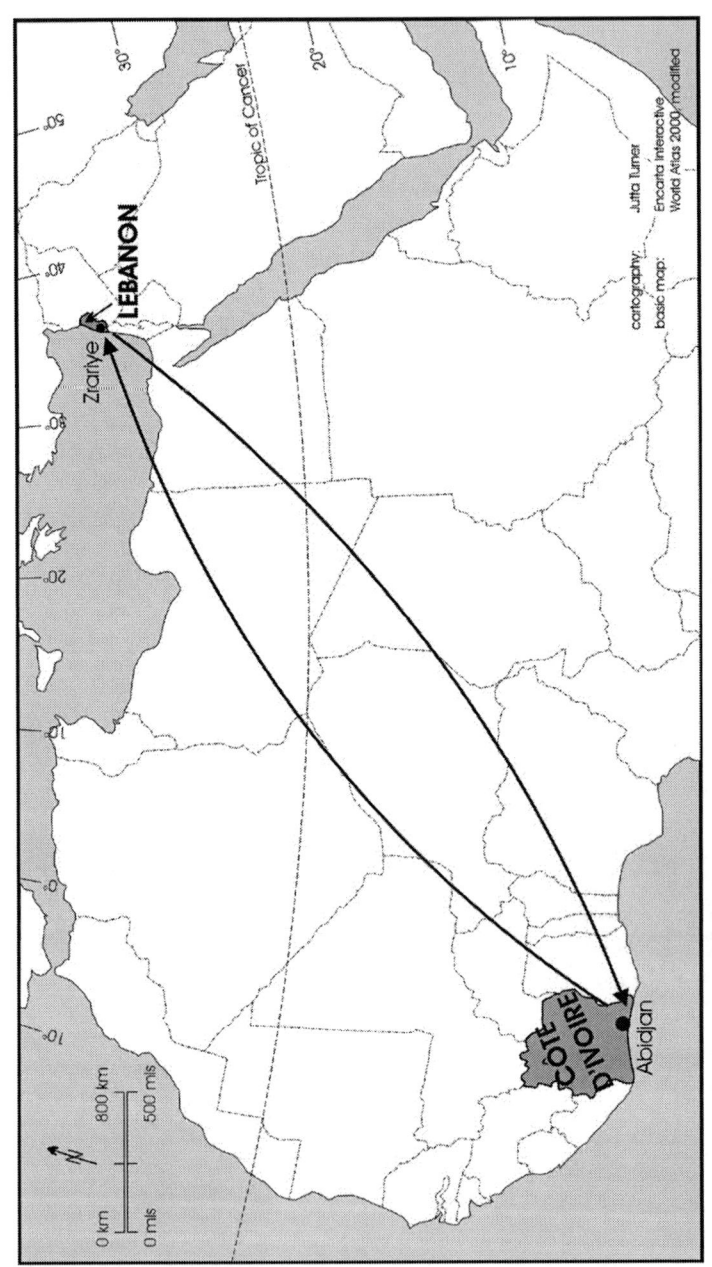

The movement between Lebanon and Côte d'Ivoire

Preface and Acknowledgements

The book emerged primarily from a study that was conceptualised, carried out and written between 1994 and 1997 when I was a doctoral fellow at the "Market, State, Ethnicity" Graduate School of the Sociology of Development and Social Anthropology Research Centre at the University of Bielefeld. It was submitted as a dissertation to the Faculty of Sociology in July 1998. The German Research Council *(Deutsche Forschungsgemeinschaft)* and the state of North Rhine Westphalia *(Nordrhein-Westfalen)* made this study possible by providing financial support for the project in particular and the Graduate School in general.

The dissertation was based on fourteen months of anthropological fieldwork in the South Lebanese village of Zrariye (June-December 1995 and March-August 1996) and its migrant community in Abidjan, Côte d'Ivoire (January-February 1996). After leaving Graduate School and moving on to new research projects, I managed to return to the village at least once a year for various lengths of time between 1997 and 2002. At times I stayed only for a couple of days, occasionally for a week, sometimes two or three. These return visits allowed me to witness change in the lives of women and men, some of whom I have now known for ten years. At the same time, I was able to observe my own ongoing changes in perception and approach in both personal and professional locations. My comprehension of what I experienced constantly shifts as my locations change. This new understanding is not static but reflects where I am at a specific juncture in time and place. Thus, what I had ascertained about Zrariye's translocal connections before I came to stay there for a year was frequently quite different to what I later wrote down when the year came to a close. By that time, I was far from the village and involved in discussions and debates on globalisation and localisation in Bielefeld University contexts. The pre- and post-fieldwork periods influenced the writing of my dissertation significantly, as did my sojourn in the village. But once again, these understandings have changed over time. As more and more books were published in the field of transnational migration – most of them emerged after I had submitted my thesis – I was able to relocate my own findings in the context of these debates and reflect them in a more comparative light. This present volume is a step in the process of changing locations, reflections and reformulations. It is my version of Zrariye people's emergent translocal realities and agencies as filtered through my own experience.

My thanks go to those who guided this project from its inception. I would like to express my gratitude to my supervisors, Prof. Dr. Gudrun Lachenmann, Prof. Dr. Hans-Dieter Evers and Prof. Dr. Günther Schlee, for their support and the critical comments and suggestions they made. They helped to clarify my arguments at various stages of the research project and sent me in fruitful directions.

The book profited greatly from inspiring and ongoing discussions with my colleagues at the Centre for Modern Oriental Studies *(Zentrum Moderner Orient)*, Berlin, all of whom I thank. In particular, the debates in the project groups "Locality and the State" and "Translocality" helped me to rethink my own work and understand differences and variations in the emergence of "translocal villages".[1] My special thanks go to my colleagues Dr. Achim von Oppen and Katja Hermann for creative criticism and intellectual support.

In Lebanon, I received advice and critical feed-back from various researchers of the American University of Beirut, the German Orient Institute of the German Oriental Society *(Orient-Institut der deutschen morgenländischen Gesellschaft)* and the *Centre d'Études et de Recherches sur le Moyen-Orient Contemporain* (CERMOC).

My profound gratitude goes to the women and men of the translocal village in Zrariye, Beirut and Abidjan. They gave me their time, their words, their voices and very much more.

I would especially like to thank Salma Kojok for her friendship, support and for the ongoing discussion on "Lebanese migration". I would also like to thank Fatima Haidari and Abir Bassam, who helped me where they could and acted – at various times – as my Arabic teachers and fieldwork assistants. I am grateful to the late *Hajj* Nahme Mroué and the late *Hajjeh* Zahra Zorkot, who always gave my son and myself a home in Zrariye. Their house feels empty since they passed away in December 2000 and June 2001 and visits to Zrariye have not been the same since. Furthermore, I want to thank members of the Mroué family throughout the translocal village. I received tremendous help from Hassan Mroué and his wife, Fatima Khansu. Ahmad Mroué and his wife Dalal invited us to their home in Abidjan. Khadisha, Fatima and Zaynab Mroué and their husbands and children in Zrariye and Beirut provided assistance wherever possible. Many thanks to all of them. They supported me in the difficult task of combining research and motherhood, as did my parents, Antje and Paul Peleikis, during the writing process. I also want to thank my brother, Jörg Peleikis, who came to my aid so many times when computer problems threatened to cause chaos. I especially want to thank Ali Mroué, who introduced me to the village and was of invaluable assistance.

It took me a long time to finally sit down and rewrite my original dissertation manuscript. I am grateful to several people who gave me the final push and motivated me to "get it done". A very warm "thank you" goes to Karin Werner of the *transcript* publishing house for her faith in the book project and her endless patience. I am grateful to Prof. Dr. Keebet and Prof. Dr. Franz von Benda-Beckmann, who head the Project Group "Legal Pluralism" at the Max Planck Institute for Social Anthropology in Halle, where I am currently based. In the final process of rewriting this book, they showed great consideration and released me from other tasks.

I owe special gratitude to Sunniva Greve, who went through my English text with great care, competence and commitment. Moreover, I would like to thank Kerstin Frei, who has been a tower of strength over the last few years and worked closely with me on the final copy editing. She impressed me with her attention to detail and the many valuable comments she provided, as did Dr. Friederike Stolleis, who was also a great help in transliterating correctly. I also want to thank Jutta Turner for drawing the maps.

I am very grateful to my friends, who understood and accepted my "retreat" during the final stages of rewriting and were supportive when it was needed. Special thanks go to Kerstin Müller for the much appreciated "distraction breaks".

Finally, my thanks go to Michael Beumer, who assisted tirelessly in preparing the manuscript. I am more than grateful for his encouragement, patience and emotional support, especially in times of trouble and occasional distress. Last but by no means least, I want to thank my son, Djamil Paul, who accompanied me on so many journeys. I hope he will always manage to move within his worlds.

Note concerning transliteration

In general, the transliteration of Arabic terms follows the English transliteration system. However, an effort was made to stay close to the Lebanese vernacular. I have omitted diacritics except for the 'ayn. All Arabic words, except for proper names and standard English forms, are italicised.

All photos taken by Anja Peleikis.

1. The Local and the Translocal: An Introduction

> In the age of speed we no longer have a home. We constantly have to build one, like the three little pigs in the fairly tale, or have to carry it on our backs like snails. (Melucci 1997: 62)

Walking through post-war Beirut and its devastated city centre in the summer of 1995, I felt torn between images of the past and the future. Pictures of the vibrant pre-war city, on the one hand, with its buildings in the ancient Roman, Islamic and Ottoman styles as well as those from the French Mandate and post-independence periods emerged through the skeletons of haunting ruins. On the other hand, I was confronted with the envisioning of a post-modernist city and the impressive ventures that reconstruction plans conveyed on large billboards throughout shattered Beirut. Suddenly, my eye was caught by a huge advertisement with the words "The Global Village, literally at your fingertips". A telecommunication firm advertising for the "First National On-line Data Network" had taken up the expression "global village", made popular by the media theorist Marshall McLuhan in the early 1960s. It was intended to account for the new cultural situation worldwide and express the increasing global interdependence through modern mass media. McLuhan made the term "global village" prominent with his theory that the new electronic interdependence recreates the world in the image of a "global village". (McLuhan 1962: 31)

In contrast, Patricia Nabti proposes the use of the term "global village" for the field of anthropology on Lebanon (1989, 1992, 1995). Her aim is to convey a concept of the village that combines the intensity of its overlapping social networks with the global dimensions that have developed as a result of emigration. Nabti traced dispersion from one Lebanese village empirically over time and uncovered a vast international network of people in over forty different countries. Thus, her topic is not to see the world as a village but to study a village that has virtually expanded into the world:

> Because of the wide dispersion of its emigrants, I have chosen to identify Bishmizzine as "a global village" since it is simultaneously a spatially bounded, hence territorial village whose geographical boundaries serve as the source of community identity, and a completely unbounded "non-territorial community" whose "socially determined space" encompasses the whole globe. (Nabti 1995: 2)

This statement raises crucial questions about the interrelations of "social space", "place" and "identity". These issues have recently attracted attention in the context of describing and analysing changes in the social world and put established sociological and anthropological conceptualisations under strain.

Giddens, for example, depicts the difficulty of operating with society as equated with the nation state (1990: 64). Gupta and Ferguson (1992) have stated that the distinctiveness of societies, nations and cultures is based on a seemingly obvious division of space. It is often implicitly taken for granted that they occupy "naturally" discontinuous spaces, which is best exemplified in the school atlas representation of the world as a collection of yellow, green, red and blue countries that make up a global map with no vague or fuzzy spaces. It is taken for granted that each country embodies its own distinctive culture and society, such as when a tourist visits Thailand to experience "Thai culture" or the United States to live "American culture" (Gupta and Ferguson 1992: 7). Classical "ethnographic maps" have tried to illustrate the spatial distribution of peoples, tribes and cultures as transcending nation states. Thus, the Nuer are depicted in "Nuerland" and the Igbo inscribed in "Igboland". Nevertheless, in all of these cases, space is the unquestioned central organising principle. But what happens, one is tempted to ask, when people start to move outside these fixed spaces that even social science has ascribed to them? What happens when the Lebanese move all over the world and the Igbo move out of "Igboland"? Throughout human history, people have been on the move. Today, in an era of rapidly expanding mobility, whether of migrants, refugees, tourists, or business men and women, the cultural certainties and fixities related to space are in an even greater state of turmoil and profoundly questioned. Gupta and Ferguson expressed this in the following words:

In a world of diaspora, transnational culture flows, and mass movements of populations, old-fashioned attempts to map the globe as a set of culture regions or homelands are bewildered by a dazzling array of postcolonial simulacra, doublings and redoublings, as India and Pakistan apparently reappear in postcolonial simulation in London, prerevolution Tehran rises from the ashes in Los Angeles, and a thousand similar cultural dreams are played out in urban and rural settings all across the globe. In this culture-play diaspora, familiar lines between "here" and "there", center and periphery, colony and metropole become blurred. (Gupta/Ferguson 1992: 10)

Similarly, "little Beiruts" have begun to emerge all over the world, in Abidjan/Côte d'Ivoire as well as in Dearborn/USA, Berlin/Germany and Sydney/Australia. Famous Lebanese dishes such as *tabbuleh, kufteh, mlukhiyeh* and *bamiyeh* are served in Lebanese households all over the globe. Music by the famous Lebanese singer Fayruz and the *dabkeh* dance is not confined to an area mapped out as "Lebanon", a small, compact, closely-knit country with a population of four million people and encompassing barely 4,000 square miles but spread among Lebanese migrant communities all over the world. In addition to the mobility of "cultural traditions", Lebanese religious, political and social expression, and its associated conflicts are disseminated beyond local and national boundaries. Accordingly, people from the South Lebanese village under study, with their social, political and economic practices, are no longer tied to one territorial location but are scattered around the four corners of the globe.

These empirical observations question anthropological definitions of "local communities" hitherto taken for granted. As a rule, concepts of locality and local communities have predominantly been associated with a bounded entity, where people's interaction is marked by face-to-face relations and repetitive enactment of daily practices. In this context, "local communities" often stand for a disappearing world of traditions, solidarities and values, a relict from a pre-modern era (cf. Albrow 1997: 39). The influence of these assumptions, which go back to the works of Durkheim and Tönnies, can be retraced in a wide range of empirical studies on "local communities". The classical studies carried out by members of the "Chicago School" on local communities in the United States between 1920 and 1970 (cf., for example Trasher 1927, Wirth 1928) are worthy of mention here.

"Community studies" developed as a tradition in post-war Britain, where the local community was generally depicted as a homogeneous neighbourly small world (cf., for example Rees 1950, Brennan/Cooney/Pollins 1954, Stacey 1960). This image has, in fact, been reproduced in a large variety of community studies that ignore non-resident visitors, outside travel, national events, and above all, population inflows and outflows (Albrow 1997: 41).

Ahead of their time and contrary to this kind of community study, Elias and Scotson (1965) focused particularly on questions of mobility and migration in their study on Winston Parva (Britain). They rejected images of communities as ideal pre-industrial villages with no mobility. Albrow calls the work of Elias and Scotson "a forerunner of globalization research" because they treated geographical social mobility as normal, thus opening up paths to reconceptualise the sociological category of "community" (Albrow 1997: 42). But despite this somewhat new approach to the understanding of community put forward by Elias and Scotson, the concept lost much of its prominence after the 1960s, as it was seen to be inherently bound up with a discredited functionalism and "guilty of being traditional and premodern" (Day/Murdoch 1993: 83).

Despite the unpopularity of the term "community", questions concerning place and location as a significant dimension of social relationships remained important in social science and found renewed interest especially in the 1980s (Day/Murdoch 1993: 85). Researchers like Philip Cooke, involved in studying socio-economic restructuring in Great Britain, suggested the term "locality" as a strong candidate for replacing community and thus filling the conceptual gap (Cooke 1989: 10-19). Cooke and his colleagues, working in the British project dealing with the changing urban and regional system, principally regard "locality" as the space within which the larger part of most citizens' daily working and consuming lives is lived (Cooke 1989: 12). By studying individual and social mobilisation on a local level in modern society, they demonstrated how locality can be a base from which subjects exercise their capacity for activity within and beyond that base (Cooke 1989: 12). Thus, it is Cooke's main concern to give voice to people's local interests in the light of regional, national and global political forces.

In the context of recent debates on globalisation and transnational migration, it was Arjun Appadurai who put forward the argument that locality can no longer be perceived as a given social reality placed in a bounded site. In contrast, he suggests that one should focus on the question of how locality is in fact produced (1995)[1]. In his view, producing locality is a constant struggle. Different social actors are continuously involved in ongoing negotiations to define and produce locality (1995: 213). By emphasising the role played by migrants and tourists in the process of locality production, he leads up to the question of "What is the nature of locality as a lived experience in a globalised deterritorialised world?" (Appadurai 1991: 196). He argues that due to global technological communications, people can virtually be involved in struggles about locality, despite living their everyday lives in different places all over the world. Appadurai speaks of "virtual neighbourhoods" that are created through new forms of electronically mediated communication.

These virtual neighbourhoods are able to mobilise ideas, opinions, social linkages which often directly flow back into lived neighbourhoods in the form of currency flows, arms for local nationalisms, and support for various positions in highly localised public spheres. (Appadurai 1995: 219)

By sending e-mails, chatting on the phone, sending video- and audio-tapes, people can exchange news, information, ideas and gossip that bypass local, regional and national boundaries and leave influential marks in the process of constructing localities from a distance. In fact, it is an irony of the times that, on one hand, genuine places and localities become ever more blurred and indeterminate, while on the other hand, ideas from culturally and ethnically distinct places become more salient (Gupta/Ferguson 1992: 10). Indeed, (imagined) homelands, remembered and revisited places of origin, have become more and more important for the dispersed, in a world that increasingly seems to deny such firm territorialised anchors. Malkki has shown, for example, how Burundi refugees who lived in exile for many years constructed their "homeland" from a distance (1992). Depicting how places are constructed from a distance has challenged the anthropological habit of equating people and a unity of place.

Taking the empirical case of the South Lebanese Shi'ite Muslim village of Zrariye and the migration of its inhabitants to Abidjan/Côte d'Ivoire, my study will show how people are involved in constructing and producing their village "away from the village". I will argue that as a field of social relations, the village has developed into a "translocal village-in-the-making" that emerges from the narratives and practices of social actors dwelling in different places and moving between them. A variety of communication means makes it possible to keep in touch constantly and redefine kinship, neighbourhood, friendship, and generational and gender relations beyond local, regional and nation state boundaries. Belonging to one of the village's patrilineal kin groups is the essence of the translocal circuit. These patriclans are no longer tied to a specific geographical place but unfold their power, control and dominance in the emerging translocal sphere. In calling this social space a "translocal village-in-the-making", I want to clarify that it cannot be taken as a fixed, stable or bounded social reality. The translocal village is in the making and remaking, as it emerges from the various practices and narratives of social actors. It appears as a contested social arena where actors continuously relocate themselves and others, remake their "place of origin" through narration and practice, and struggle for loyalties, power and spaces to manoeuvre. I will show that for the translocal villagers involved, their place of origin continues to be of great importance, since it has become a vital economic, political, social and psychological resource in an age of mobility, change and insecurity.

Exchanging and sharing narratives of place, whether traumatic, nostalgic or political in nature, has the potential to create and redefine local kinship groups and identities, as well as to revitalise local struggles and create a sense of common history for people "at home" and "abroad". Finally, shared and contested struggles over place contribute to the overall process of producing translocal social fields. Thus, it is my interest to show that even in times of globalisation and transnational migration, people always find themselves in some relationship to the places they move through. They are never "nowhere". In this context, I understand "place" not so much as a fixed and stable given but rather as a process of construction and reconstruction. People understand, narrate and engage with "their places" in different ways, depending on the specific time, place and historical situation as well as on their gender, age and class, and on their social and economic environment.[2] It is, therefore, my specific interest to explore how narratives of place and processes of place-making are linked to movement and migration experiences. How does people's perception of their "place of origin" change from a distance and/or over time and how do places change through people's movement? Finally, it is my interest to analyse perceptions of place and migration through a gendered lens. How are narratives of place gendered and how are gender relations expressed in places?

Ethnographic description of male and female associations with different spatial domains in one place has been a staple topic of anthropological research. Researchers described houses, for example, that were physically or conceptually divided into two parts, as distinct male or female spaces (cf., for example, Bourdieu 1973; Humphrey 1974; Pellow 2003). Spatial dimensions were used and interpreted to theorise about gender differences. In this context, Shirley Ardener has argued that the organisation and uses of space express the hierarchy of social structural relationships (1993). Rosaldo has argued that women's subordination to men can be found in their primary association with the "domestic sphere", while men are associated with the "public sphere" (Rosaldo 1974). Since then, the study of gendered spaces has moved away from fixed territorial and symbolic associations to consider more complex understandings. With her research on factories mainly run by men, for example, but employing a large female workforce, Ong has shown how "non-domestic" space is gendered (Ong 1990), while Friederike Stolleis has demonstrated how "female private spaces" can be temporarily transformed into "female public spaces" (Stolleis 2002).

In my study, I want to investigate the question of how gendered identities are negotiated from a different angle. Particularly interested in understanding how female identities are produced and reproduced in translocal social contexts, I will explore the ways in which gender and place are mutually constituted within the translocal social fields that link people "at home" and "abroad".

Rethinking Migration

Up to the late 1980s, migration studies were mainly interested in answering the question of why people leave their country of origin and migrate, and what problems arise for them and for members of the countries they move to (and to a lesser extent for the country of origin) (Pries 1999: 20-21). Migration was generally considered as a one-time, unidirectional and permanent process from one (national) society to another, caused by the imbalance of push-and-pull factors acting on the individual from the place of origin and the place of destination (Todaro 1969, 1976).

Accordingly, primary attention in classical migration research was paid to the social problems and processes associated with the (irreversible and assimilative) integration of migrants in the new society and the consequences this had for the country and region of origin (Pries 1999: 27).

This direction in migration research was strongly questioned in the late 1980s. In studying people's everyday involvement in migration processes, more and more researchers began to realise the multifaceted dimensions of migration. Anthropologists like Nina Glick Schiller and her colleagues, Linda Basch and Christina Blanc-Szanton, called attention to the fact that migration processes across borders cannot be exclusively seen as a more or less permanent state (1992). They have shown that a significant proportion of immigrants who settle in the United States still maintain home ties. By focussing on the social networks that extend across international borders, they questioned the long-held assumption on migration as a move between essentially autonomous (national) societies. Within the "assimilist" framework, immigrants to the United States have primarily been seen as people who uproot themselves, leave home and country behind them and face the painful process of incorporation and integration in a different society and culture. In their studies on "transnational migration", Glick Schiller, Basch and Blanc-Szanton (1992, 1995) have shown that in contrast to the "uprooted" migrant image, many generations have upheld persisting connections to their home countries, even when these are geographically distant. Pointing to this empirical evidence, they proposed "transnational migration" as the new paradigm for the study of migration across the borders of nation states.

Transnational migration is the process by which immigrants forge and sustain simultaneous multi-stranded social relations that link together their societies of origin and settlement. (Glick Schiller et al. 1995: 48)

In this way, transnational migration approaches try to understand the ongoing and continuing ways in which current-day migrants construct and reconstitute their simultaneous embeddedness in more than one society. Since the initial works by Glick Schiller and others, transnational migration studies has emerged as a vital and flourishing field of research, as evident from the large number of books and articles published in the last couple of years[3].

Coming from various disciplinary and national backgrounds, researchers have taken different approaches to theorise and analyse the concrete social relationships that immigrants maintain and construct across borders. Different concepts and terms have been introduced to describe the old and new transnational social realities in an increasing globalised world. As there is an absence of a clearly defined set of terms that can be utilised in research, I will point to various authors and their terminology to clarify the concepts that will run through my study.

"Transnational migration" was first of all promoted by Nina Glick Schiller et al. (1992), who specified that the term would be deprived of use, if taken as a synonym for any movement across international borders (Glick Schiller 1999: 96). Not all migrants are transmigrants and transnational migration cannot be equated with the immigrant sense of longing for home, if this sentiment is not translated into continuous movement across borders. For Glick Schiller and many others, the main dimension of transnational migration is expressed in people's ongoing movement back and forth between places in different nation states, in which they are incorporated as social actors. By maintaining or establishing familial, economic, religious, political or social relations beyond international borders, transmigrants establish "transnational social fields". Glick Schiller defines "transnational social fields" as an unbounded terrain of interlocking egocentric networks. It is a more encompassing term than that of network, which is best applied to chains of social relationship specific to each person (1999: 97).

As the term "social field" focuses on human interaction and situations of personal social relationships, this concept facilitates analysis of the processes by which migrants are linked to their home societies and become involved in the receiving countries (Glick Schiller/Fouron 1999: 344). Glick Schiller prefers the term "transnational social field" in contrast to the widely used expression of "transnational community", which was made popular in particular by scholars related to the British "Transnational Communities Programme", led by Steven Vertovec.[4] Similar to the arguments that were put forward in the general debate on the usefulness of the term "community", Glick Schiller argues that "community" stresses affinity, solidarity and cultural homogeneity and leaves unmarked the exploitative class relations and divisions of wealth and status that stratify a population (Glick Schiller 1999: 97). Further, the term "transnational community" evokes an imagery that fosters the false impression that immigrants create their own autonomous cultural spaces outside of either sending or receiving states (Glick Schiller 1999: 97).

Moreover, the term "transnational community" has been used to describe very different units of analysis. Some scholars use the word "transnational community" to refer to a specific locality in which local relationships expand across borders (cf., for example, Goldring 1996; Levitt 2001; Smith 1998; Georges 1992). Others refer to the term to relate to a specific region migrants identify with in transnational contexts, such as Mixteca in Mexico. This region has become an important point of reference and identity for transnational migrants in the United States (Nagengast/Kearney 1990). Furthermore, some researchers use the term "transnational community" in its broadest sense when talking of groups of people originating from the same nation state and engaging in transnational activities, such as "the Sudanese transnational communities in Cairo" (Häusermann Fábos 2000) or Mexican migrant communities in the US (Roberts/Frank/Lozano-Ascencio 1999).

Apart from "transnational community" and "transnational social field", the term "transnational social space" was introduced and made prominent by Ludger Pries, in particular, in the debates on transnational migration (1996, 1999, 2001). Pries' argumentation is embedded in the broad discussions of sociological and geographical concepts of space and has called attention to recent reconfigurations of space. He argues that until recently, sociological migration research has mainly worked with an elaborate concept of "container space" where the move from one "container space" to the other was studied (1999: 20). Pries states that this "container model" can no longer be applied.

At present, extended geographic spaces (of the "nation state" and its "territory") do not necessarily coincide with the relevant social spaces. He states that this congruence of geographic and social spaces has begun to diminish intensely (1999: 27). Transnational social spaces, then, are understood as new social "interlacing coherence networks" (Elias cit. in Pries 1999: 26).

They are spatially diffuse or pluri-local at the same time comprising a social space that is not exclusively transitory. The social space serves as an important frame of reference for social positions and positioning and also determines everyday practices, biographical employment projects, and human identities, simultaneously pointing beyond the social context of national societies. (Pries 1999: 26)

Despite the wide variety of terms that have been introduced to describe transnational migrant experiences all over the world, it seems that most of the scholars in transnational migration share a fairly similar starting point despite the different disciplinary backgrounds and national contexts they were trained and worked in, and from where their distinct terminologies originated (Al-Ali/Koser 2002: 2). Accordingly, most of the scholars in transnational migration are interested in what Michael Peter Smith and Luis Guarnizo (1998) have called "transnationalism from below", which examines people's everyday grounded agency across nation state borders. Other scholars share the opinion that there is a distinction between transnationalism and globalisation, although the concepts may overlap. Generally speaking, contemporary transnational processes reflect globalisation but are more limited in scope. The term "global" is best reserved for processes that are not located in a single state but happen throughout the entire global world (Glick Schiller 1999: 96). Transnational migration processes are a dimension of globalisation that expands beyond the borders of particular states but are at the same time shaped by the policies and institutional practices of a particular and limited set of states (Glick Schiller/Fouron 1999: 344).

Further, transnational migration approaches differ from the transnational cultural studies that focused primarily on the growth of global communications and media (Featherstone 1990, Hannerz 1992). Many of these cultural study theorists praised transnational migration, which was depicted as an active strategy by ordinary people to escape control and domination and simultaneously weaken the power of nation states. This argument has been deconstructed by a range of well-researched studies that demonstrate how transnational social networks develop beyond a specific nation state but are at the same time strongly influenced by the legal, social, political and economic contexts of the nation state in their home country as well as in the place of migration (cf., for example, Basch et al. 1994; Glick Schiller/Fouron 2001a). In fact, the specific relation of transmigrants to the various nation states and the borders they transcend is an important topic in transnational migration studies that became apparent through the work of Nina Glick Schiller. Drawing on the example of Haitian migrants in the United States, Glick Schiller and Fouron (2001) show how migrants become involved in nationalist projects in their ancestral homeland and how political leaders in Haiti try to reincorporate them into their politics. Glick Schiller and Fouron call these processes long-distance nationalism.

Long distance nationalists may vote, demonstrate, contribute money, create works of art, give birth, and fight, kill, and die for a "homeland" in which they may have never lived. Meanwhile, those who live in this land will recognize these actions as patriotic contributions to the well-being of their homeland. (Glick Schiller/Fouron 2001a: 20)

Taking the Lebanese case, we are confronted with very similar social realities. We know that during the civil war, militias and political actors were supported financially and morally by refugees and migrants abroad. In the post-war era, Lebanese politicians and politically motivated religious figures are some of the frequent travellers who visit Lebanese abroad and appeal for financial and moral support for their nationalist and confessionalist projects. They also motivate migrants to travel home for elections and become involved in local and national politics. Drawing from this, one can argue that the overall reconstruction process of post-war Lebanese society profoundly transcends nation state borders and is strongly influenced by the Lebanese who live all over the world. Hence, it is not possible to fully comprehend Lebanon's reconstruction practices and policies on a local and national level without understanding how they are intertwined with the agency of transnational Lebanese migrants.

However, without ignoring the relevance of long-distance nationalism and confessionalism, I will approach the overall topic of transnational migration by concentrating first and foremost on questions of producing (trans-)locality.

However unique the case of Zrariye may sound, it stands for many Lebanese villages with a high percentage of transnational migration. Nevertheless, constellations of transnational migration and place-making do differ from village to village, since they developed from a background of different political, confessional, historical and migratory contexts. Thus, wherever possible, I will include comparative data, such as on the multi-confessional village of Joun, located in the southern part of the Shuf mountains.[5]

Gender in the Translocal Village

Transnational and translocal migrants are not gender-neutral, although there is a tendency in theoretical accounts on migration to hide this fact. Migration is always gendered. Up to the mid-1970s, women were totally invisible in migration studies. When they finally emerged, they were described merely as the dependants of active male migrants, expressed in the common phrase "migrants and their family" (Morokvasic 1983: 16). Weyland stresses the male bias in many publications that implicitly understands migration as a male issue (1993: 7). Referring to Egyptian migration to the Gulf States, Weyland shows that despite the absence of literature, a substantial number of Egyptian female migrants work abroad as professionals or unqualified workers (1993: 7). In recent years, the need to provide a gendered account of migratory processes has been increasingly recognised. Despite this recognition, many contemporary studies on migration, including transnational mobility, have been somewhat gender blind. The works that tackle gender issues have shown how the gender variable structures transnational migration and influences migrant lives (cf., for example, Salih 2002a/b; Glick Schiller/ Fouron 2001b; Glick Schiller/Fouron 2001a: 130-154; Georges 1992; Al-Ali 2002).

Given the empirical case of South Lebanese migration to West Africa, a high number of transmigrants are women. Today, many South Lebanese women follow their husbands into migration rather than staying behind. This contradicts examples from Egypt and Sudan where the majority of women stay "at home". In my study, I want to focus on the gendered nature of South Lebanese migration to West Africa and describe the specific experiences of female migrants, remigrants and the women who stay behind. By giving a detailed picture of women's lives, I want to contribute to the main question raised in the context of transnational migration. Does gender as it is lived sustain gender hierarchies and inequalities, or do these transnational gender experiences help build more equitable relations between men and women?[6] I will argue that, on the one hand, maintaining connections with the home locality and being part of translocal kinship, religious and political networks can renew old gendered structures. On the other hand, I want to show that gender relations, norms and orders are constantly being redefined, contested and negotiated, thereby opening up potential spaces for female manoeuvre.

Clifford gives the example of Mexican women who migrate to the United States independently of their men. While they often do so out of desperation, under strong economic or social compulsion, they may find their new diaspora predicaments conducive to a positive renegotiation of gender relations (Clifford 1994: 314). Aihwa Ong (1995) illustrates the complexity, moral ambivalence and female "strategic ways" that Clifford speaks of. Describing the lives of two Chinese American women, Ong portrays two specific female "strategies". Whereas one woman relocated and anchored herself in the overseas community and in her family in Beijing, the other was more affected by American middle-class aspirations and sought to remake her identity by defining a private self and her own place in the United States (Ong 1995).

With an actor-centered approach, this study aims to analyse the multiple means and strategies used by South Lebanese Shi'ite women in building their lives and identities in a translocal village and the constraints and changes they experience. I will argue that the intensified process of globalisation has threatened and uprooted many of the local gender identities once taken for granted. New identities have to be forged. I will endeavour to analyse the multiple identification processes that take place in a translocal village and through which it is at the same time constituted. Translocal Lebanese women and men are engaged in redefining and reconstructing their local gender identities.

The meaning of proper religious practices and attempts to redefine gender relations and behaviour for Muslim women are, for example, the subject of ongoing negotiations. Women take up these controversial discussions themselves by manifesting their religious and gender identities in the form of fashion and specific life-styles. At the same time, ideologies concerning the question of how a woman "should be" are in fact "used" to demonstrate a particular kinship or confessional identity. Ideas about women are thus used as symbols in the political and religious struggle for power and loyalty. But as I hope to show, women are not only symbols, they are social actors manoeuvring between choices and constraints. Using the gender-relations analysis as my lens I will examine the overall practices of subjects who position themselves in complex relationships that constitute the translocal village-in-the-making. It is, therefore, the task of this book to explore – at least partially – the ways in which gender and place are mutually constituted in the translocal social fields that link the village of origin and the place of migration.

2. From Experience to Text

> To press the point: why not focus on any culture's farthest range of travel while also looking at its centers, its villages its intensive fieldsites? (Clifford 1992: 101)

Mobile Fieldwork

Ever since the days when Malinowski pitched his tent among the Trobriand dwellings and later outlined his concept of fieldwork in "Argonauts of the Western Pacific" (1922), fieldwork practice has become the constituent characterising element of anthropology. Long-term fieldwork was preferably carried out in remote villages and small-scale localities, which were seen as manageable units and enclosed sites particularly suited to carrying out ethnographic work. They provided the ideal ground for centralising research and served as a focus to represent the "cultural whole" (Clifford 1992: 98). Various anthropologists have recently argued that this approach tends to marginalise or even erase blurred boundary areas and historical realities, causing them to slip out of the ethnographic frame (Clifford 1992). As all movement or mobility tends to be restricted to the village and the surrounding area known as the field, social realities that transcend the village context are often excluded from research. Clifford mentions, for example, that anthropologists have a tendency to ignore the various means of transport and communication that link villagers to the world beyond the local level (Clifford 1992: 99-100). He further states that at times researchers focus too narrowly on the field, thereby forgetting the importance of the *préterrain*, all those places anthropologists have to go through and be in contact with just to get to the village, and that inform their knowledge production as well (Clifford 1992: 100). In the same vein, Shore verifies that pre- and post-fieldwork encounters have a significant influence on the research process, as well as on knowledge production and ethnographic writing (Shore 1999: 45). In line with Clifford's argumentation, van der Veer (1995) remarks that even in modern ethnographies dealing with situations where there is evidence of considerable migration, the village community has often continued to be the sole focus of research. He wonders whether the anthropologist is perhaps the only person not involved in the constant movement to and from "the village".

Moreover, Appadurai reminds us that people were undoubtedly more mobile than the static typological approach of classical anthropology would suggest: "[...] natives, people confined to and by the places to which they belong, groups, unsullied by contact with a larger world have probably never existed" (Appadurai 1988: 39).

In another article, Appadurai describes an encounter experienced by his wife, the historian Carol Breckenridge. On revisiting one of her main sources of information in a temple in Madurai (India), she was told that the priest was no longer there. He had moved to Houston (USA) to serve the same deity he had worshipped in Madurai. Confronted with this reality, Breckenridge was compelled to broaden and recontextualise her experiences in Madurai, which for some of the central actors now also included Houston (Appadurai 1991: 201).

With regard to Lebanon, we should recall the numerous places the Lebanese have travelled to and settled in over the last hundred years. Many people told me their "story" of encounters with Lebanese people in far-flung places throughout the world. People who travel constantly come upon the Lebanese, who are themselves extensive travellers. With this in mind, my research is based on the context of travelling. It did not begin when I entered the village, but of necessity included experiences that took place prior to this, as during my trips to Africa and Lebanon from 1990 onwards. When I was changing planes in Paris on my way from Germany to Lebanon in 1995, for instance, I was blatantly exposed to Lebanese "culture-as-travel-relations" in the waiting lounge. I watched a young Lebanese woman talking to her partner and ostentatiously showing off her new sunglasses, "look what I bought, darling!" She spoke so loudly that everyone could hear her, "they were $ 180 at Nina Ricci's!" Her husband then photographed her in front of one of the expensive airport shops. This incident illustrates a distinct form of conspicuous consumption that must be taken into account when analysing Lebanese social relations. On yet another trip I sat next to a Lebanese shop-owner who was living in Abidjan. He told me he had attended a business conference in Germany and had then spent a few days in France. The day I met him he was on his way to Lebanon to visit his parents and intended to fly to the Far East two weeks later to buy stationery for his shop in Côte d'Ivoire. Observing the young Lebanese woman and the business man, and all the other Lebanese travellers between Africa and Europe, and Europe and the Middle East gave me valuable insights into Lebanese "travelling culture" and multiple migration processes, which I would never have gained had I confined my research exclusively to the local constraints of the village.

Hence, in order to grasp Lebanese migrant realities, it was necessary for me to take up their concept of "migration as travelling" as a principle of fieldwork. When people talked about the movement between the village under study, Zrariye, and other parts of the world, they generally talked of *al-safar* (journey). Whether someone goes on a short trip to visit their children in Abidjan or a young, newly-married woman leaves to be with her husband for a longer period is irrelevant. The idea is the same: people travel, they depart and arrive, they bid farewell and are welcomed, they are constantly on the move, their lives depending on multiple and constant interconnections across international borders. First and foremost, they do not fit into the image of migration as a single wave of direct migrants on their way to their destination economies, leaving their countries, uprooted, and finally being integrated into a new country. They are much more travellers between the worlds.

In comparison to Patricia Nabti, who followed the migrant path from the north Lebanese village of Bishimizzine to a variety of different host countries (Nabti 1989), I did not try to trace Zrariye migrants to their various places of residence. In contrast to Bishimizzine, where over 80 percent of migration was directed at four countries (Nabti 1992: 41), the majority of Zrariye migrants has moved exclusively between Lebanon and the Côte d'Ivoire. This led me to choose the specific example of South Lebanese migration to West Africa as a case study to be presented and analysed. Nevertheless, I tried whenever possible to get in touch with villagers who had been to other parts of the world. I talked to migrants in the village who live in Senegal, Guinea-Bissau, Guinea, Nigeria and Zaire. Others live in the United States, Canada, Brazil, Kuwait, Dubai, and Saudi Arabia, as well as in Italy, France, Finland and Germany. I had the opportunity of visiting several Zrariye migrants in Germany. Moreover, I had e-mail contact with students of Lebanese origin studying in the United States, Canada and France. Extensive e-mail correspondence helped to verify and discuss my findings, and even gave me valuable new comments.

My initial research plan was to focus exclusively on the changes in the village in Lebanon. Discussions that took place during my first year at the Graduate School of Development Sociology and Social Anthropology at Bielefeld University made me think more and more of Lebanese migration as a dimension of globalisation, and realise that I needed to adapt my fieldwork practice to the ongoing movement between Lebanon and Africa. I was motivated to follow the migrants and visit them in their host country in Côte d'Ivoire. I spent the first six months of fieldwork in the village of Zrariye (June until December 1995). There I had the opportunity of meeting various migrants, whom I later visited in Abidjan. In fact, it was tremendously important to learn about specific family relations and the general village social structure, which later helped me to understand the migrant discussions in Abidjan. Despite my relatively short stay in Abidjan (January to March 1996), I met a large number of Zrariye migrants I had either already met in the village or who were relatives of people I knew there. Furthermore, I was able to personally take advantage of migrant networks and stay in the house of in-laws who introduced me to the Lebanese community in Côte d'Ivoire, and especially to people from Zrariye. This gave me an insight into the situation of the Lebanese in West Africa, enriching my experience from previous trips there in 1991 and 1992, where I had talked to Lebanese in Senegal, Guinea Bissau, Guinea, and Togo.

I spent the last period of my fieldwork (April to July 1996) back in

Zrariye, with a two-week break at the end of April/beginning of May when an unpredictable Israeli air-raid forced the majority of South Lebanese villagers to flee to Beirut.

This multi-sited field research approach made me realise that globalisation increasingly confronts researchers with the changing social situation of many of their informants, thus challenging them to redefine their concepts of the field, the practice of fieldwork, and the understanding of anthropologists as fieldworkers.

Generations of anthropologists were – and still are – trained with the idea that going into the field means leaving home, which was considered a "First World" place where one's University is located, for a specific amount of time – ideally at least a year – to live with the other in a remote place somewhere in the "Third World". The field becomes the site where data is collected under difficult conditions, mostly in isolation, whereas home is where analysis is carried out and ethnography written up, in the academy, in libraries, in the midst of theoretical conversations with one's own kind (Gupta/Ferguson 1997: 12). These two forms of activity are not only distinct from one other but thought to be sequential. One generally writes up after coming from the field. Thus, the field and home are inherently conceptualised as spatially separated and characterised by their temporal succession. This sharp contrast between the field and home is often expressed in stories about entry into and exit from the field. Nowadays, colonial-style heroic tales of adventurers battling the fierce tropics are out of fashion, but, as Gupta and Ferguson have shown, no matter how playful, parodic, or self-conscious present-day stories of entry and exit may be, they still function in constructing a difference between the field and home (Gupta/Ferguson 1997: 13). As the anthropologist's home is usually depicted as being somewhere in the "West", the archetypal fieldworker generally takes on the appearance of the Euro-American, white, middle-class male who carries out fieldwork in places that are most other. This binary opposition between home and the field runs into difficulty when it comes to groups of anthropologists to whom home is not the "Eurocenter" (cf. Lavie/Swedenburg 1996: 1) and the rest of the world not the most other place.

Challenging this image of the world, as present-day globalisation and transnational studies do, means, therefore, that we must also challenge the traditional image of fieldwork. The question that needs to be asked in the era of globalisation is where the anthropological field is located.

Directing this question to my own research, I wonder where my field is when I study the gender and migration patterns of the Lebanese who move around the world, and whom I have met in Africa and Lebanon, as well as in Europe and North America? Where is the field when I write about my experiences in Germany, but am involved simultaneously in data collection via informal exchange with Lebanese per e-mail or in discussions with

Lebanese living next door? Where is home when I present an anthropological paper at the American University or the German Orient Institute in Beirut in front of a Lebanese and international audience? Where is home and where is the field when my informant, a Lebanese historian trained at a Côte d'Ivoire University, lives in Beirut and is on her way to Germany to give a lecture at the Research Centre where I work?

Rather than presenting the field and fieldwork as bounded in time and space, more and more anthropologists have challenged this view in the current era of global interconnectiveness and introduced far more dynamic and flexible perspectives. Following Shore, I would argue that in contrast to the traditional idea, the anthropological field is progressively emerging as a fluid, loosely connected set of relations, sites, events, actors, agents and experiences on which anthropologists are trying to impose some form of conceptual order (Shore 1999: 45). Such an approach would also reveal the multiple ways in which colonialism, imperialism, multinational capital, global cultural flows, and travel bind the spaces of home and the field, once understood as distinct and separate (Gupta/Ferguson 1997: 13).

Gupta and Ferguson challenge the concept of the field as a spatial site by following the notion of the field as a political location (1997: 35). They understand fieldwork in this context as a "form of motivated and stylized dislocation" (1997: 37):

Rather than a set of labels that pins down one's identity and perspective, location becomes visible here as an ongoing project. As in coalition politics a location is not just something one ascriptively *has* (white middle-class male, Asian-American woman, etc.) – it is something one strategically works at. We would emphasize, however, that (as in coalition politics) shifting location for its own sake has no special virtue. Instead the question of what might be called location work must be connected to the logic of one's larger project and ultimately to one's political practice. Why do we want to shift locations? Who wants to shift? Why? (Gupta/Ferguson 1997: 37)

Feminist scholars in particular have expressed the need for shifting locations by asking: "Who produces knowledge about colonised peoples and from what space/location? What are the politics of the production of this particular knowledge?" (Mohanty 1991: 3).

In fact, the debate on the "politics of location" taken up by Gupta and Ferguson was primarily developed in recent feminist scholarship. It was initiated by Adrienne Rich who pointed out in her essays on location politics that North American feminism has primarily been dominated by white, middle-class women. This "location" has often failed to acknowledge that women in other contexts and in different places may have separate and very different agendas. In the face of this situation, Rich proposes a "politics of location" whereby white feminists explore the meaning of "whiteness", recognise their location, and name the ground they have come from and the conditions they have taken for granted (Rich 1986: 159).

Caren Kaplan remarks that despite Rich's efforts to account for the politics of location, she remains locked in the conventional opposition of the global-local nexus as well as the binary construction of Western and Non-Western (Kaplan 1996: 166). Kaplan acknowledges the importance of the politics of location but questions Rich's examples, which focus primarily on the difference between white middle-class women in the US and poor women of the "Third World" far away. Kaplan explains that in times of globalisation the issue of accountability not only lies between North and South American women, but also between women located in one specific place. She refers here to the coalition work with coloured women in the United States (1996: 166).

This draws our attention back to anthropologists and fieldwork as "motivated dislocation". If we follow this understanding of fieldwork, we have to do away with the distancing and exoticisation of the classical anthropological field, which was thought to be the detailed study of a limited area. Instead, we should work for an understanding that blurs the boundaries of here and there, home and the field, and give way to both forging links between different knowledges that are possible from different locations and tracing lines of possible alliance and common purpose between them. In this vein, let me reflect in the following on my specific locations during fieldwork. Further, I will illustrate the kinds of constraints and advantages my social placement created for my ethnographic project at a specific point in time and will make clear how these changed under varying circumstances.

Researcher, Woman, Mother, Daughter-in-law and (Ex-)Wife

> Anthropological writing may be scientific; it is also inherently autobiographic. (Fabian 1983: 87)

During my time at Graduate School in Bielefeld, I was often asked to talk about my specific situation as a daughter-in-law while carrying out fieldwork in a South Lebanese village. When I did I sometimes felt embarrassed, even annoyed. Above all, I wondered why only my social position was at stake. What about the other graduate students? It was taken for granted that my social circumstances as a daughter-in-law, wife and mother in the field would somehow influence my research, whereas no one seemed to think the social position of the other Ph.D. students as single European men or women, for example, could have a bearing on their fieldwork situation. Is it not so that all our anthropological research endeavours are influenced by our personality and social location in the community, which in turn shape the fieldwork process and its product? I suggest that various components of the researcher's identity, such as gender, age, class, ethnic/national origins, marital/parental status and many other identity dimensions are brought into play in the field. Specific and changing social locations influence the overall context of fieldwork and writing. In this, I do not understand social location as a fixed and stable position, but as multiple and constantly changing. In the words of Katy Gardner:

Individuals are placed on shifting ground where no single identity is possible. Instead, personhood is endlessly fragmented; we have permeable boundaries and are endlessly transformed in each new interaction. The positions one speaks from are located in and contingent upon specific contexts. The researcher and her informants are both changed, and agents of change. (Gardner 1999: 52)

Following this approach, I will try to reveal how my own personal and intellectual change has altered my perspective on the field. This account can only be partial and selective, but may help to render the complex and changing relationships in the field more apparent.

When I came to Zrariye with my one-year old son, Djamil, in June 1995 to stay for a year of anthropological fieldwork, it was not my first visit to the village. I went there for the first time in January 1993. At that time, I arrived not as an anthropologist but as the newly-married wife of a villager who himself had been absent for almost 20 years. While my husband, Ali, was on a return visit to his family after spending most of his life in West Africa and Europe, I was just getting to know his extended family and doing my best to be liked and accepted. At the time, I did not even think of carrying out research in Lebanon and was still involved in writing my M.A. thesis on gender and power relations in Guinea-Bissau. It was in that small West African country that I met Lebanese for the first time. Walking through the city of Bissau in 1991, I realised that the majority of small shop-keepers were actually Lebanese and not, as I had presumed, Portuguese descendants of the former colonial rulers. Not only the shopkeepers were Lebanese, but the pharmacy, restaurant and coffee-shopowners as well. Between 1991 and 1993 I made several trips to West Africa and learned more about the Lebanese communities in Dakar/Senegal, Lomé/Togo, Abidjan/Côte d'Ivoire and Conakry/Guinea. I was amazed by the wealth some Lebanese had accumulated, and during my first two visits to Lebanon was able to trace their wealthy connections to their country of origin. Many rich migrants have invested in the building of huge, individually-styled villas, which form a sharp contrast to the rest of the South Lebanese countryside as well as to the social and economic landscape. These buildings caught my eye as I travelled throughout the country in 1993 and made me curious about the nature of Lebanese migrant connections to West Africa. Having been accepted at the Graduate School of Development Sociology and Social Anthropology at Bielefeld University

Figure 1: Learning gender: Djamil and his grandfather

allowed me to develop my ideas further and embark on a research project on the transnational connections of Lebanese migrants to West Africa.

For various reasons, I decided to carry out research in the village of Zrariye. First of all, it is a "typical" South Lebanese village with a high migration rate to West Africa. Secondly, it is situated in an area of South Lebanon that was not a "hot spot" of Israeli targets at the time, thus giving me a feeling of security. I also thought that the social contacts I had developed during my visits in 1993 and 1994 would help to make the first few months in the village easier.

But what influence did my social locations as a mother, daughter-in-law and wife have on my research? During the fieldwork I carried out in Guinea-Bissau/West Africa in the context of my M.A. studies, I learnt just how influential social location can be to the research process. I was a young, single woman at the time and did not have a child. In the beginning, this constituted a barrier to the "women's world", since the Jola Baiote only accept a female person as a real "woman" when she has given birth to a child. This put me in a quandary since I wanted to observe female rituals. Only after the Jola women had transformed me into the mother of a fantasy child was I permitted to participate (Peleikis 1994: 2-3). This experience led to my arguing that the social location of researchers is never a fixed one, but permanently subject to renegotiation by both researchers and their informants. This also proved to be true for my long-term fieldwork in Lebanon.

In Zrariye, I was constantly negotiating my position as a married woman, daughter-in-law, mother, European woman, and anthropologist from a German University. These multiple identities were neither fixed nor stable but continuously negotiated and renegotiated through interaction with people in the translocal village.

Reflecting on her own situation as a married anthropologist in the course of fieldwork in her husband's community, Anita Häusermann Fábos noticed that marriage, as an institution and a process that interacts with fieldwork experience, deserves attention for its knowledge production about self and other (2000: 285). Some accounts have been published in this context, reflecting the situation of anthropologist couples who embark on a research project together. In these cases, both partners came from the "Eurocentre" and were white, middle-class anthropologists carrying out fieldwork as a couple or family (cf., for example, Smith Oboler 1986). Very much less has been written on the topic of anthropologists who have a spouse originating from their research community.[1] Häusermann Fábos makes clear that it has now been accepted in anthropological discourse that ethnography is a joint project between the anthropologist and the research community. There is, however, still a reluctance to admit that crossing the line between "us" and "them" can lead to interaction on a more intimate level (2000: 286). Having a spouse from one's research community represents a level of intimacy that has often evoked harsh criticism by the academic community. Some anthropologists consider emotional involvement with people directly connected to our work and study as jeopardizing our ability to analyse and describe another people's way of life dispassionately (Gearing 1995: 209). Furthermore, having emotional relationships with individuals from the research community is usually described derogatorily as "going too far" or "going native", and may reflect unspoken assumptions of loss of capacity to be objective (Gearing 1995: 209; Häusermann Fábos 2000: 287).

As marriage legitimises sexuality, it openly questions the public taboo on sexual encounters and emotional relationships with the other during fieldwork. Despite the fact that numerous stories about the escapades of certain anthropologists circulate under cover in every Department of Anthropology, they do not normally surface to public ears, let alone to the self-searching reflexive analyses of fieldwork encounters. Basically, erotic relationships or sexual involvements in the field are considered a contravention of the unwritten ethnographic code.

According to Wengle, most anthropologists stick to this convention and remain celibate in the field (Wengle 1988). If anthropologists dare to break this taboo publicly, acknowledging their relationships to people in the field, and maybe even getting married and having children, they often have to face strong criticism, or worse, tackle obstacles to their careers. Jean Gearing, who married her main informant during fieldwork in the West Indies, describes how her American colleagues reacted with shocked surprise: "Even now, when I tell new anthropological acquaintances that I married my key informant, I am often greeted with an uncomfortable pause, as many colleagues struggle to cover their initial dismay" (Gearing 1995: 210). Close relationships with members of the research community are unthinkable in mainstream anthropology, since in terms of self and other, the main discourse of anthropological fieldwork preserves distance, difference and distinction as the normal state of cross-cultural affairs.

It is thus evident that engaging in close relationships with people from one's research community thoroughly questions the subject-object, self-other, researcher-researched binaries on which much of anthropology rests.

Instead of seeing this as a general problem, several authors have shown that precisely this blurring of boundaries strengthens the potential for a universal reflection on the anthropological self-other dichotomy, as well as on exploitation, racism and boundaries (cf., for example, Gearing 1995; Kulick 1995; Willson 1995)[2].

Anita Häusermann Fábos, for example, shows how the process of learning to be a proper wife contributed to her reflection on the gender and ethnicity research she had carried out (2000: 289). Through her marriage to a man from St. Vincent/West Indies and the reactions she received, Jean Gearing was able to reinforce her argument that the class/colour line is less rigid in St. Vincent than it is in the supposedly "advanced" United States (1995: 211). She showed that the marriage of a white, American, middle-class woman to a black, working-class Vincentian man not only blurred the boundary between "us" and "them" but questioned the implicit assumption of Euro-American cultural superiority (Gearing 1995: 211).

These examples suggest that blurring boundaries, engaging in close personal relationships and taking up the role of wife or husband in the research community, for example, can provide new and challenging social locations from which fresh insights and reflections might be derived in the research process. Being a wife or mother or daughter-in-law in a research community is thus not merely an ascribed social status that influences research, but can be a chosen location for the study of social relations and a process that undergoes change with the passage of time. Let me explore this from my own experience.

Learning to be a Daughter-in-law

I carried out fieldwork in the village my husband comes from and lived there with our son in my parents-in-law's household for about a year. Being a daughter-in-law and a mother were two key positions that influenced my research and the perspectives I developed on Lebanese transnational migration to West Africa. I was also a wife. But since my husband remained in Germany for most of the time I was in Zrariye, husband-wife relations were not often directly visible in the field. Thus, marriage in my case was not the predominant social position from which I gained an understanding of social relations in the course of my fieldwork. This was to change, however, when my husband and I separated later on. The fact that my husband was working in Germany did not cause much astonishment. There are numerous cases of wives who stay behind with the children when their husbands migrate. They occasionally join their spouses when the latter are settled in the place of migration. People naturally asked me why I – as a German woman – came to live in Zrariye, while my Zrariyen husband remained in Germany. They are familiar with cases of foreign women who come to live in Lebanon when their husbands return to their village of origin. People appreciated the idea of my wanting to learn Arabic and become acquainted with village life. Actually, being able to communicate with them in Arabic and trying to behave according to their expectations – or more correctly, what I thought were their expectations – made people consider me more as a daughter-in-law, an "insider", than as a European woman or "outsider". I, on the other hand, engaged in the process of learning to be a proper daughter-in-law. When I came to live with my parents-in-law, all of their eight children had moved out of the house. Two sons were living in Africa, another son, my husband, lived in Europe, and only the fourth son lived in the village with his wife. Two daughters lived in Beirut and visited their parents regularly, one daughter was married in Jordan, and the remaining daughter still lived in the village with her husband. Migration and internal migration as a result of the civil war had scattered the family. The parents, often called as *Hajj* and *Hajjeh* were in their 70s and 80s and spoke often of their happiness that I had come to live with them, and that they were able to see their grandchild on a daily basis. Their daughter, son and daughter-in-law often came to help in the house with everyday life. I helped as much as I could, trying at the same time to live up to the model of what I believed was a "good daughter-in-law" in Lebanese families, e.g. helping to look after the parents-in-law. I saw what was expected of Fatima, the other daughter-in-law who lived in the village, and sometimes felt embarrassed when I realised that they expected much less of me. Occupying the same social position as daughters-in-law led to Fatima and I becoming close friends. We were able to share our experiences, our thoughts and our feelings towards our parents-in-law, some of which we had not even shared with our husbands. Through interaction with Fatima, I acquired a great deal of knowledge about gender relations, about relations between the generations, and about female friendship. Furthermore, through my overall experience with my family-in-law, I became aware of the centrality of the family as a core unit in Lebanese society – in political, economic, social and religious terms. I experienced – and sometimes suffered from – the privileges males and elders (including older women) have and learned that young people are taught to respect and defer to their older kin.

It was in these very close relationships with my in-laws and siblings that the boundaries between the self and the other regularly became blurred. Pat Caplan has pointed out this flexible dynamic interrelationship, which for her is so characteristic of fieldwork relationships:

[...] I have become aware that being an ethnographer means studying the self as well as the other. In this way, the self becomes 'othered', an object of study, while at the same time, the other, because of familiarity, and a different approach to fieldwork, becomes part of the self. (Caplan 1993: 181)

I noticed that my position and identity as a "detached, observing anthropologist" came to my aid on several occasions. It became a distancing strategy, a position I fled to when I felt I was becoming too involved in family matters. Calling on my anthropologist identity, the one that observes and makes notes about what is happening, helped me to cope when the other had become part of myself, and I more and more an ordinary family member. I realised later that in moments like this I was, in fact, afraid of losing my objectivity and scientific rationality. On looking back, I now see that it was precisely the moment I really felt like them, got involved in family and village matters, argued, shouted, and laughed with them, that I gained the most valuable insights. Through this emotional involvement and my particular locations I found myself able to develop the "situated knowledges"[3] and partial perspectives that form the basis of this book.

Being a (Working) Mother

When I lived my year in Zrariye, my son was between one and two years old. Since then he has been to the village almost every year and has developed ongoing friendships with neighbouring children and his cousins, which are remobilised on every return visit. He learned his first Arabic words in the village and now, at the age of nine, he has become quite fluent in it, switching easily between his worlds. Being a mother offered me a distinct location from which I could gain insight into social relations and migration experiences that were of special interest to me. Trying to combine fieldwork and motherhood, I often had the same impression as Joke Schrijvers who wrote of her fieldwork with children in Sri-Lanka: "[...] I primarily remember my enthusiasm at the discovery that in rural Sri Lanka these two spheres of activity were not seen as a problematic combination" (Schrijvers 1993: 144).

No one questioned my ability to combine work, research and motherhood. They knew I had come to the village to write a book and continue my university career and, as education has a high social status in Lebanon, gave me great support in achieving this goal.

A glimpse at their everyday life reveals that working mothers can rely on family support as a rule. Many women work in the fields, in shops or as teachers, while their children are looked after by their grandmothers, aunts or older sisters. I also received tremendous help from my in-laws and learned that helping each other in the family is a matter of course, particularly if the mother is working outside the home. Still, carrying out fieldwork with a child was not as easy as I thought it would be. Before going to live in Zrariye, I imagined it would not be difficult to find a young female student to look after my son for a few hours a day. This proved to be a false assumption. I was lucky I did have the family to rely on, since it would have been extremely difficult to find a Lebanese girl or woman to take care of my child. Working in someone else's household is considered to be extremely low-prestige work, and no father would allow his daughter to do so. I suddenly realised that migration had led to difficult circumstances for most of the working women in the village. If numerous family members migrate, the ones who stay behind will probably be confronted with the difficulty of finding someone to look after the children. This turned out to be one of the reasons why many families employed girls from Sri Lanka to take care of the children and the household.

All in all, having my child with me facilitated making contact with other women. Initially, I adapted myself to their visiting patterns, going out in the mornings and late afternoons to see the neighbours. I took my son with me, who played with their children. Chatting about children often "broke the ice", allowing us to move on to other topics of discussion. In these situations I followed a non-directive approach and was quite open to their agenda. I soon realised that my migration topic with all its facets was their topic as well. In many instances, they initiated discussions related to migration, remigration and change in the village.

Besides this, being a mother contributed to a better understanding of inter-generational relations and conflicts between younger and older women. Observing how different women reacted to me and my interaction with Djamil, and watching them with their children told me a lot about their child-raising practices and ideas on children's role in society. Interestingly, my own methods and points of view were appreciated mostly by my mother-in-law and women of her generation, while younger women of my age often looked at me with dismay. They were surprised to hear that I had given birth in a "birth house" equipped only with midwives and not, as they had expected, in a hospital. They could not believe that I had breastfed my child, something they clearly considered traditional, while they themselves thought it extremely modern to prepare bottles of "Nestlé" milk for their children. When I spoke of my experience, the older women often felt motivated to start talking of their own experience, remembering how they had given birth at home with the support of a midwife and how hard it was to feed all the children, work in the fields and prepare food for the winter. By revitalising their memories on giving birth and raising children, the older women presented a detailed picture of their life-worlds, and how they remembered them some 50 years later. For me it was a perfect opportunity to learn about their lives in a changing world.

Changing Locations

> Each venture is a new beginning. (T.S. Eliot)

I continued visiting the village and learning about people's lives for years after submitting my thesis. Following Shore, one could say that my fieldwork in Lebanon did not so much draw to a close as that it underwent a metamorphosis (cf. Shore 1999: 44). It was composed of "pre-fieldwork" visits in 1993 and 1994, graduate school experiences before and after the "main fieldwork" in 1995 and 1996 in Zrariye, Abidjan and several other places in Lebanon and Côte d'Ivoire, as well as continuous visits between 1997 and 2001. These ongoing visits allowed me to witness change in the lives of the women and men I had got to know over a long period. As their lives unfold, my own interpretations have shifted. This has made me aware yet again that what and how we learn is endlessly influenced by our personal locations and identities. Whereas anthropologists traditionally followed a clear sequence in fieldwork, beginning with preparations at home, continuing with fieldwork abroad, and concluding with writing "at home", they now tend to come back to the field, update their findings, and observe the changes that occurred with the passage of time. This often leads to a much more historicised perspective on the field, as revealed in the words of C.W. Watson:

Anthropologists [...] often return to the field, pick up the threads and find themselves weaving a very differently patterned cloth from that which they wove so confidently during their previous encounter. (C.W. Watson 1999: 1)

This proved true in my case as well. The fact that my location had changed contributed to pinpointing other social realities and led to the transformation of some of my knowledge.

When I returned to the village in 1998 after a year's absence, the village seemed to be the same from the "outside", with its eye-catching villas and unfinished houses. As always when I came back, people told me about the weddings and divorces that had taken place in my absence or who had had a baby and who had died, all of which made me realise once again the change that comes with time. More than ever before, my personal relationships had now suddenly become a topic of interest and curiosity. When I walked through the village and greeted people as I used to do during my fieldwork, many of them looked at me with curious eyes – or was I the only one, occasionally insecure and self-conscious, who interpreted them as curious? One woman came straight towards me, shook my hand and said quite frankly, "I hear that you and your husband have separated. Why? That's impossible. You have to get together again!" I was speechless and wondered how the news had arrived at the village so fast. But, I said to myself, wasn't I the one who wrote about the emergence of the translocal village and its close links to the migrant communities? How could I have doubted that our news would reach the village immediately? I began to understand that I was the one who had now become the topic of translocal Zrariye gossip. I became painfully aware of the potential disadvantages of translocal connections. Some translocal actors experience translocal linkages negatively, if they are compelled to suffer social control beyond boundaries. When migrants are linked in the way Zrariye people are, it becomes more and more difficult for individual actors to break out of the translocal networks even if they themselves are not active in keeping the connection. Others will know about them and pass on the news.

I was in fact hesitant to talk about my personal situation. I was afraid of their reaction, scared that they would judge me according to some stereotype image of "European women". I was afraid they might destroy my own image of the "good anthropologist" who had adapted perfectly to the social position of a daughter-in-law, wife and mother, the ideal social location for women of my age in Lebanese society. I was afraid they would pity me and see me as the poor divorced woman who was forced to return to her parents' house, while her children stayed with the father. I certainly did not want to be in this position. I felt torn apart. Would they understand and respect that I had not gone back to my parents but was living on my own with my son, who spends half of each week with his father? Would they realise that it is possible to remain cooperative parents after divorce? Interestingly, my new social status as a divorced woman made some of the women talk more openly than before about divorce and what it means to them. I was sitting once with 31-year-old Zaynab who had married at the age of 15 and was recently divorced. She complained that she had to go back to her parents' house and that her children lived with their father. When she asked me what it was like in Germany, I explained my personal situation, which she commented as follows: "It is better in Germany. Woman who get divorced can live alone, here we have to go back to our parents. That's the problem. The biggest problem is that the children normally stay with the father. In Germany you can get divorced and still remain friends." What followed was an exchange about marriage and divorce laws and practices in different contexts. Zaynab would probably not have come to me if she had not known that I too was divorced. In short, social roles can change over time and can have an immediate effect on fieldwork and reports, books and articles that are written later. Pat Caplan revealed this clearly in her reflections on fieldwork in a Tanzanian coastal village over a period of twenty years. Being in the position of a young unmarried woman, or a married woman and mother made a difference to her research and to people's reception of her, as well as to her research topics and interests (Caplan 1993).

But the biggest question after my separation remained: what consequences would this have for my relationship to my in-laws? I was afraid I might have to give up my Lebanese social world, my relationships in the village, and that my parents-in-law might refuse to see me again. I realised that the pictures that sprang to mind were informed by my time in the village, on the one hand, where divorced daughters-in-law usually no longer come to see their ex-husband's family. On the other hand, I have to admit that these images were also informed by my own European framework and the prevailing prejudices that came to my ears: "Be careful, do not go back to the village, they will kidnap your son". I realised that the alarm bells ringing in my head were my own cries of warning and not the attitude of the two old people I had lived with and grown so close to. I returned with my son Djamil for visits and saw how sad *Hajj* and *Hajjeh* were at the news that their son and I had separated. *Hajjeh* cried and expressed her disbelief: "But both of you wanted it, the marriage was not arranged!"

But they hugged me and said that they always wanted me to come back to the village and visit them, either with Djamil or on my own. I was deeply moved by their behaviour, which was beyond norms and values and beyond their image of me as a daughter-in-law. Stronger than at any other time, I could feel instantly that they liked and accepted me as "Anja", beyond whatever role I wanted to live up to. I could feel the depth of our relationship, which had grown over the years.

I returned for visits in 1999, in the summer of 2000 and in November 2000. I was at a conference in Beirut when I received the tragic news that *Hajj* and *Hajjeh*'s eldest son Muhammad had died in England at the age of 45. My ex-husband travelled to London immediately to arrange for the body to be flown to Lebanon. On the day it arrived in the village, I came to pay my respects to the family. I had met my brother-in-law only once during a visit to Africa, where he had lived most of his life. He was the eldest son of *Hajj* and *Hajjeh* and had not returned to the village for many years. During my time in the village, I often heard my parents-in-law talking about their beloved son, yearning for him to visit them. Muhammad had rarely come back to the village, however, and they had not seen him in years. For reasons unknown to me, he was one of those migrants who had broken with the village and partially with his family. Although he himself had not kept the translocal connection, the translocal family took care of him after his death. The whole village came together to say a last "goodbye" to him, who in the memory of the villagers was a lively, charming young man before he emigrated to Senegal in the 1970s. When the coffin arrived at the village, it was carried to the house of *Hajj* and *Hajjeh* where the corpse was laid out and washed. Women were screaming and crying and everyone said farewell before the body was buried in the cemetery. This was the most difficult part for *Hajj* and *Hajjeh* and the whole family, who had waited so long for their son to return. It sometimes seemed to me as if their entire motivation in life derived from waiting and not giving up before they saw their son again. Now, he had finally come home – but not alive. "We brought him up. We educated him and then he left. And we waited all those years, waited for the day he would return", *Hajjeh* remarked in a bitter resigned voice and continued "This is his last journey. God give him a safe journey". In an even quieter voice, *Hajj* repeated: "He travelled, he travelled, he went away and we will go, too, *Hajjeh*!"

A month later, on a calm December day, one of the last of the month of *ramadan*, *Hajj* was sitting where he always sat in the evenings after dinner, enjoying a cup of coffee. All of a sudden, his five year-old grandchild began to scream as *Hajj* fell sideways and was dead immediately. *Hajjeh* could not bear the pain of losing her son and her husband. Six months later, she followed both of them after months of suffering from a protracted illness.

Telling and Writing Lives: The Politics of Representation

> Ethnography is a movement from "subjectively meaningful experiences emanating from our spontaneous life" (Schutz 1962: 211) in the field into academic text – ranging from scribbled fieldnotes to polished, published articles and books. (Lavie 1990: 34)

Much of the empirical data on which this study is based was acquired through participant observation, everyday conversation, and non-structured interviews.

While living in the household of my parents-in-law, I broadened my relationships with people in the village at first along kinship and neighbourhood ties. Since paying a visit to migrants on arrival or before their departure is a social "must" for neighbours, friends and relatives, I would hear the latest news and gossip from those who came to welcome me or say good-bye. A mediator between the Lebanese from Zrariye living in Germany and their families who lived in South Lebanon on many occasions, I used to carry tapes, presents and money in both directions. I always made an effort to return their visits in the first weeks after my arrival, where visiting patterns provided a good opportunity of gradually extending my social interaction on a daily basis. At the same time, I used to observe the women who came to see my mother-in-law. They would make little comments of approval when they saw me helping with the household – a mere gesture measured according to Lebanese daughter-in-law standards. Nevertheless, I was gradually more or less accepted into the female neighbourhood. Watching these women carry out their day-to-day activities and listening to their ordinary conversations, I could well imagine the importance of absent family members. They showed me photographs of their children and grandchildren who live abroad and talked about their absent relatives as if they were next door. I knew all about the migrants living elsewhere before I ever met them personally. During my visit to Abidjan later on, people were amazed how well-informed I was about rumours and stories circulating in the translocal village. This was presumably the signal that I somehow belonged to their Zrariyen social world, since they then appeared more comfortable about including me in their chats and discussions, although they had not known me for long.

In Zrariye I lived in a mixed neighbourhood with families from several kinship groups, so that I got to know both women and men belonging to different extended families. As most of the neighbours were in their 40s, 50s or older, I asked them about their grown-up children and their places of residence. These "data-sheets" gave me a reasonable overview of migration schemes and confirmed my assumption that the majority of Zrariye migrants are in fact in Côte d'Ivoire.

To grasp the transnational experience and its significance for South

Lebanese social life, it was essential to understand that it is not independent of other social fields. Different social actors – those who move and those who stay behind – are linked in some way to the translocal experience. Realising this, it was important to interview the migrants as well as their relatives and friends "at home".

In an attempt to gain a better understanding of people's personal positions in the translocal circuits between South Lebanon and West Africa, I favoured a biographical and actor-centered approach. Literature reviewing the life-history approach in the social sciences is extensive (cf., for example Bertaux 1981; Bertaux/Kohli 1984; Fischer/Kohli 1987; Langness/Frank 1981; Rosenthal 1995; Schütze 1983). However, there is a danger here of giving too much space to methodological individualism, either granting the individual a high degree of singularity or, on the other hand, of treating him or her as the exclusive token of a type (Gupta/Ferguson 1992: 15). Contrary to this, my interest was to follow a social biography approach based on the personal accounts of mutually familiar narrators. Conducting life-history interviews with different members of an extended family gave me an intimation of the interdependence of their lives and disclosed the retrospective understandings people have of their migrant experiences. It also provided me with many different, even contrasting versions of the same events and experiences.

My primary interest in carrying out biographical interviews was to understand how women and men reflect on their personal lives and their movements between South Lebanon and Africa. My aim in collecting details about people's lives was to establish similarities and differences according to gender, age, religion and social status. While observing women in their daily lives and talking to them in Zrariye and Abidjan, I tried to decipher a variety of "identity types" as conceptualised by Berger and Luckmann: "Specific historical social structures engender identity types, which are recognizable in individual cases" (Berger/Luckmann 1966: 174). In doing so, I had no fixed, static or closed entities in mind. On the contrary, by presenting the life-stories of several women, I particularly wanted to voice the complexities, ambiguities and conflicts that make up their lives, showing both similarities and differences, and the historical contexts in which their lives are embedded. To protect women's privacy I have changed their names. Although the various life stories presented here are individual cases, they stand for the lives of a wide range of South Lebanese women.

This life-history analysis not only gave me an appreciation of people's past experiences but also of their present concerns and future plans. Several authors have shown that telling a life-story has more to do with the present than the past, since constructing it allows the individual to represent aspects of the past that are relevant to the present and to guide the present with future-oriented intentions (cf., for example, Fischer 1978). In this context, it is essential to bear in mind that a life-story is not an immediate representation of the informant's life or its direct equivalent. In contrast, the narrative "is" not the person itself, but a version of the self, constructed by the subject for presentation to the anthropologist. Each account is an arbitrary imposition of meaning on the flow of memory, highlighting some causes and ignoring others: "That is every telling is interpretative" (Bruner 1986: 7). Crapanzano notes that the interplay of "demand and desire" governs much of the content of life-histories. Consequently, the dynamics of the interview must be taken into consideration in any evaluation of the material collected (Crapanzano 1984: 956).

A major question raised in debates on ethnographic representation refers to how the process of knowledge production during the fieldwork encounter should be included in the written text (Moors 1995: 19). The argument that anthropologists are writers was the starting point for considerable reflection on textuality and the fieldwork encounter (Geertz 1988; Clifford/Marcus 1986). Anthropologists have been experimenting with new forms of writing in an attempt to close the gap between fieldwork and ethnography. Many have argued that ethnography must include both the dialogue and the interaction between the anthropologist and those represented. The idea was to avoid an anthropological monologue by creating a text in which several voices can be heard. The issue of anthropological authority remains, however, and the shift to polyvocality could serve to mask authority and obscure power relations.

With reference to Moors, I understand ethnographic writing first and foremost as a means of creating images (1995: 20). Writings on women in the Middle East have tended to emphasize dichotomies, which in turn tend to create a hierarchical and essential difference between women in the West and those in the Middle East. Presenting life-stories should be seen as an attempt to create "counter-images" that provide a possibility for understanding and empathy (Moors 1995: 20). In this context, it is my wish to present a variety of stories that include various, sometimes even contradictory forms in which different women – and men – relate to significant aspects of their lives. While it is true that I retell their stories, they themselves set the limits within which I was able to work. They made the initial selection by deciding to talk to me and by choosing what they wanted to tell.

3. The Emergence of a Translocal Village

> Poverty's children, where are they now,
> Torn autumn leaves?
> Where is my village that was,
> Those named paths
> Now asphalt roads?
> ('Araidi cit. in Lavie 1995: 421)

Places and Emotional Landscapes

The village of Zrariye[1] lies in the south of Lebanon. Part of the Saida district (*mohafazah*), it is situated on a hill plateau approximately 300m above sea level in the triangle between the southern towns of Saida (Sidon), Sour (Tyre) and Nabatiye[2], between the Mediterranean coast in the west and Mount Hermon (*Jabal al Sheikh*) in the east. Comparative maps by Taraf-Najib show the configuration of the village between 1920 and 1986 (Taraf-Najib 1992), where its development can be traced from an essentially nuclear village with a cluster of houses surrounded by agricultural fields to a small town with residential areas expanding to form new neighbourhoods (*harat*). The original compact village centre cluster identifiable in old village maps still partly exists and includes the main mosque, some shops and a public square (*saha*). Houses were built close together, with kinship groups forming a neighbourhood (*hara*). In the 1940s, villagers began to relocate outside their family cluster. This was due to lack of space for new construction in the densely built up centre as well as to a tremendous change in the style of building over the years. In the past, the village centre was dominated by tightly-knit clusters of rather uniform, small, flat-roofed houses made of clay and yellow stone. At that time it was possible to go from one house to another by walking across the roofs. Today, people generally prefer to build individually-styled houses, especially successful migrants, who use their capital "made in Africa" to create personal "palaces".

The village continued to expand, although many villagers from the poorer social strata migrated to Beirut in the 1950s and 1960s. The civil war frequently forced them to return to the village and start building houses – sometimes illegally on state-owned land. According to Taraf-Najib, the village population was approximately 2,000 in 1950 (1992: 45). The village headman (*mukhtar*) claimed that there were around 16,000 people living there in 1995. However, the dynamics of internal and international migration make it exceedingly difficult to estimate the actual population of the village. Deciding on who should be counted poses a problem. Should those who spend the weekends and summers in the village but live in Saida and Beirut be included or should only the "full" residents be counted? What about the migrants overseas, many of whom own a house in the village? Some come regularly for visits, while others cannot afford the journey home. Yet they all refer to themselves as members of the village.

For the old *mukhtar*, it is obvious that anyone registered in his books as a member of one of the local patrilineages belongs to the village, regardless of her or his current place of residence. This view is shared by villagers living "at home" or "abroad" and, since all personal affairs are registered in the village, mirrors Lebanese personal status laws reinforcing strong ties with the paternal birthplace. Polling cards and the documents required to register births, marriages and deaths can only be obtained from the local headman. The same applies to people who no longer reside or have never lived in the village but whose patrilineage has always been registered there. Whenever migrants in Beirut or abroad require a certificate, they are obliged to go to their village of registration or authorise a family relative to procure it for them.[3] Although it would entail endless official complications, people are permitted to change their place of registration. However, as the paternal village of origin stands for more than mere registration practices, they rarely do so. Belonging to the same patriclan and the same village of origin still mobilises (trans-)local identification processes despite the fact that many of the social actors involved live their lives in very different places. The question arises as to why people cling to these places of origin, reapproaching and redefining (trans-)local identities in a globalised world that offers an immense variety of identification opportunities?

I contend that for many Lebanese migrants, travellers and war refugees living in uncertain and at times difficult political, social and economic circumstances in different parts of the world, their village of origin, the place they ultimately come from, becomes an important fixed point of reference and identification, providing imaginary stability in a world of increasing mobility, change and insecurity. This holds true for migrants as well as for those who stayed behind in Lebanese villages and cities. Their life-worlds also changed dramatically as a result of the disintegration of local agriculture, rural-urban migration and, above all, civil war.[4]

I would argue that by constantly imagining, sharing and negotiating the understanding of what their "village" or "place of origin" means, of what it was, is and could be, people "at home" and "abroad" are involved in jointly producing and making their "village". By doing so, they actively strengthen their sense of belonging and can enjoy social proximity despite living hundreds or thousands of miles away. People "here" and "there" narrate, remember and sense places and landscapes in and around the village. What looks like a river, a hill, a field of wheat or olives from the outside may be much more than that. These elements are also expressions of moral and emotional landscapes, which unfold in language, names, stories, myths and rituals[5]. The meanings crystallise into shared symbols and can link people "at home" and "abroad" to a sense of common history and (trans-)local identity.[6] In this way, places capture the complex emotional, behavioural and moral relationships between people and their territory. They are representative of people, their actions, and their interactions and, as such, become malleable memorials for negotiating and renegotiating human relationships (Kahn 1996: 168).

Talking about place becomes a code for communicating important messages, such as a reminder of social obligations that have gone unfulfilled or of moral responsibilities. When, for example, old Zrariyen men talk about their olive fields, the quality of a particular yield or of harvest time, they are also referring implicitly or explicitly to the current situation: the fact that agriculture has lost its value and that migration has caused a labour deficit, resulting in the use of cheap labour from Syria to work the land. The narratives of working the olives has now become the shared symbol of a vanished past, when most of the villagers lived in the village and worked the land themselves. In migrant and village narratives, the South Lebanese hills, with their terrace cultivation of olive trees, wheat, and orange and lemon plantations near the Litani river, are often depicted with nostalgia. People recount how they used to walk the four kilometres to the Litani river where they learnt to swim and enjoyed family picnics. The land and the landscape around the village often appear as places of happy childhood memories, of rootedness and stability in a current world of constant change. Following Pierre Nora's terminology, the land, the fields and the South Lebanese landscape in general have become sites of memory (*lieux de mémoire*), shattered fragments of a lost or destroyed social life-world (Nora 1989: 11). The social milieu of agriculture has vanished as a consequence of rural-urban and international migration and of war. But for many (trans-)locals, the village itself, the land and the landscape have since become nostalgic places of memory.

Producing Nostalgic Places of Memory

> I close my eyes
> and smell the ripe olives.
> (Suheir Hammad, cit. in Hammer 2001: 474)

The Lebanese "at home" and "abroad" use various forms and media to express their sense of nostalgia "for the village". They talk about the times of yore, remember events and activities, refer to songs, sometimes to poems and novels, and nowadays, even express their love for their village on websites in the Internet. Clever Lebanese businessmen detected a market in people's nostalgic attachment to their village and began offering photographs of places of memory online:

> Every Lebanese emigrant is nostalgic to his Lebanese origin, the scenery, his neighborhood or village. We at 3D Stickers Technoprint created a special department fulfilling this nostalgia and making Lebanon nearer. Upon your request, we will commission a professional photographer to take pictures of your desired location in Lebanon. For only $ 200 (US Dollars – shipping included), we will select the best 10 pictures, process them using our special dome technique and send it to your address by airmail to any location in the world.[7]

Similar to photographs that trigger cherished memories, books and songs have the ability to arouse sense memories, such as the smells and tastes frequently associated with early childhood. Fayrouz, Lebanon's most famous singer, has the unique power of activating emotional memories connected with local Lebanese life. The lyrics of her early songs from the 1950s and musical plays of the 1960s have a particularly strong appeal to this sense of nostalgia for village life.[8] Many of the songs contain detailed descriptions of "traditional local life" and refer to the land, to the people living in traditional village houses and to celebrations in the village square *(saha)* (Weinrich 2002: 259-265).

The metaphors in the lyrics alluding to nature repeatedly hint at a yearning for the old days in the village, aroused by the use of traditional folk tunes (Weinrich 2002: 230-231). In her Ph.D. thesis, Ines Weinrich has shown that a diverse audience continuously redefined the lyrics of Fayrouz songs. Migrants clung to "the village" as a means of restoring memories of their own personal village of origin. During the Lebanese civil war, displaced persons embraced the nostalgia of the lyrics to escape its harsh reality, while the same words inspired urban intellectuals to recapture their own childhood past in some Lebanese village (Weinrich 2002: 262-265). Impressively, Fayrouz songs still have the power to unite the Lebanese both in Lebanon and abroad, beyond social, political and confessional boundaries. When Fayrouz sings of the "the village of childhood", Lebanese villages rise to people's minds instinctively, whether they are Maronite, Greek-Orthodox, Shi'ite, Sunni or one of the many confessionally heterogeneous localities, despite the fact that the lyrics mainly allude to a "traditional Mount Lebanon village" with no reference to other regions (cf. Weinrich 2002: 255)[9].

Thus, Fayrouz stands out as an exceptional "national icon" with the power to create a sense of shared Lebanese identity and nationality beyond confessionalism. "More than just a singer's name, Fayrouz is a concept whose connotations are ethnic and nationalistic as well as musical and poetic"

(Racy 1996).[10] Nizar Qabbani, a well-known Syrian poet, hints at the unifying potential of her songs in the following comment:

> When Fairouz sings, mountains and rivers follow her voice, the mosque and the church, the oil-jars and loaves of bread; through her, every one of us is made to blossom, and once we were no more than sand; men drop their weapons and apologize. Upon hearing her voice, it is our childhood which is being molded anew. (Qabbani cit. in Zaatari 2001)[11]

In fact, Fayrouz became the unifying voice for all the Lebanese who lived through both external and civil wars. Her patriotic songs seem to be healing ointment for the war-torn Lebanese. When in 1994 Fayrouz gave a concert for the first time in sixteen years in Lebanon at the end of the civil war, the Lebanese felt a sense of unity – if only for the length of the concert in Martyr Square.

The topoi of "the village" as a place of longing, nostalgia and happy childhood memories and as a symbol of national unity and identity not only appeared in the repertoire of Fayrouz and the Rahbani brothers but are also used in the Lebanese context for different periods and genres. The literature of the *mahjar* ("immigrant poets") is one example. Having come as migrants to the US at the beginning of the twentieth century, poets such as Ameen Rihani, Gibran Khalil Gibran and Mikhail Naimy initiated the New York Pen League in 1920, which was known as *al-rabitah al-qalamiyah* or the *al-mahjar* (Ostle 1992). Writing from a distance, these authors often returned nostalgically to the sites of their childhood and to romantic villages in Lebanon and Syria.[12]

Since the emergence of nationalist discourses and movements in the region (at the turn of the twentieth century), the narrative of the "traditional Mount Lebanon village" has also become a dominant symbol of Lebanese Maronite nationalism. Here, the "village" is used as a metaphor for the Lebanese nation. Propagated almost exclusively by the Maronites, "Lebanese nationalism" ideology was conceived for the benefit of their confessional particularism and aimed at maintaining their political dominance (Reinkowski 1997: 505). So-called local Mount Lebanon village traditions and folklore are reimagined in this context to serve as a constitutive element of nationalistic ideas and ideology.[13]

It is evident from this example that discourses on "the village" cannot be understood solely in the context of people's personal lives, in their yearning for a place of origin and of childhood in the face of migration, displacement and alienation from lost life-worlds, but must also be analysed in that of disparate political, economic and social interests and power struggles. This aspect will be explored in more detail in the following, taking a very different example to illustrate how discourses on "the village" are used politically: namely, village websites on the Internet. I will argue that, on the one hand, these websites are a means of holding together and living family relations in a globalised world and, on the other hand, a strategy of local politicians to attract migrants in the pursuit of their own political and economic interests. The following example concentrates particularly on the village websites of Joun, which is a multi-confessional (Shi'ite, Greek-Catholic, Maronite) village situated in the southernmost part of the administrative district of Mount Lebanon in the Shuf mountains (cf. Peleikis 2001 a-c).

By going through this wonderful website I saw myself walking the street of my village long time ago with my cousins. That was the best time of my life.
It gives me a big pleasure to belong to the big family of Joun. I will always have the wonderful days in my memory and my heart that I spent in this dear village. These memories I will pass on to my children and grandchildren.
Proud to be a Jouni. It is a wonderful page that reminds me of my village.[14]

The author of the above expresses his love for his village of origin in the website guestbook. Lebanese village and city websites have mushroomed on the Internet in the last couple of years.[15] Some of them were created by migrants for the specific purpose of keeping the memory of the village alive and of getting in touch with people from the village now scattered all over the world. As their homepage indicates, this was the motive expressed by people originating from the Lebanese village of Kalamoun:

We are a group of people from the beloved village of Kalamoun, who identified a great need to communicate with each other and exchange news and information related to our village. Many of us who are originally from Kalamoun, currently live or reside in various parts of the world. This, in fact, contributes to the importance of using an effective communication medium, such as the Internet, to keep the warm memories about Kalamoun alive in our hearts. Our message is simple and clear: we CARE about each other.[16]

The idea of reuniting people via the Internet, who originate from the same village but now live in all corners of the world is also expressed by the webmasters of the Tannourine village website:

The Tannourine White Page is a free service providing Cyber Tannourine's community and friends around the world a resource that could possibly reunite friends, create new friendships, and make Tannourine's feel closer to Tannourine.[17]

While some of the websites were initiated and designed by Lebanese living outside Lebanon, most of them are actually designed by order of a particular

Lebanese municipality. It seems that the use of the Internet as a representative platform for the municipality is especially common in villages where local politicians acquired their computer and Internet knowledge in the US or Europe and subsequently introduced it to their own Lebanese communities. This is the case with the village of Joun, for example, where the local mayor had lived in France for many years.[18] Other villages were latecomers to the Internet, as for instance Zrariye, where it has not yet been introduced in the service of local politics. I would argue that this is because migration from Zrariye is directed towards Africa, where different local administration strategies were experienced and readapted.

The village websites designed by the municipalities inform the public primarily about the (new) municipal council, its work, projects and plans. On the other hand, the detailed and colourful descriptions of the village and its uniqueness are particularly striking. On the municipality website of the village of Joun, specific reference is made to the landscape and its incredible beauty, to individual archaeological and architectural sites, as well as to the impressive history of the village and its famous personalities:

Got a burning desire to explore the peaceful hill and valleys of Joun and a green nature well preserved? Or wander among the tales of history and its events? Then you've landed at the right place. Just turn away from the main road and in minutes you will have it all. Joun: A Charming nature and the myth of the adventure. Experience the best of the Lebanese mountains, enjoy the virgin nature of Joun. The most fascinating sights can be yours to enjoy.[19]

The comments on the Joun website referring to the beauty and singularity of the village are an attempt to motivate people to come and see it. I would argue that the websites are deliberately designed in a "nostalgic mode" to appeal to translocal villagers and convince them to pay a visit to their village of origin and become economically and politically involved, and that nostalgia in this case can be seen as a political strategy. The language of nostalgia on the Joun website abounds with metaphors of peace, purity and tranquillity, which at the same time invokes a sense of adventure. A politicised nostalgic mode is clearly used to create a selective version of the past that both hides and ignores the painful memories of war and the destruction and disintegration of recent years. The village appears as a place of unique charm, adventure and happiness – at least on the Internet. The nostalgic memory site created on the Internet gives way to a sense of new beginning and local belonging, and the binding together of people beyond local and national boundaries.

The "guestbooks" of the individual village websites give "virtual visitors" an opportunity to comment on the page, on the work of the municipality and to get in touch with other translocal villagers and express their specific relation to the village of origin:

I was very happy and elated to visit your site. I am from Joun. Ain Hyroun brought back happy childhood memories. Good job! Please include more high quality pictures and perhaps, short video clips...

                              Mustafa Shamsedin <MShamsedin@scana.com>
             Columbia, USA – Saturday, August 10, 2002 at 15:44:33 (UTC)

hallo there i love you all guys as much as i love my place joun i missed every one; hope to see everyone in a good shape as i know them alllllll. theres no place like home.

                                   zein mekkawi <zeinmekkawi@hotmail.com>
                 paris, javel – Sunday, March 31, 2002 at 16:23:02 (UTC)

It seems that Lebanese villagers – from Joun in this case – have found an additional place to negotiate the meaning of their own village. Whereas the meaning of a particular place, village or landscape has usually been negotiated by villagers from various social backgrounds in public and private places "in the village", this activity now also takes place in a "virtual village square" on the Internet. Moreover, it was usually men who gathered at the village square and produced a common understanding of their village and thus a shared local identity, while women produced their meaning of the village in the course of private meetings and visits. Similarly, villagers go on the Internet to meet at the "virtual village square" for a chat and to exchange ideas. It is above all the younger and more educated generation, men and women alike, that uses the new means of communication to produce a shared image of "their village of origin".

    The production of "place" is evidently a highly flexible process that depends on various factors, such as gender, generation, social class, and political and economic interests. Hence, place is never inert. People always engage with it, rework it, appropriate and contest it. In this sense, place is not so much an artefact as a process of construction and reconstruction. Different ideas and narratives of "place" are used by social actors at different times for different political, social or economic reasons. This can lead to discord and conflict, as I observed in Joun, where municipal actors and local villagers use different images of their village for different reasons.

    Municipal leaders in Joun, many of whom were migrants to Europe and the US, exert their influence by spreading the image of a "nostalgic place". By comparison, Zrariyen municipal leaders and "successful" migrants are interested in dispersing a self-defined "modern" image of their village. As "successful migrants" who managed to accumulate a certain amount of wealth in Africa, they demonstrate their "new image" of the village by building large individually styled villas and attempt to "modernise" the village, e.g., by paving as many roads as possible with asphalt. They consider the old agricultural Zrariye "traditional" and "backward", whereas in Joun the "nostalgic" regard for the village motivated the municipality to rebuild some of the old village walls and steps. It would be highly rewarding to observe in detail how the disparate migrant experiences of Joun's local politicians in the US and Europe and those of Zrariyen local politicians in Africa influenced their view of their own locality, and how these images were used for their respective political purposes. According to my research so far, ideas of local politicians in both Joun and Zrariye are contradicted by various social actors who have conflicting images of their place of belonging. Local farmers in Joun, for instance, who disagree with the municipal approach of remaking the village along nostalgic lines and are fighting for fairer work opportunities. Or people in Zrariye who reject the "modernist" approach of the municipality and boycott new construction sites. Similar to other places in Lebanon, the struggle for locality is an ongoing process in Joun and Zrariye. As a result of the diverse (trans-)local and (trans-)national connections between these places and their social actors, it is expressed quite differently in each village – despite the short distance of 50 km between the two.

Producing Traumatic Places of Memory

> The olive grove was always green.
> At least it used to be, my love.
> Fifty victims, at sundown
> Turned it into a red pool ... fifty victims.
> (Darwish 1973: 291)

The Lebanese wars deeply altered the meaning of places, public spaces and landscapes, as pointed out by Samir Khalaf (1993: 108):

While prominent public spaces lost their identity, other rather ordinary crossings, junctures, hilltops, even shops, became dreaded landmarks. The war produced its own lexicon and iconography of places.

As a result of the recurrent shifting targets of hostility during the war years, people were constantly displaced from villages and cities, and from their familiar and reliable landmarks. They were forced to abandon their homes and neighbourhoods and flee to safer areas, while their houses and places of everyday life were destroyed in the fighting or deliberately blown up to prevent their returning. People were literally displaced from their local past, their family histories and habitual social relationships. During the war years, many people left the country temporarily or for good, while others moved around within the country in the hope of finding relative safety and shelter. They had to cope regularly with the loss of family and friends and reorganise their daily lives under strained conditions, frequently in unfamiliar or even unknown places and regions.

No sooner have they suffered the travails of dislocation by taking refuge in one community than they are once again uprooted and compelled to negotiate yet another spatial identity or suffer the added humiliation of reentry into their profoundly transformed communities. (Khalaf 1993: 95)

People became displaced but were still place-bound, as Edward Casey made clear: "More even than earthlings, we are placelings, and our very perceptual apparatus, our sensing body, reflects the kinds of place we inhabit" (Casey 1996: 19). I would thus argue that being in new, often insecure places in the course of displacement or migration influences and changes people's perception of their home locality. In a world of forced displacement, loss and disruption, the village of origin develops into a distant, unattainable, idealised home locality, an emotional landscape and projection site for the need to feel at home, rooted and at peace (cf. Peleikis 2001a: 417). The production of "nostalgic places of memory" may indeed help people to cope with war and post-war realities and give them a sense of hope when peace seems all too far away. Attachment to nostalgic places of memory can suppress – at least for some time – the pain of sensing that these places have been transformed, at worst into "traumatic places of memory".

The Zrariye village square *(saha)* can be narrated simultaneously as a "nostalgic and a traumatic place of memory". It is narrated in a nostalgic mode, for example, when people recall their youth and how they danced the *dabkeh* (traditional dance) at the *saha* on feast-days. At the same time, the village square is deeply inscribed in people's memory as a "traumatic place of memory" that tells stories of war, pain and loss. Above all, it tells the story of the 11th March 1985 when Israeli soldiers invaded the village and the local men were forced to stand in the village square in unbearable heat for an entire day. Sixty-three Zrariyen men were killed, 150 arrested, dozens injured and 40 houses blown up.

Where do people's "traumatic places of memory" find their expression? Are they hidden and silenced behind nostalgic narratives or are they expressed in personal narratives, in literature and song, and placed in memorials, land and landscapes?

People in Zrariye rarely talked about their "traumatic place of memory", about the massacre that occurred in the village square in 1985. The experience itself may have prevented them from doing so, since "trauma is the impossibility of narration" (Assmann 2001: 57). In the same vein, Judith Hermann has shown that the normal response to atrocities is to banish them from consciousness (Hermann 1997: 11). She also states that "atrocities, however, refuse to be buried" (Hermann 1997: 1).

During the annual *'ashura* rituals, I felt that the "unspeakable" had forced its way into the open, as people's painful emotions and traumatic memories were powerfully embodied, placed and symbolically transformed in the village square. An impressive performance of the historic battle of Karbala (680 AD) between the prophet's grandson, Husayn, and the forces of the caliph Yazid takes place at the village square each year on the 10th of the month of *muharram*. Over the centuries, various writers have embroidered this historical battle and created a number of plays portraying the ten-day battle that ended tragically for Husayn and most of his family. These narratives *(ta'ziyeh)* revealing Husayn's martyrdom are read and recited throughout the Shi'ite world both privately and in the public sphere during the ten days of annual mourning. Moreover, amateur and professional theatre companies reenact the events of *muharram* in 680 AD in Shi'ite villages and towns each year, thus bringing it even more forcefully into the present.

In Zrariye, where the villagers rehearse the passion play with great intensity, the performance of Husayn's death in the village square on the 10th day of *'ashura* marks the climax of mourning. The square is decorated with tents and palm leaves to create an atmosphere of the desert scenery around Karbala, which has now become an important Shi'ite pilgrimage site in today's Iraq. In the Zrariyen performance, the actors playing the "good" characters – members of Husayn's family and his followers – wear predominantly green costumes, and sing and recite in soft, melodious voices, whereas the "bad" characters – Husayn's enemies – are dressed in reds and yellows and perform in a raucous manner. Hundreds of people from the village and the surrounding areas come to watch the performance at the Zrariye square. Migrants even come home to participate in the *'ashura* rituals, especially the performance of Husayn's battle.

By staging this historical drama, the heart of Shi'ite collective memory is brought into the local consciousness. It is not merely a commemoration of a particular historical tragedy but the artistic expression of the universal struggle between good and evil, between the oppressed and the oppressors. The audience can easily identify with Husayn, as his battle becomes their own difficult battle against injustice and suffering. Finally, by performing or watching the passion play at the village square, villagers can reappropriate this "traumatic place of memory" and transform it into a place of rebellion and martyrdom. The constant victimization, powerlessness, trauma and suffering endured in the South of Lebanon are transformed by these rituals and give way to a sense of self-esteem, self-control and the power to resist.

"*Kullu yawmin 'ashura, kullu ardhin Karbala*". ("Every day is *'ashura* and every land is Karbala"). These sentences were conveyed on large posters during the *'ashura* rituals in Zrariye in 1996, only a month after Israeli military forces had entered Lebanon with a vengeance during a military operation under the code name "Grapes of Wrath". Despite Israel's claim that its target was the *Hizbollah*, countless civilians were wounded or killed in the course of the operation and the economic infrastructure destroyed. The attack that caused the highest number of casualties and left the greatest imprint on people's minds was that of April 18th 1996, when a UN compound in the South Lebanese village of Qana was hit. The Fijian compound had given shelter to 5,000 people seeking refuge with international peace-keeping troops. More than a hundred innocent people were killed and many more injured. This horror site was later transformed into a sanctuary for the dead and finally into a local Shi'te and national memorial. In contrast to many other traumatic places in Lebanon whose histories remain untold, silent or buried, Qana has become a "Karbala" for the Lebanese Shi'ites, a place of mourning and of resistance. It even rose to become a national symbol of resistance to Israeli occupation and aggression. Lebanese throughout the country and beyond it come to visit Qana, the grave of more than a hundred villagers. It has in fact become more than just the name of a place. It has become a symbol of shared suffering and a metaphor for a "community of fate and resistance".

The Lebanese take Qana with them on their journeys, migrations and movements and thus remake and reproduce the meaning of this fierce attack on South Lebanon in their current places of residence – in Africa, Europe, America or Australia. By discursively recreating the events of Qana over time and in different places, they effectively redefine and strengthen their (South) Lebanese and/or Shi'ite translocal and transnational identities. The Lebanese migrants who were in Lebanon during the attacks in 1996 passed on the information and their experiences of that day to their friends and families. Video films about the disaster and the subsequent moving funeral, where more than a hundred coffins were buried at the place of destruction, made their way to Lebanese communities all over the world. Lebanese political organisations, NGOs and private individuals created websites displaying pictures of the atrocities, accompanied by detailed eyewitness reports, articles by journalists and comments on the events by national and international politicians.[20] Most of these websites were created years after the attack with the obvious intention of spreading a political interpretation of the massacre and above all of not forgetting, as most of the pages clearly state: "Qana 96, so that we don't forget".[21]

Letters to the editors of the specific websites give an impression of who reads and comments on the Qana websites. As frequently confirmed by interviews with visiting migrants in Lebanon, they are actively looking for information about "their country of origin" and thus produce and spread the meanings of places. The younger generation in particular, who grow up in Lebanon and elsewhere with this means of communication, use the Internet to learn about their "origins". Ruba Haidar, a 16-year-old Lebanese Canadian, is an outstanding example of how young people get involved in making, negotiating and spreading the meaning of places like "Qana". She lives in Canada but was in Lebanon on the eve of the Israeli attacks in 1996. Two years after the massacre, she wrote to the editors of the Qana website of Lebanese Future TV:

Date: Sat, 25 Apr 1998 11:39:50 -0400
From: Ruba Haidar
My name is Ruba Haidar. I am 16 years old. I am Lebanese Canadian. I was in Lebanon during Qana's massacre, and it stained my heart to see what happened to my people. I wrote this poem to express my feelings. I present it to Qana's people. (I read it before my highschool's staff, which proved to be very moving and made some teachers cry, and it won a prize). I am doing my part to spread awareness in Canada, and thank you for the beautiful web page on Qana (I will give the address to all my teachers). I would be very grateful if you would put this poem in Qana's WebPages for all to read. Thanks again.

A Cry To The South
A blazing fire burns in the south
A shrilling cry from an innocent mouth
An end to a life that has hardly begun
Oh south! Why does this have to be done?
Oh where has the glory gone?
The terror in a UN camp,
where mothers with their children lay
So high the mounds of body parts
The butchers yard on Qana's day
The many tears drowned the scattered hearts.
It left such hardness in children's eyes,
With blood it marked the sacrifice.
The eyes that will never see,
A more repulsive tragedy.
A child chokes in his bitter tremble
As he calls out for his mother's care;
But she can't hear you child
Who are you left to?
What did you ever do?
For them to hurt you.
Oh South! the rain that falls on you
Is the forlorn tears that cry for who
Ever lies beneath your soil.
And they who hurt your bless'd land
Will be stopped beneath the people's hand
And let dear peace uncoil.

By: Ruba Haidar[22]

This young Lebanese Canadian girl, who describes her feelings about the events in Qana in her poem, is also involved in discursively creating images of the Lebanese South, depicted here as a war-torn land where "blazing fire burns" and rain is the "forlorn tears that cry for who ever lies beneath its soil". The poem expresses the long history of South Lebanese suffering and sacrifice and talks of people who have had to bear incredible loss.

The images come from a young girl who grew up in "safe" Canada, but who is connected through her family to a wider transnational Lebanese community. Confrontation with the events in Qana during a visit to Lebanon inspired her "Cry to the South". In this context, Qana has become a metaphor for an emotional landscape expressing pain and loss, lived and relived by generations of Lebanese "at home" and "abroad". I would argue that the topoi of personal and communal suffering, so deeply inscribed in Shi'ite collective memory, also contributes to the sense of belonging to an imagined "community of fate" beyond nation state boundaries. This grieving is bound up with people's traumatic memories of massacres and where they occurred. While, on the one hand, these places are actually "in place", they are also portable possessions that move with people and become a tool for their imagination. Hetherington claims that "places are like ships" (1997: 185-9). "They are not something that stays in one place but move around within networks of agents, humans, and non-humans" (Urry 2000: 134). Similarly, Doreen Massey has put forward the idea that instead of thinking of places as areas with surrounding boundaries, they can be imagined as articulated moments in networks of social relations and understandings (Massey 1994: 154). She continues her argument by remarking that a large number of these relations, experiences and understandings are constructed on a far greater scale than what we happen to define for that moment as the place itself, whether it be a street, a region or even a continent:

And this in turn allows a sense of place which is extroverted, which includes a consciousness of its links with the wider world, which integrates in a positive way the global and the local. (Massey 1994: 155)

These statements on "place" bring me back to the village of Zrariye and its translocal inhabitants, struggling and negotiating the images and meaning of their village. In the following, I would like to give space to the accounts of two elderly people, Imm and Abu Ali[23], two Zrariye villagers who never migrated but lived in the same village all their lives. Throughout most of the war years, they remained in this one place and saw their village change, just as they themselves had changed. They saw people migrating and returning, and conjured up their own ideas about "places of migration" in relation to their dwelling-place. Their conception of the translocal village is filtered by their gender and generational experiences. The following is an example of how people engage with their dwelling-place and how this is dependent on the specific time, on gender, age and class, and on the specific historical, social and economic environment.

Producing Gendered and Generational Narratives of Place

In the course of his life, Abu Ali has witnessed history in the making: the collapse of the Ottoman rule (1918), the French Mandate period in Lebanon (1920-1946), the British Mandate in Palestine, Lebanese independence (1946), the creation of the State of Israel accompanied by the exodus of the Palestinians and their subsequent entry into Lebanon (1948). Abu Ali lived through sixteen years of Lebanese civil war (1975-1991) and experienced the Israeli invasion of Lebanon in 1982 and the "slaughter of Zrariye" (1985), when Israelis made a fierce attack on his home village. During my stay in 1995/1996, the Israeli threat was still a daily reality for the white-haired old man and his wife, Imm Ali. The noise of Israeli military helicopters and planes day and night reminded him of the Israeli air raids during the civil war and later in 1993 and 1996. Whereas most of the villagers fled to Beirut, Abu Ali stayed where he was in the village. No one could bring him to leave his house, his animals or his olive groves. He explained that he had not wanted to encounter the same fate as the Palestinians who left their homes and villages, never to return. He remained inextricably bound to Zrariye, the place he was born and grew up in, where he married and lived a family life. It is also the place his children moved away from to embark on new lives in different places, and finally it is the place where he grew old:

I grew up with my mother because my father died when I was very young. When I was fifteen, I began to work here and there. Later I bought a donkey and began work as a small trader. I used to go to Palestine by donkey. It took me two days to get there. I used to bring back oranges from Jaffa and sell them here. You know, at that time there were no orange plantations here. It was only when the Palestinian refugees came here after 1948 that oranges were grown. When the first migrants came back with money, they began to invest in fruit plantations and build irrigation systems.

I sometimes brought grapes back from Palestine and sold them at the market in Nabatiye. A lot of the time I was too busy to come to Zrariye to see my family. I sold various things: cows, sheep, thyme (za'tar), wheat and tobacco. Smuggling was very profitable. I smuggled tobacco to Palestine. You know, tobacco had to be sold to the state at that time. Selling it to Palestine was far more lucrative. On the way back, I smuggled women's scarves by hiding them under the donkey's saddle. They were cheap in Palestine and very expensive here.

Buying and selling, that was my life. Later, when the Jews created the state of Israel and we couldn't go to Palestine anymore, this kind of trade became impossible. On the contrary, many Palestinians had to flee to Lebanon, where they still are today. I continued as a trader in Lebanon and bought some land in Zrariye from the money I had earned. I didn't inherit anything from my father, you know. I had to work hard for what I have. I couldn't buy as much land as the migrants who came back from Africa with plenty of money. They bought a lot of land from the As'ad family who used to own all the land. But *al-hamdu li-llah* (Thank God) I worked the land – olives and wheat – and had enough to feed my family and send my children to school.

Abu Ali's story so far illustrates the life of a small-scale trader in *Jabal 'Amil*.[24] Born in 1911 as a member of a peasant patriclan that is said to be one of the founding families in the village, Abu Ali spent the first few years of his childhood in the Ottoman-ruled province of Syria – which included the confines of present-day Lebanon. The end of the First World War marked the disintegration of the Ottoman Empire. The Syrian provinces were divided up between the French and the British, whereby the territory known today as Lebanon being part of the French mandate. On 31st August 1920, the French established Lebanon as a separate state distinct from the rest of Syria. They expanded the borders of the former "Mount Lebanon region" to include the coastal cities of Beirut, Sidon, Tyre and Tripoli as well the Shi'ite populated areas of the south and the Bekaa plain. This territory, with its sizeable population of Sunni and Shi'ite Muslims, Christians and Druze, was then referred to as "Greater Lebanon" (*Grand Liban*) to distinguish it from the smaller Mount Lebanon region that was mainly populated by Christians and Druze.[25] The creation of Greater Lebanon was essentially the result of French efforts to establish a stronghold in the Middle East and those of their Maronite allies, in particular, who wanted to lead an independent Christian-dominated state under French protection.

The French drew up a constitution in 1932 and ruled Lebanon until 1943, when the country gained independence. The "National Pact" of 1943, an unwritten agreement between Lebanon's powerful Maronite and Sunni families, distributed positions of authority in government according to religious affiliation, based on the 1932 census. Since the Maronites were the largest confessional group by a narrow margin in 1932, it was decided that the President would always be a Maronite, the Prime Minister a Sunni and the president of the parliament a Shi'ite. Thus began the establishment of the multi-confessional make-up of the country in the state's confessional system (*ta'ifiyeh*). Up to the present day, government posts and other key positions are distributed along confessional lines, a system that has permeated all facets of public life, administration, law and education. In his book "The Culture of Sectarianism" (2000), Ussama Makdisi has shown that this confessional system, based on a belief in age-old, primordial confessional identities, was not a "natural" given but had in fact been "produced" by social actors since the middle of the nineteenth century. This occurred at a time when the

Figure 2 & 3: In Zrariye

"traditional" social order was being heavily questioned and during a period of transition in the Ottoman Empire, of growing European political, missionary and ideological influence, and of internal struggles for social and political power.

> The beginning of sectarianism did not imply a reversion. It marked a rupture, a birth of a new culture that singled out religious affiliation as the defining public and political characteristic of a modern subject and citizen. (Makdisi 2000: 174)

Makdisi thus argues that this new modern confessionalist definition of political identity was produced by the interaction and at the interface of colonial (European), imperial (Ottoman), and local (Lebanese) actors (Makdisi 2000: 7). In this sense, European imagination contributed substantially to the invention of imagined confessional communities by creating a coherent typology of separate Maronite, Druze, Greek-Orthodox, Shi'ite and Sunnite communities.

Thus, when I refer in the following to Lebanese Shi'ite, Maronite or Sunnite groups and identities, it should be kept in mind that confessional identities are not static but similar to other identities in a continuous process of being (re-)produced. I use the term confessional as distinct from religious, since a religious identity expresses a person's beliefs and practices, whereas a confessional identity is first and foremost a political one. Here, religious heritage, symbols and habitus are used to legitimise differences that find their institutional expression in the Lebanese political system of confessionalism.

Once the confessional political system had been established, the Shi'ites were kept at arm's length from political power. Historically, they had leanings towards Palestine as, for example, Abu Ali's economic activities show. However, the frontier divisions of 1920 and the creation of Israel in 1948 cut them off from their true capital, Haifa (Picard 1986: 163). Since the Palestine war (1948-1949) and even more so after 1968, their land has become the battlefield for the Israeli-Arab conflict (Picard 1986: 163). In comparison to other parts of Lebanon, the South was one of the last regions of the country to be integrated into the capitalist economy. As early as the seventeenth century, the Patriarch of the Maronite Church of Mount Lebanon entered into communion with Rome, effectively converting the entire Maronite community to Catholicism. The Maronites fell under the protection of the Catholic King of France and the strong ties between France and the Lebanese Maronites were established. In fact, all but the Shi'ites evoked foreign interest, particularly in the nineteenth century. As mentioned earlier, the Maronites had traditional links with France. Russia increased its interest in the Greek Orthodox community. The Druze were the object of British interest, and the Sunnis identified with the Ottoman Empire (Olmert 1987: 190). One aspect of

European patronage was the cultivation of protégés, local merchants with intimate knowledge of the local market who could disseminate European commodities and seek out goods for exchange. These developments concentrated on Beirut and the Mount Lebanon region, which became Lebanon's leading commercial and cultural centres – "Lebanon's window" to the world (Olmert 1987: 190).

The integration of Mount Lebanon and the Beirut area into the European-centred market economy from the end nineteenth century onwards largely excluded Shi'ite South Lebanon. The vast majority of the Shi'ite peasantry lived on meagre plots with poor soil and very limited water resources. Most of the working population were sharecroppers, working in a landlord's fields for an agreed share of the crop (mainly grains and olives). Well-suited to the dry plateaus of southern Lebanon and grown as a cash crop, tobacco was the only crop to have expanded production since the 1930s.

As Abu Ali mentioned in his life story, most of the land in Zrariye was owned by the As'ad kin group, which, along with the Usairans, the Zains, Khalils and others, belonged to the leading landlord families of that time. The leadership of the *zu'ama* (notables, patrons, sing. *za'im*[26]) was – and still is to some extent – the organising principle in the socio-political order throughout Lebanon. Today, *zu'ama* use their wealth, inherited status and contacts to create a clientele that forms the basis for their electoral support. The clientele is bound to the *za'im* by a network of transactional ties, whereby economic and other services are distributed to clients in return for political loyalty. In Zrariye, the Mroué kin group was a client of the *za'im* associated with the As'ad family. Some members of the Mroué patriclan were themselves *zu'ama* in relation to other kin groups or individual members of their own family.

As long as Abu Ali can remember, village politics were largely determined by the conflicts between the Mroué and Fakhry families. Members of the Fakhry family were the first to migrate at the beginning of the century and the first to come back with accumulated capital. As political and social power rested on land ownership, they marked their new position in the village by investing in land, which they later used for market-oriented fruit and vegetable plantations *(basatin)*. Buying land in the village surroundings became possible as the economic power of the landlords weakened and they were forced to sell – mainly to returned migrants who had accumulated the means (Taraf-Najib 1992: 36). I asked Abu Ali if he himself had ever thought of migration:

No, I never really thought of migrating. Once, when I was a young man, I borrowed some money for the passage to *"Ameriki"* to a friend of mine. People were poor at that time and although there was lots of land, it was exclusively owned by one rich family, which is why there was no benefit to the poor peasants. I was a trader and had a little money. I gave it to my friend and everyone said "you'll never get the money back". My friend never returned to the village after he went to Africa. But a year later, he sent me back twice as much money.

Abu Ali made clear that similar to many others he battled for quite some time before taking the final decision to leave the country or not. Many farmers were so poor and the economic pressure for survival so tough that they took the risk of facing the unknown and left. Abu Ali chose to stay. As a trader, his situation seemed a little better than that of the farmers around him. He explained later that his decision not to migrate was influenced by his family circumstances, since he was the eldest son and therefore responsible for his mother's well-being after his father's death. Over the years, however, he realised that migration was the only possibility for people from a poorer background to acquire money and status. He saw the first migrants return with accumulated capital and observed how their money changed the overall social, economic and physical appearance of the village.

According to Halawi, Shi'ite migrants engendered a Shi'ite "bourgeoisie" that was in a position to take over the socio-economic development of towns and villages across South Lebanon and the Bekaa from the state (Halawi 1992: 74). By the late sixties, in fact, the impact of this new Shi'ite wealth had been strongly felt in the South and in the village under study, where most of the public construction has been sponsored by migrants for the last thirty years at least. They had the main roads and village square paved with asphalt. They took control of the water supply, bought generators to sell electricity to individual households and, finally, built the mourning halls and the mosques. Abu Ali explained:

The oldest mosque in Zrariye was built about seventy years ago. It was a common project among the villagers. Everyone, rich and poor, young and old, participated in the construction. Some people had donkeys and used them to transport stones and sand. At that time, there was no money coming in from Africa, which is why everyone had to participate in the construction process. Nowadays it is different, every wealthy migrant builds a mosque with money made in Africa.

There are now six mosques in Zrariye and all of them, except the oldest one, were built as private projects by one or several rich migrants. In fact, migrants, remigrants and family members who profited economically from migration have developed as the "new rich" in the village, bringing fresh cleavages into the social make-up of the village, drawn between economically successful (re-)migrant families and those less prosperous.

Amery and Anderson, who carried out research in a Lebanese village in the Bekaa, found out that remittance income from abroad constitutes almost 50 % of the total annual income of the households surveyed (Amery/Anderson 1995: 52). My qualitative data from Zrariye is substantiating proof of this high number. Zrariye residents have grown firmly dependent on the remittance income from family members living abroad. They receive money or gifts and are thus able to obtain higher social standing. Contributing to the construction of public buildings, building impressive private houses and filling them with imported electronic devices, and driving flashy cars are all forms of raising a migrant's social status and that of their families in the village.

Imm and Abu Ali still live in a small old village house. Despite the fact that their sons migrated to Africa, their success was limited and their businesses characterised by setbacks. Although they now send money regularly to their parents in the village, it is just enough to cover their daily expenses. Both parents talk frequently about their sons' businesses, pray for their success, send tapes and write letters asking about their financial situation. They dream of one day building a new house in the village and often imagine what it would look like. Although impressed by the villas of the "new rich", they picture a small comfortable house for themselves. While talking about the "new rich", Imm and Abu Ali repeatedly referred to Abu Muhammad, the most famous migrant in the village, whose economic success brought him social status and political influence in Zrariye and beyond.

Abu Muhammad is one of the new influential people in the village whose importance is not derived from a prominent position in the "traditional" local patron-client system but from his economic success in migration. In fact, this success turned him into a "new patron", providing him with social and political privileges and a whole network of "new clients". Abu Muhammad comes from a rather poor background and worked as a taxi-driver in Zrariye. When his uncle died in Abidjan in the 1960s and his cousins were very young, his father sent him to Africa to care take of the business. He was one of the first in Abidjan to invest in the manufacturing of plastic goods. He had heard about the Lebanese who produced injection-moulded shoes and sandals in Brazil and brought the idea and the machines to Abidjan. His idea paid off and today he is the owner of a large family enterprise including three plastic factories and several shops. He has now returned to Zrariye, having passed the business on to his three sons. Accompanied by his wife, he still travels at least twice a year to Abidjan to advise his sons and "be close to the family" as he explained.

Abu Muhammad lives with his wife in a spacious villa in Zrariye, which looks very attractive from the outside. However, the real clue to their high standard of living is the interior, with its marble floors and expensive furniture. They brought two Africans back with them from Abidjan, one of whom is employed in the house and one as a gardener and chauffeur. Abu Muhammad has recently been busy supervising the construction of three "palaces", the new holiday homes of his three sons. These gigantic villas are beginning to protrude at the entrance to the village near the main road, close to the "Zrariye" sign, meaning that everyone who passes through the village will be obliged to take note of them. Architectural fantasies know no bounds in South Lebanon, since there were no building regulations to curtail the frantic construction plans developed during and shortly after the war. I saw so-called palaces that reminded me of the White House, the Acropolis and even of castles on the Loire. The climax to one of Abu Muhammad's architectural creations is a royal crown inspired by the trademark for Winston cigarettes. Another one has the word *ALLAH* (GOD) written on top of the roof.

Abu Muhammad's ascent from poor taxi-driver in Zrariye to millionaire and influential personality in South Lebanon is an exceptional case and not the usual migrant reality. Most South Lebanese migrants spend their whole life in West Africa, saving every penny to build a house in Lebanon. This dream frequently remains unfulfilled, as people find themselves without the means to finish the houses they had begun to build. In one particular place, five immense concrete skeletons bear witness to this fact. The plan of four brothers and a sister was to turn the land of their parents into a modern family compound, with each one living in a spacious villa. However, having invested their fortune in the concrete for five buildings, they ran out of money. These six carcasses have remained an embarrassment to their parents ever since and an obvious demonstration that their children were not in a position to complete the houses. Their failure is visibly inscribed in the village landscape, so to speak, and tangible proof that the successful migrant image they and their parents attempted to convey for a long time is no longer valid.

I would argue that these and other examples of domestic architecture provide important data on how the spatial arrangement of the constructed environment reflects and reinforces the nature of social relations in this community. Migrants, for example, inscribe their experience in the surrounding village landscape by creating an environment of extravagant palaces that, in turn, provokes reaction and affects people's social relations. Thus, physical environment and social relations cannot be understood as isolated phenomena but as bounded and mutually constitutive.

In this context, I would argue that migrants not only bring back money, artefacts and newly-acquired social status to the village, but also visions of what a rich migrant's house should look like. These ideas, trajectories and visions are a true global/local mixture of appropriated African, European and Lebanese elements that, once inscribed in the local landscape, write the experience of migration into the physical surroundings. There are interesting similarities between these villas and some of the houses of rich Africans in countries of Lebanese migration. It can be assumed that in planning their own houses back in South Lebanon, Lebanese migrants are partly inspired by "African fantasies in concrete". Large houses in South Lebanon traditionally belonged to the *zu'ama*, the landowners and patrons. Thus, building lavish, at

Figure 4 & 5: Villas of the "new rich"

times even colossal villas gives new rich migrants the opportunity to "perform" their identity and express their new social status and desire for power. Interestingly, returning migrants in the various regions of Lebanon have applied a variety of architectural styles to these houses. Comparing Zrariye and Joun, the two villages I worked in over the last few years, I would argue that houses of returned migrants tell very different migration and local village histories. In Zrariye, for instance, the villas of the new rich tell the migration stories of poor peasants who became rich traders and businessmen in West Africa. In Joun, on the other hand, where it is traditional for a large number of educated people to migrate to Europe, migrants frequently return with new values of modernity or antiquity and, instead of building brash villas, prefer to restore the old houses in the village.

Since migrants in Zrariye build their houses on family land, inconsistencies with neighbouring houses automatically arise, expressing the contrast in the lives of their inhabitants. An urban-style three-storey house in whitewashed concrete surrounded by a white wall will be found juxtaposed to a small peasant house with goats and sheep grazing in the front yard and cows in the adjoining stable. When Abu Ahmad, the owner of the white-washed villa, drives his new Mercedes into the concrete parking space at his house, he sniffs at the stench coming from the stable and curses his "dirty peasant" neighbour, Abu Mahmoud, who has just passed by on a donkey. Both of these Zrariyen villagers have their roots in two village kin groups that belong to the group of small-scale peasants. Whereas the owner of the villa profited from being a member of an old migrant family and his father's investment on his return in large fruit plantations, his neighbour, Abu Mahmoud, remained a small-scale peasant with no access to new income from migration.

It thus emerges that migration changes people's relation to the land, to their dwelling-place and to their constructed environment. Historically, Zrariyens were linked to the land by village life and their work as small-scale peasants, as sharecroppers in the fields of rich landowners or as owners of small plots. Kin groups were associated with distinct neighbourhoods and the land they owned. Social status and political power derived from the land, which to a large extent belonged to the land-owning families who profited economically from the work of the peasants. When people grew prosperous as a result of migration, they began to invest in land, which in turn gave them the necessary influence and social status to become "new" patrons. At the same time, they transformed their relation to the village land. Far from working the land they bought, they turned it into fruit and vegetable plantations and let other people do it for them. Many migrants remained abroad and experienced "their land" merely from a distance. In this process, Zrariye's land gradually developed into happy childhood memory places and nostalgic narratives of the old peasant days. At the same time, migrants have been actively involved in inscribing their own life experiences into the village landscape through private and public buildings, distinguishing themselves from Zrariyens who did not profit from the new money inflow and still depend on the land for subsistence. In the eyes of successful migrant families, working the land has become an intensely "backward", "traditional" activity.

Abu Ali is one of those rarities who still work their wheat and olive fields. Although he receives remittances from his sons in West Africa, he needs more to survive. Thus, Abu Ali, his wife and the children who still live in Zrariye work in the fields, harvesting olives and wheat as they have done all their lives. Abu Ali's life, his security and his identity have always been strongly attached to the land, the hilly countryside around Zrariye. He worked the land and moved progressively through it as a small-scale trader. When he bought a donkey as a young man, he felt partially liberated from the grim work in the landowner's fields. Trade gave him the opportunity to accumulate money and buy his own land. He still rides his donkey to the olive fields. But while the donkey used to be a symbol of workforce and mobility in Abu Ali's youth, it has now become a sign of utter backwardness. Mercedes and BMW have become the icons of mobility and modernity on today's village roads. Not only do the donkey and the flash cars represent the old and the new symbols of mobility, they also express the relation of men in particular to their place of origin. While women primarily relate to their village through their life at home with their children, men's relation to the village is expressed by their movement, by trade and by migration. In this context, Imm Ali's narrative of Zrariye focusses chiefly on her life at home and the changes she witnessed over time.

Imm Ali is in her 70s. She was born, raised, educated and married in the village. She gave birth to nine and educated them. Her relation to her dwelling-place is mediated through her memories, her age, her class and her gender:

I married Abu Ali at the age of sixteen.
The first child was a girl, Fatima, then Zaynab was born and the third was a boy, Ali, thank God (*al-hamdu li-llah*). When I was pregnant with the fourth child, I was carrying a box of tomatoes once. I wanted to make *sharab* (tomato puree). I fell and lost the baby although I was seven months pregnant. During the next pregnancy I noticed blood. People told me to lie down but I couldn't because I had to bake bread, I had to wash, I had to cook and I had to feed the animals. After a while, I felt a movement in my stomach. "*Al-hamdu li-llah*, it was alive". The second boy, Muhammad, was born healthy.
In the end, *al-hamdu li-llah*, I had five boys and four girls. I breast-fed them all. It was not like nowadays. They say "*yallah* (let's go) bring her milk", "bring her *NIDO*" (milk powder from Nestlé). "*Haram* (pity for her) leave the mother alone." "She will get tired and thin from breast-feeding." I breast-fed all my children and they were healthy. I

rarely went to the doctor with them. I don't know what's happening today. Young people run to the doctor all the time. They have plenty of food but they are ill. We used to be healthier. We cooked *mjaddara* (a lentil dish), *ful* (a beans dish), *hommos* (chickpeas) and *burghul* (smashed wheat). Nowadays, people live on meat, meat and meat again with rice and get ill all the same. We used to get milk from the cow and I made yoghurt, butter and cheese. We had a cow, chickens and a goat and we had olives and olive oil.

I baked the daily bread. It was not like now when you go to the *dukkaneh* (small shop) every day and buy bread. We only bought sugar, some matches and tea from the shop. We lived from what we had. Every woman baked the daily bread for the family. There was no running water. We had to walk for over an hour to the *'ain* (well). We didn't have a gas-cooker at home. We had to walk far to fetch the fire-wood. Ah, life was difficult but it was also sweet.

Neighbours used to come together every morning and evening. We talked and told each other stories. We didn't offer coffee or black tea. No, we made herbal tea from herbs that we collected in the countryside. It was very pleasant. Everyone was poor but no one was alone. Nowadays, we hardly see each other. Everyone is out for themselves. People are very selfish. Women worked a lot, unlike today where young women only want to sit, drink coffee and have a Sri-Lankan maid. We had to fetch the daily water, bake bread, cook, collect fire-wood and take care of the animals. We went to the fields to grow wheat and picked the olives. We had small gardens and grew all sorts of vegetables. We lived on the land. Now, it's "plastic generation" (*jil al-naylon*). We worked hard and it was not easy to raise our children. Although life isn't easier nowadays.

Imm Ali's relation to her village was marked by her daily work-load, which included baking bread, fetching water from the well, preparing food for the winter, cooking, and looking after the children. Her identity as a village woman is strongly linked to these female activities, which in her eyes were difficult and tiring but proved women's strength and sense of responsibility. Women carried out some of these activities together, such as fetching water, for example, or spending time at the river washing clothes. Here they exchanged daily news and village gossip, turning the place temporarily into an exclusively female space through their practices and interaction. At certain times, women worked with their husbands and children in the fields, for instance harvesting olives. These examples show that women's relation to their village was also actively constructed by their manifold tasks. Imm Ali describes the tremendous changes in labour relations over the years, which in turn changed women's relation to their dwelling-place.

Most of the families in Zrariye and especially those with "successful migrant connections" have turned away completely from subsistence production and, instead, buy everything they need for their daily consumption. They might still own olive and wheat fields but they prefer to employ people to work in them or rent the land to sharecroppers. Women in these families no longer have to work in the fields. Families with limited remittance resources still cultivate the land for their own use, mostly olives and wheat, and treat their remittances as an additional source of income. Thus, the value of women's economic activity and production "outside the house" in the village fields has turned into consumption values, leisure and work inside the house. The more prosperous a family, the more time women have for "leisure". This has become an important marker of women's status in successful migrant families.

The desired state is one of leisure, where one can maintain white skin and soft hands as city women do. Women following this line, moreover, should have time for more feminine pursuits like interior decorating, sewing and more elaborate cooking. [...] There is no doubt that leisure has a high value among women who have never known it, and to them seclusion does have desirable connotations of privilege, urbanity and class distinction. (Myntti 1978: 15-16)

In fact, "leisure" and "consumption" have become extremely desirable attainments in the lives of many women in translocal Lebanese contexts. Imm Ali describes the move to "leisure" and "consumption" as follows:

In the past, we spent 2000 LL. [in 1995 equivalent to two German marks] to get married. Today, a wife wants a television set, a radio, a tape recorder and a video recorder. She wants dresses, a big car and everything for her house. Many women no longer want to cook. They only want to eat in restaurants. Before, we used to walk six hours to reach a place and another six hours back. Today, people can't even walk a quarter of an hour, they have to go by car for a 100 meters. A wife needs a car, a chauffeur and a Sri-Lankan maid. The woman only wants to sit around, while the Sri-Lankan has to do everything.

Imm Ali refers to the fact that the *mahr* (dowry) has increased dramatically and that more and more assets are required as a precondition for marriage. She declares that young women today have no desire to carry out household tasks and that, on the contrary, their sole aim is "to do nothing". Imm Ali also mentions the growing number of Sri Lankan housekeepers in the village. Having a house-maid has become an important symbol to express a "successful" migrant life-style and is a sign of social status.

Imm Ali's narrative clearly indicates the change that occurred over time in women's relation to their dwelling place. In Imm Ali's youth, a woman's place was not only in the house but in the village fields, where she worked alone or with her husband. In today's world, women have the opportunity of moving around the translocal village between Zrariye and Abidjan, and frequently do so. In this translocal space, however, they are often more confined to activities in the house and to a female neighbourhood.

Moving through Places

> At daybreak we come down to the harbor
> Where ships have spread sails for departure.
> And we cry, "O beloved sea,
> As near as the eyelids of our eyes,
> We are eager for the voyage".
> (Yusuf al-Khal, cit. in Warnock Fernea/Fernea 1997: 3)

Migration is an option for young people from Zrariye as soon as they become conscious of the global dimensions of their family, their village and their society. It becomes even more salient when they observe the perennial flow of migrants visiting the village. Significantly, cases of successful migrants serve as an outstanding example for the village youth. West Africa still has the image of being the place with potential, where it is possible to become prosperous and powerful, and be someone. Massey et al. describe communities where "migration becomes deeply ingrained into the repertoire of people's behaviors and values as a culture of migration" (Massey et al. 1993: 452-453). It could in fact be argued that having been profoundly influenced by this, Zrariyen village life and, indeed, Lebanese society as a whole has become an expression of the "culture of migration".

In an attempt to understand the significance of migrational development, I will focus on the historical background of Lebanese migration to West Africa, using the case of Leila's family as an example.[27]

My grandfather was born in 1885 in Zrariye, South Lebanon. In 1907, he wanted to follow his brother to America and took the boat from Beirut to Marseille where he had to undergo a medical check-up on arrival. They found out that he was suffering from trachoma eye disease so he didn't get a health certificate. Since he didn't want to return to Lebanon, he decided to take a ship to Dakar (Senegal) because he knew of someone who had gone there. That's how my grandfather, one of the first from Zrariye, came to West Africa.

This is how Leila, a 45-year-old Lebanese woman, who was born in Dakar (Senegal), grew up in Lebanon and married in Abidjan (Côte d'Ivoire), began the story of her family dating back to her grandfather's migration to Africa.

Leila's grandfather, Z. Fakhry, was one of approximately 600,000 people who emigrated from the Ottoman-ruled province of Syria between 1860 and 1914 (Bierwirth 1994: 44). Although some of these emigrants remained abroad, a large number returned to their country of origin (Hashimoto 1992: 66). Thus the simple dichotomy of countries into those "exporting" and those "receiving" population, as applied by international migration scholars for decades, does not present an adequate picture of the complexity of Lebanon's historical migration flows. Migration research has all too often focused exclusively on the causes of migration, with very little attempt being made to assess the consequences of emigration and its impact on Lebanese society for any one specific period. This stems from the false notion that migrants, particularly Lebanese migrants, are no longer members of the homeland and society they leave behind, the assumption being that a butterfly does not revert to the state of a caterpillar (Chia cit. in Hashimoto 1992: 65).

Leila's grandfather returned to Lebanon in 1918 and got married. A few years later, he returned with his wife to Dakar where their five children were born. One of them was Leila's mother, who married a migrant in Dakar and gave birth to Leila in 1951. Four years later, Leila's father made the decision to remigrate.

I came to Lebanon at the age of five. We lived in Zrariye where I also went to school. I married at twenty-three and went back to Africa. Not to Dakar where I was born, but to Abidjan where my husband lived and where we have been living ever since.

Leila's case exemplifies that of many Lebanese families, whose diverse mobility does not fall easily into the simple category of one-way migration flow. Likewise, Leila's family history demonstrates that migration does not of necessity imply a permanent rupture from the start or the abandonment of old cultural patterns. On the contrary, it can be stated that the movement between worlds and the creation of social migrant networks have been in progress since the early days of migration at the end of the nineteenth century.

In the period prior to the First World War, most Lebanese migrants were Christians from "Mount Lebanon". The majority were either peasants or people from low socio-economic groups, "pushed" into migration by economic, political and demographic pressure (Bierwirth 1994; Issawi 1992; Khalaf 1987b).

By 1900, the population of Mount Lebanon was estimated to have reached 400,000 or an average population density of 200 per square mile (Hooglund 1987: 5). Most of the people lived in villages and worked in agriculture, where the growing scarcity of land became a real threat. Dividing a family farm between several children had the effect of reducing inherited land to mere subsistence plots. To avoid the impoverishment of their children, many families began to encourage their young sons to seek their fortunes outside the village, in Beirut or in the "New World". This demise was not brought on by land scarcity alone but also by a serious decline in the silk industry, the most important area of local production. The impact on the economy of the mountain was crucial and accelerated rural emigration. Entire families and village communities were dependent on silk as the primary source of livelihood. When the Suez Canal opened in 1869, Japanese and

Chinese silk was brought to Europe cheaply and led to the collapse of the price for raw silk (Khalaf 1987b: 26). Despite the depression and rising emigration that accompanied this decline, Mount Lebanon made considerable economic progress and was integrated in the world economy through trade, transport, communication, and finance. Foreign trade favoured Christian Lebanese disproportionately. Acting as agents for European traders, a new mercantile, almost entirely Christian middle class began to emerge in Beirut.

The first migrants who left Lebanon at the end of the nineteenth century were Christians who had been exposed to Western education and were thus more aware of the opportunities abroad at the time. They were soon followed by people from other confessions, such as the Druze and Sunni and Shi'ite Muslims. While peasants and members of the poorer strata left Lebanon primarily for economic reasons, the intellectuals[28] and other educated groups sought liberation from the repressive political atmosphere under the Ottoman rulers, who had subjected them to all kinds of censure, oppression and even persecution (Khalaf 1987b: 27).

It can be said that political conflict was the essential stimulus to emigrate from the Syrian province of the Ottoman Empire, under whose rulers the Shi'ite population of southern Lebanon and the Bekaa valley had suffered in particular. Unlike the Maronites, the Greek Orthodox and even the Druze, who were protected by foreign powers, they had no external champions and were subjected to persecution by the Sunni Ottomans (Bierwirth 1994: 57). Muslims were increasingly forced to use the Turkish language, while Christians were allowed to maintain their own schools, often sponsored by European and American missions (Bierwirth 1994: 58). Likewise, Christians from Mount Lebanon were exempted from military service, while Muslims faced Ottoman conscription. Thus, many young men took to migration rather than be forced to serve in the Ottoman army.

Christian communities began to achieve political dominance in the twentieth century, at first under French Mandate (1920-43) and subsequently in the National Pact regime, and introduced economic disparities that continued to grow along confessional and regional lines. As Christians, and particularly Maronites, broadened their control of the Lebanese State, more and more official development projects and funds were directed towards the Christian-dominated areas of Beirut and Mount Lebanon. Simultaneously, rising taxes were burdening the peripheral provinces with largely Muslim populations (Bierwirth 1994: 69). Educational policies show evidence of yet another aspect of regional imbalance. Bierwirth states that only 13 out of 650 schools were located in Muslim or Druze areas under French Mandate (Bierwirth 1994: 69). The outcome of such an imbalance is the tremendous disparity in income distribution and other benefits of progress along confessional lines. This growing socio-economic discrepancy became a prominent factor in the drift towards migration. Realizing that they had only limited opportunities in their homeland, many Shi'ite peasants chose to migrate and try their luck abroad. The succession of wars that beset Lebanon between 1975 and 1991 accelerated emigration during that 16-year period. It has been estimated that approximately 990,000 Lebanese left their country at that time (Labaki 1992: 610).

In conclusion, having identified some of the primary reasons that led to Lebanese migration, I do not want to overlook or minimize the role of seemingly small, private tragedies or fortuitous circumstances that may have finally triggered people into emigration. As Khalaf stresses, the cause of (early) emigration was often no more significant than the death of a farmer's horse, a quarrel between a single-minded son and a stubborn parent (1987b: 27); or in other cases, an interest in exploring the world and in adventure. This is well illustrated in Nadra Filfili's autobiography, where he documents his reasons for leaving Lebanon (Filfili 1973).

The Lebanese in West Africa

Why did the southern Lebanese Shi'ites migrate to West Africa, when most other Lebanese groups were travelling to the "New World", to North and South America, and even to Australia? The story of Leila's grandfather and his migration to Senegal presents us with an answer. Unable to fulfil the strict health requirements for immigration to the United States introduced after the First World War, many southern Lebanese migrants were forced to abandon their dream of "America". The onward passage for west-bound Lebanese migration went through Marseille, where many poor Lebanese found themselves with insufficient funds to cross the Atlantic. Fares to West Africa, on the other hand, were comparatively cheap. Eager to secure business there, French shipping lines and their trade agents for West Africa gave glowing reports of the situation (Winder 1961: 298). It has also been suggested that the first immigrants to West Africa may well have been put on board a ship by unscrupulous Marseille shipping agents, only learning that they were heading for St. Louis or Dakar and not New York or Sao Paulo after the ship had weighed anchor (Winder 1961: 297). Be that as it may, for most migrants anything was preferable to returning unsuccessfully to their homeland. Hanna states:

Almost all these emigrants were members of large, poor families. Each in raising money for his voyage had exhausted all the family's savings, had sold personal belongings, or borrowed money. All the family sacrificed in the hope that the one member emigrating would be able to send remittances. An emigrant contemplating return from Marseille had to think of all those facts and the disillusionment and disappointment he would cause to all his family. They decided West-Africa was easier to face than their hungry families and disgrace to their countries. (Hanna 1958a: 393)

It is very likely that the first Lebanese arrived in Senegal in the 1860s (Cruise O'Brien 1975: 98), at which time Dakar was a transit port for liners connecting France to South America (Boumedouha 1992: 550). Leila's husband recounted his ancestor's experience in this context:

> My grandfather arrived in Africa in 1910. His plan was to emigrate to South America. He got ill on the way and had to leave the ship in Dakar. He postponed the passage to South America and actually never took it up again!

Several authors argue that it was in the interest of France, the Mandate power in Lebanon and colonial ruler in West Africa, to bring the Lebanese to Africa where they were needed as middlemen for the colonial economy (Kojok 1993; Boumedouha 1992: 550). The Lebanese were regarded as potential intermediaries who could act as go-betweens to foster business between the major European companies operating on the coast and African farmers inland. Beginning in 1902, when the governor general of the AOF *(L'Afrique Occidentale Française)* Roume, sought prospective emigrants through the French Embassy in Beirut, the colonial administration officially supported the settlement of Lebanese people in its West African colonies (Boumedouha 1992: 550).

As poor uneducated peasants from South Lebanon, the newcomers began their lives in West Africa practically penniless. They had little or no capital, skills or access to credit and had neither the language nor the qualification to find wage employment. Thus, these early migrants began dealing in very small imported items. They were known as "coral men" by the local people in Senegal and Sierra Leone, which reveals the line of business they initially undertook at the end of the nineteenth and beginning of the twentieth century.

> In those early years one would find them in the cities, round the corners of the trade "stream-line" streets, sitting on small boxes in front of boxes a little larger on which they displayed imitation coral beads and other cheap articles. (Hanna 1958b: 34)

By paying little or no rent for shops, working hard as hawkers and peddlers, making a small profit and living cheaply, the early Lebanese traders were able to survive and expand. Up until the First World War, many Lebanese avoided the hinterland,[29] but when news of potential business became known and transport facilities improved, many of them gave up their existence as street vendors and traders on the small pavement locations of the coastal cities and moved inland. As the colonial economy expanded, large colonial companies exporting groundnuts from Senegal and later coffee and cocoa from Côte d'Ivoire, for example, had to rely on middlemen to buy the products directly from the peasants in the fields and transport them to a provincial trading centre (Cruise O'Brien 1975: 99). The Lebanese, who were ideal for this function, thus found a lucrative niche in the colonial economy. They also took over the trading posts of the many French small-scale traders who had left for military service in the First World War. Isolation, poor living conditions and the required mobility of the inland trader were as unattractive to French expatriates as were its meagre profits. Pointedly, it has been argued that the Lebanese quickly gained several advantages over European and African small-scale traders. It has also been suggested that the Lebanese had less expenses than European and African traders, since running family businesses required lower overhead costs than those that had to hire employees. When the single Lebanese male trader was joined by his wife and children, the business developed along a family employment structure that involved little expenditure for local labour.[30] While keeping the running and employment costs down, they were willing to accept very low profits initially in order to enlarge their clientele. Notably, they learnt West African languages, were prepared to bargain with African customers and, more equipped to judge risks, gave credit more readily (van der Laan 1975: 222). The embeddedness of economic activities in African society and their accompanying financial obligations towards relatives left Africans at a significant disadvantage compared to the Lebanese. African traders were thus confronted with the following predicament:

The dilemma faced by traders arises out of their moral obligations to share proceeds with kinfolk and neighbours, on the one hand, and the necessity to make profits and accumulate trading capital, on the other. (Evers/Schrader 1994: 5)

As strangers, the Lebanese were in a position to solve the "trader's dilemma". By leading a separate life from the host society, they were not integrated in the moral economy and thus had no difficulty in claiming debts and accumulating capital.[31] Evers states that trade requires solidarity among the traders and social/cultural distance from the customers (1990: 19). This mutual support among Lebanese traders has been mentioned in various sources. Firstly, the Lebanese made use of their community networks to spread information relevant to their businesses and helped out the needier in their group with credit (Cruise O'Brien 1975: 111). The wealthier Lebanese relied and continue to rely on smaller scale members of the migrant community to run their businesses. Consequently, they prefer to sell their goods to fellow Lebanese retailers and to buy products from them rather than deal with Africans. Sponsoring is another practice that ensures mutual support. Newcomers start by working in shops owned by relatives for a certain period of time and when they set up their own businesses, they, in turn, usually help out other newcomers with credit. This type of sponsoring contributed strongly to the growth of the Lebanese community.

From the very beginning of migration, as we have seen, the Lebanese were primarily engaged in trade. In West Africa they work predominantly in trade-related fields to this day, which is why they were called the trade diaspora, as were the Chinese in Southeast Asia and the Indians in East Africa (Curtin 1984). Robin Cohen has also referred to these groups as "auxiliary diasporas", since they profited from colonial expansion but were composed of ethnically different camp-followers of military conquests or minorities, permitted or encouraged by the colonial regime (Cohen 1997: 84). They were known by others as "middlemen" in colonial times since they conducted trade between the colonisers and Africans. However, as van der Laan has stated, this term can be misleading. Taking the example of the rice and kola trade, in which the Lebanese were heavily implicated, he points out that buyers and sellers were African and that no French or English colonisers were involved (van der Laan 1975: 222).

The discussion on trade and middlemen minorities has been the subject of sociological and anthropological interest for a long time and goes back to the works of Max Weber on "pariah capitalism". Indeed, extensive literature has been devoted to the study of these minorities in various societies.[32] Edna Bonacich (1973) argues that "middlemen minorities" have their origin in "sojourning", indicating that their members had not originally planned to settle permanently in the host countries.[33] This had a number of important consequences. Motivated by their desire to eventually return home, sojourners were more willing to suffer short-term deprivation, to save their income and thus accumulate capital. They also chose specific occupations that did not tie them to the host country for long periods. Trade was an ideal solution. Conspicuously, in the hope of a future return to Lebanon, sojourners were interested in keeping their ethnic traditions alive, such as endogamy and the establishment of separate Lebanese schools for their children.

As early as 1908, Simmel drew attention to the fact that in many societies, trade was carried out by "strangers". He and subsequent scholars emphasized that these trading minorities are mostly migrants whose integration into the host society is prevented by active discrimination. In fact, the vulnerability of these groups has been described as their most salient feature: pogroms, expulsion, expropriation and even genocide are frequent events or threats.[34] Hence, the possible reaction to hostility from other groups is to organise the community in the "protective cocoon of an ethnic enclave" (van der Berghe 1975: 199). Locality, ethnic ties and a widespread kinship network are more often than not the basis of this protective community organisation. Politically they are described as disfranchised and are excluded from playing a significant role in host societies. Despite being considered wealthy, they cannot easily convert this asset into direct power, although many have developed strategies to influence the political sphere in their host countries from "behind the scenes".

The Lebanese in Côte d'Ivoire

Although the first Lebanese immigrants arrived in West Africa as early as the 1870s and had established significant migrant communities in Senegal and Guinea by the 1900s, an interest in settling in Côte d'Ivoire did not emerge until much later. Although only three Lebanese were registered there in 1921, the figure gradually increased to 183 in 1929, and 322 in 1935 (Kojok 1993: 47-50).

The rapid expansion of its export economy during the 1920s sparked the real beginning of Lebanese migration to Côte d'Ivoire. The period from the mid-1920s until the Second World War was described as the first phase of Lebanese immigration (Kojok 1993: 3; Bierwirth 1994: 138). It mostly included young men who had recently arrived in West Africa in search of new opportunities. Commercial businesses were beginning to establish trade centres at posts in the interior. They needed men to work as intermediaries between large colonial companies and the African producers and consumers. The first wave of immigrants grasped this opportunity to become lower-level commercial intermediaries, small-scale retailers, produce buyers or transporters. Over time, they became involved in larger-scale retail and wholesale and managed to displace many of the big European traders during the Great Depression. The success of the first generation of migrants and the demand for labour as a result of the economic boom after the Second World War as well as during the first two decades after independence led to an increase in the number of Lebanese immigrants to Côte d'Ivoire between 1945 and 1960. By 1953, their numbers had risen to over 2,000 (Bigo 1992: 513). This second phase of immigration was now composed first and foremost of men and women[35] with kinship links to the first migrants.

The high influx of Lebanese to Côte d'Ivoire around the time of Independence not only originated in Lebanon itself but was also a result of the growing number of Lebanese arriving from other West African countries to open their own trading counters. Kojok argues that the sons of first-generation Lebanese in Senegal often left for Côte d'Ivoire in search of new openings and challenges, at a safe distance from the strict eye of their fathers (1993). The networks created were not restricted to one particular host country but extended to several countries in West Africa. In recounting the history of her family's migration, Leila spoke of her uncle, L. Fakhry, who was born and brought up in Senegal. He migrated from Dakar to Abidjan during the 1950s and built up one of the largest import-export companies in Côte d'Ivoire.

My uncle always had problems with his father. He wanted to work independently and sought adventure. That's why he decided to leave Dakar and take a chance in Abidjan. He became very successful.

Contrary to other West African countries such as Senegal, which pursued a strategy of economic nationalisation after Independence (Cruise O'Brien 1975; Boumedouha 1992), the reassuring stance and predominantly liberal ideology of the Côte d'Ivoire regime encouraged Lebanese business activities (Bigo 1992: 514). By 1965, there were circa 7,000 Lebanese people in Côte d'Ivoire. Ten years later, the number had risen to about 15,000 (Bigo 1992: 514).

The confessional proportions of the Lebanese community in Côte d'Ivoire changed dramatically during the second phase of migration. Whereas Christians were well represented in the first phase, the vast majority of newcomers after the Second World War were Shi'ite Muslims following in the footsteps of their predecessors. This can be partly explained by the political and economic developments in Lebanon itself. The Lebanese government had devoted a large share of its resources to the Christian-dominated parts of the country, leaving the Muslim Shi'ite areas severely neglected. Meanwhile, the booming economy of post-war Côte d'Ivoire promised newcomers golden opportunities, made accessible through the assistance of earlier migrants, who often provided them with a helping hand on arrival. It has been observed that specific kin groups from certain villages and towns in Lebanon tended to cluster in specific locations abroad. Accordingly, most of the Lebanese in Dakar (Senegal) come from Tyre, Zrariye and Nabatiye (South Lebanon). The migrants in Accra (Ghana), on the other hand, come from Tripoli (North Lebanon), whereas those in Kano (Nigeria) have their origins in the southern Lebanese village of Jouayya. The first migrants in Calabar and Lagos were mainly from Mizyara in North Lebanon, while migrants from Haris in South Lebanon departed for Sierra Leone (Falola 1992: 121; Taan 1988: 154; Khuri 1965: 385).

Most of the Lebanese in Côte d'Ivoire come from a very small region in South Lebanon. There are patrilineal kin groups, e.g., extended families or, as expressed in Arabic, people from the same "house" *(bait)*, e.g., from the same patriclan, such as the Mroué, Fakhry and Zorkot from Zrariye and the Attié and Dahlalah from Qana. Historically, these patriclans tended to cluster in a particular area of Côte d'Ivoire. The Fakhry went to Grand Bassam, the Ezzedine to Gagnoa and so forth. Recently, however, with the growth of Abidjan and the arrival of many new migrants, these regional concentrations in Côte d'Ivoire have become less significant.

Since the beginning of the Lebanese wars in 1975, the movement of Lebanese to Côte d'Ivoire has increased dramatically. While Senegal closed its borders to Lebanese war refugees, entry formalities were kept to a minimum in Côte d'Ivoire. This made it easy for war-torn Lebanese to flee their country and follow in the footsteps of earlier migrants to Côte d'Ivoire, which had become the symbol of success, wealth and peace for many southern Lebanese Shi'ites.

Bigo estimates the number of Lebanese in 1985/86 as being up to about 80,000 and Bierwirth mentions the figure of 90,000 (Bigo 1992: 515; Bierwirth 1994: 9). Ascertaining the exact size of the Lebanese population in Côte d'Ivoire is indeed extremely difficult (Bierwirth 1994: 3; Bigo 1992: 515). Estimates vary from 25,000 to as many as 300,000. The fact that no comprehensive national census has been carried out in almost two decades explains this discrepancy. Current assumptions often have more to do with hidden agendas than with a lack of statistical data (Bierwirth 1994: 3). Those who feel threatened by Lebanese economic influence tend to grossly exaggerate the figures, while the Lebanese themselves try to minimise them. Despite their dominant economic position in Côte d'Ivoire, the Lebanese make up only a small percentage of the national population.

During my fieldwork period in Lebanon in 1995/1996, migration to Abidjan continued to be a vital factor in the future plans of young men and women. With the aid of relatives and economic assistance from their parents, numerous young men leave the village of Zrariye each year, despite a deterioration of the job prospects in Abidjan and a somewhat more promising future in post-war Lebanon. In the face of growing hostility towards the Lebanese in Côte d'Ivoire, those who have lived there for a long time tend to have a split mind on the issue. On the one hand, they are under a moral obligation to help newly-arrived relatives fresh from Lebanon but, on the other hand, must try to counter the risk of being rejected in Côte d'Ivoire should their community be seen as increasing.

The first Lebanese migrants in Côte d'Ivoire generally made their living as petty merchants, traders and small shopkeepers. However, business activities have meanwhile diversified and socio-economic rifts within the community have widened. The retail business remains an important activity for the Lebanese in present-day Côte d'Ivoire, where there is bound to be a Lebanese shopkeeper in almost every town and sizeable village. Whereas shops in smaller places offer a wide range of goods, many small and medium-sized Lebanese retailers in the towns specialise in a particular branch, such as textiles, plastics, household articles, spare parts for cars and so forth. Some retailers have moved exclusively into wholesale. Many others keep sufficiently large stocks to be able to sell *en demi-gros* to African traders, who then resell in smaller bulks to market dealers.

Over the last twenty years, Lebanese entrepreneurs began to invest the capital they accumulated from commercial enterprises and move into new fields such as manufacturing. Wealthy Lebanese invested in various industries that include building material, textiles, soap, perfumery, beauty care products and plastics. Produced in Lebanese factories, these consumer goods bear the label "made in Côte d'Ivoire" and are primarily intended for the domestic market, with some being exported to other West African countries. Further Lebanese investments found their way into services such as bakeries, fast-food *(falafel and shawarma)* shops, supermarkets, restaurants, pharmacies, hotels, video shops, petrol stations, and property and insurance companies.

It is striking that a certain branch is often dominated by people who originally come from the same village. Lebanese from the village of Qana dominate the textile business in Abidjan, for example, while Zrariyens run the plastic industry. They produce plastic commodities of all types and colours ranging from polyethylene bags, to plastic cups and plates. They normally specialise in injection-moulded plastic shoes, slippers and sandals.[36] Some of the Zrariyens produce the shoes, owning anything from one or more machines to large modern industries with fifty machines, while others from the same village sell them in small shops mainly located in market areas throughout the city. On the lower end of the scale, businesses are small family enterprises where the husband runs the factory and the wife or son takes care of the shop. One particular street in the market district of Adjamé in Abidjan abounds with plastic shoe shops, all of which present the entire spectrum of plastic shoe models, bearing imaginative brand names such as "Fayrouz", "Madonna", "Maradona", "Etoile", "World Cup 96", "Jaguar" or "Romario". As most of the shopowners originally come from Zrariye, the street is popularly known as "Rue Zrariye". On a more advanced level, rich entrepreneurial families often own several factories and employ large numbers of African workers.

The fact that a range of individual commercial branches are dominated by people from one village or from the same extended families must be seen in the context of kin sponsorship. As mentioned earlier, kinship ties are the key factor in directing Lebanese migration to West Africa. Relatives lend assistance with visas, entry formalities, plane tickets and usually a place to stay, occasionally providing employment for a year or more. Evidence of this can be seen in the plastic factories and shops of Zrariye migrants, where fresh arrivals learn the business from scratch. At first, they are entrusted with menial tasks such as handing goods to customers, moving commodities from one end of the shop to the other and keeping an eye on potential thieves. Working conditions in the factories are less appealing, due to high temperatures, exhaust fumes and night shifts.[37] By saving their money, new arrivals can eventually set up a business of their own, e.g., open a small retail shop or buy their first machine and start producing their own plastic goods. Once again, they can rely on the family or friends for merchandise on credit. This kind of sponsorship through established relations not only serves to attract immigration but guarantees the success of both the newcomers and the entire Lebanese community. However, sponsorship is not always an entirely felicitous situation (Bierwirth 1994: 172). A sponsor would occasionally try to prolong the tutelage period and continue to benefit from the cheap labour provided by the new arrival. By the same token, if a newcomer sets up his own business, he automatically becomes a potential rival of his former sponsor. In fact, the last few years have been marked by severe competition among people involved in plastics, whereby the dramatic growth in the community since the beginning of the Lebanese war is a major contributing factor. In addition, numerous Lebanese from other West African countries have arrived in Abidjan, having failed to set up their plastic industries elsewhere.[38]

A 28-year-old second-generation Lebanese who runs a plastic shoe factory with his father told me:

Working in this business used to be an easy affair. Sales were high and competition minimal. Nowadays, this kind of business has become more difficult. Ten or fifteen years ago when my father started with plastics, one type of shoe remained popular for a year or even longer. Now we constantly have to invent something new, new colours and new models. This shoe with neon sparkles, for example, is the latest hit in Abidjan! The problem is that as soon as a particular shoe runs well, it will be copied fast by someone else.

Larger firms often have a small workshop located beside their factories, where they employ toolmakers specialised in producing new moulds and altering older ones. In the past, these moulds had to be imported from Italy or France, an expensive and precarious investment, especially if the shoe did not sell well.

Today, the majority of plastic factories are found in Yopogon, around 20 kilometres north of Abidjan, where the government opened an industrial site in the 1980s. Many Lebanese took advantage of cheap grants and the valuable opportunity of establishing or rebuilding their factories there. A few families built their homes next to them. Others, however, prefer to commute between home and work. This contrasts with quite a few Lebanese small-scale retailers who tend to live close to their shops, if not in the same building, a phenomenon that was particularly prevalent during the colonial period when almost all Lebanese were traders and owned small shops in the business districts of many of the towns.

The development and subsequent division of cities into industrial and residential areas, into "poor" and "rich" neighbourhoods, and the arrival of countless new migrants have altered settlement schemes. People who own shops in the Adjamé market area, for instance, prefer to live nearby. With the growth of Abidjan and the development of new market locations, many Lebanese, including newcomers, moved into these districts to open up new shops. Marcory is a typical new residential area that has gradually been taken over by the Lebanese, so that both Africans and Lebanese refer to it today as "Little Beirut". Over the past twenty years, Lebanese businesses in the service sector have multiplied and prospered throughout the city: Arab bakeries, patisseries, specialised grocers, butchers, restaurants, coffee shops and Lebanese-owned Western-style supermarkets. Apart from a vast range of imported consumer goods, an extra shelf displays special products from Lebanon. Lebanese photographers, hairdressers and beauty salons as well as clothes and furniture shops are some of the services provided. Elegant fashion and furniture boutiques tend to be owned by women whose husbands are prosperous businessmen and have provided their wives with the necessary resources. Medical and dental problems are taken care of by Lebanese physicians who own three clinics in Abidjan. Many of the buildings along Marcory's main road and elsewhere in the city are Lebanese-owned. Bierwirth suggests that they probably own more than 50 % of the modern buildings in Abidjan today (Bierwirth 1994: 31).

These empirical descriptions of Lebanese locations in Abidjan's urban space show that the Lebanese in Côte d'Ivoire have partially appropriated African landscapes and inscribed their experiences into it. By giving new names to these places, such as "Little Beirut" to an Abidjan suburb or "Rue Zrariye" to a market road, they mark their presence in the city and thus to some extent Lebanese Abidjan's urban landscape. Similarly, they have africanised Zrariye's local space, for example, by building their own personal villas in an African "new rich" urban style. As people constantly move between these places, they imagine them as close to each other and narrate them as such. This is evident in the following expression used by various translocal Zrariyens: "Abidjan is like Zrariye and seems much closer to Zrariye than Beirut." Because their social networks are interwoven between the two places, people imagine Abidjan to be very close to Zrariye. Simultaneously, they inscribe this social proximity in their Lebanese and African surroundings, which in turn influences their sense of spatial and social closeness. The argument that people and their spatial environment are not separate from each other but in fact mutually constitutive is thus underlined (cf. Massey 1994: 264; Low/Lawrence-Zúniga 2003: 13). In the following chapter, I focus on the question of how people's daily lives are linked in practice between Zrariye and Abidjan. I will argue that not only people are on the move, but with them and independent of them, goods, messages, social and religious events, and organisations and institutions are also in motion.

4. The Translocal Village in Practice

> Where is Lagos? When are they coming home?
> MEA (Middle Eastern Airlines) has the connection.
>
> The wedding was in Jeddah. I was in Paris.
> MEA (Middle Eastern Airlines) has the connection.[1]

Moving People

The vast majority of early migrants who left South Lebanon and moved to unknown faraway countries at the end of the nineteenth century were young single men.[2] They stayed abroad for many years, in many cases never to return. Most of the literature available on the subject has treated migration as a single movement of direct migrants at one particular time. Contrary to models presenting the flow of migration as one-dimensional, my experience of Lebanese migration to West Africa was of a complex multi-layered process, where different actors make simultaneous decisions to migrate and re-migrate, moving back and forth between the worlds.

The men and women who set out on journeys from Zrariye are young and old, single and married, divorced and widowed, and educated and illiterate. For many of these people, migration is no longer a first, but a second, third or even fourth move. Some work in West Africa for several years and return to Lebanon with the intention of staying at home. When businesses set up in Lebanon turn out not to be as successful as planned, people often return to Africa, this time perhaps to a different country in the region. Others follow migrant networks in another direction and try to get into the USA or Europe. These young single men are not alone in being flexible enough to move to new countries or migrate from one West African country to the next. If forced by economic circumstances, nuclear families will also make this move. In this case, the wife and children usually return to the village first, while the husband attempts to set up a business in a new place and rent a house. Family relations and networks are a vital element of support when it comes to settling down in a new country. The aims and interests of migrants and travellers, whether men, women or children, differ greatly. The following cases typify the stories of migration and help to portray the variety.

Mariam is thirty-five years old, grew up in Zrariye and has three children. Shortly after her marriage, she followed her husband to Nigeria where they both worked in a plastic shoe shop. After they had lived in Lagos for a few years, the business began to fail and they returned to Zrariye. Here they opened a small fruit and vegetable shop that was mainly run by Mariam. A few years later, her husband left Zrariye once again when a relative he had contacted in Abidjan promised to organise a contract for him. Mariam had already been on her own for a year when I met her in the village. By that time, her husband had saved enough money to send the air tickets for his family to join him. Mariam and her three children are now living in Abidjan.

Rada went through quite a different migration process. She was born and brought up in Abidjan like her father and mother before her. Although her parents were second-generation Lebanese in Abidjan, they travelled regularly to Lebanon. Rada came to Zrariye for the first time after the war, where she met and fell in love with her paternal cousin Mahmoud, a doctor, and they decided to marry. Rada now lives in Zrariye and has a small daughter. She works as a pharmacist and has opened the first well-equipped pharmacy in the village.

Similar to Rada, Zuha migrated to Zrariye from Abidjan. When she was twenty-one and had finished school, her parents made the decision to return to Lebanon. One year prior to this re-migration plan, Zuha had accompanied her father to Zrariye, where he was supervising the construction of their new house. She became friends with a young female teacher from the French school in Sour (Tyre), which is famous throughout South Lebanon. While visiting the college, she heard of a job vacancy for a French teacher and applied on the spur of the moment. What had originally been planned as a short holiday trip turned out to be the beginning of Zuha's migration, the move from Abidjan to Lebanon, where she now works as a French teacher.

Fatima is also a teacher but moved in the opposite direction, from Zrariye to Abidjan, where she currently works as an Arabic teacher in a Lebanese school. She had been a teacher at a local school in Zrariye but contrary to Zuha, who teaches at a private school, her income was low. Teaching in Abidjan means earning three times as much as before. Since three of her brothers were already living in Abidjan, her father was willing to let her make the move.

Forty-five years ago, Zahra came from Abidjan to Zrariye as an eight-month old baby, the daughter of a Lebanese father and an Ivoirian mother. Whereas her father had wanted to return to Lebanon, her mother was not prepared to follow him. He then took his small daughter and disappeared from Abidjan. She grew up with her paternal grandmother in Zrariye and has lived there ever since. At the age of forty-five, Zahra travelled to Abidjan for the first time in her life. She wanted to attend the wedding of her son who had migrated there, and to meet her Ivoirian mother for the first time ever.

Najibe and Suad experienced a similar "migration fate", as they call it. Both of them came to Abidjan at the age of fifteen and were married to men much older then themselves. They suffered long years of unhappy marriage, in the course of which one of them was beaten and the other had to tolerate her husband's ongoing relationships with other women. Najibe had one child and explained: "I didn't want to have any more children from this man". Suad, on the other hand, has two children. Both women finally demanded a divorce and came back to Zrariye, where their parents live. There was no possibility of bringing their children with them. According to the law, children remain with the father and the divorced wife must return to the house of her parents.

Thirty-eight-year-old Khadija, who is unmarried, commutes between Abidjan and Lebanon three to four times a year. Her trips are of a private nature but her luggage contains masses of new clothes, which she sells to Lebanese women in Abidjan. No expenses are incurred for food or accommodation, since she can stay with her brother in Abidjan. Moreover, she has the use of one room in her brother's house as a temporary fashion boutique.

Sixty-five-year-old Imm Nabil was born in Zrariye and got married there. "Thirty years ago I made my husband travel to Abidjan", she said proudly and explained that it was her idea to move to Abidjan. She managed the family business in Abidjan for many years and paved the way for her four sons, who are still there, to expand it. A few years ago, Imm Nabil and her husband were keen to retire to their newly-built villa in Zrariye but her husband died before they had a chance to move in. She now commutes regularly between Zrariye, Beirut (four of her grandchildren study there) and Abidjan, where she still feels most at home.

Imm Ridda is the mother of ten grown-up children, eight of whom live in Abidjan. During the prosperous years of the flourishing economy, her children came back regularly to the village. Meanwhile, however, the economic situation has become more difficult, which is why Imm Ridda, now a widow, has decided to do the travelling and visit her off-spring in West Africa. She sometimes stays in Abidjan for up to six months, spending *ramadan* and other important religious feast-days with her loved ones.

It is legitimate to ask whether Imm Ridda's journeys or Khadija's selling trips can in any way be described as "migration". If migration is to be defined in the broadest sense as "a move from one place to another" (Oxford Advanced Learner's Dictionary of Current English), their journeys between Zrariye and West Africa can generally be understood as migration processes. Whether the movements between Zrariye and other parts of the country or the world are short-term or last longer, whether they are occasioned by work, family visits or religious pilgrimages to holy shrines, people of the translocal village consider them primarily as journeys. Indeed, in the context of Lebanese movements, the distinction between travelling, migration and visiting begins to blur and it becomes more manifest that the definition of migration as a one-dimensional move and a gradual shift from one ordered social arrangement to another, hitherto taken for granted, is now an obsolete concept.

Moving Families

Referring to the Lebanese case, kinship and family relationships lie at the heart of the translocal village-in-the-making. Up to now, belonging to a patrilineal kin group has been considered the primary social identity in Lebanon (Joseph 2000: 117). Individuals are believed to be born into a specific kin group, based on biological relatedness and descent through male genealogies. These patrilineal kin groups were seen as primordial, existing before the state, bequeathing members their primary identity and claiming their *a priori* allegiance (Joseph 2000: 108). In contrast, Suad Joseph has shown in the case of Lebanon that kin groups, similar to nations or religious communities, are actually "imagined communities":

> A kin group recruits its members on the basis of the naturalization of an imagined biologically based system of recruitment. Kin groups create imagined communities upheld by the power of "nature", usually sanctified by the authority of God, and, in weak states such as Lebanon, often assimilated into and institutionalized by the laws and practices of citizenship. (Joseph 2000: 108-109)

Joseph argues that the patriarchal, patrilineal kin group is founded on a kind of "kin contract", which offers emotional, social, economic and political protection, on the one hand, but demands discipline, moral responsibility and respect for the structures of patriarchal authority, on the other hand (Joseph 2000: 121). Following Suad Joseph, patriarchy can be defined as the privileging of males and seniors (including senior women) and the rationalisation of these privileges in the idioms and moralities of kinship, sanctified by religious authority (Joseph 2000: 121). The extended kinship system is reinforced by marriage practices that favour kin endogamy. The main marriage preference is for patrilineal kin endogamy, with the paternal cousin (*ibn 'amm, bint 'amm*) as the preferred marriage partner. Marrying within the father's kin group thus means marrying within one's own religious, ethnic and national group. When endogamy is combined with patrilocality, both husband and wife have their natal families close by in the same family.

Marriages of individuals from two competing kin groups are still not looked upon favourably, although there have always been exceptions, as the case of Imm and Abu Ali shows:

> I was sixteen years old when Abu Ali took me. I was still at school, studying. I wasn't a woman yet and didn't have real breasts. We married in secret (*khatifeh*) as I am from the Zorkot family and he is from Mroué. My father didn't want to give me to him so we called the sheikh and married in secret. My father was furious. Later on, however, we made peace with him.

Imm and Abu Ali did not accept the norm of kin endogamy and married against the will of the two opposing kin groups. Imm Ali in particular took an enormous risk when she dared to withstand her father's will and that of the whole kin group. A worst case scenario would be for the latter to refuse all contact with her after her marriage and deny assistance in the case of trouble with her husband, as a punishment for valuing the conjugal relationship above the primacy of extended kinship. The norm in Lebanon is that women can always come "home", meaning to the patrilineal kin – fathers, brothers, paternal uncles. She can come home if her husband treats her badly, after a divorce or after the death of a husband. A woman's final place is with her paternal kin, whose obligation it is to take care of her. This is also expressed in names. All children receive the family/kin name through their fathers and keep this name for the rest of their lives. In the case of marriage, the woman does not take on the husband's family name but retains her patri-name.[3] Furthermore, the strong link to patrilineage is reinforced when children are given the father's first name as their second name. If a girl has been called Fatima and her father's name is Muhammad Mroué, her full name will be Fatima Muhammad Mroué. Boys often receive the first name of their paternal grandfathers, followed by the first name of their father. If Muhammad Mroué's father's first name was Ali, he might call his son Ali as well. The son's name would then be Ali Muhammad Mroué. By means of this practice, the patrilineal line of descent is immediately inscribed in the name of a new-born family member, whose existence is closely tied to that of the father and grandfather and whose name will always be a memento.

Religious affiliation practices have also bolstered the primacy of kinship and kin identity. Children belong to their fathers' kin group and it is presumed that they will follow the same religious affiliation. By supporting the patriarchal authority of males and elders over females and juniors and encouraging sectarian endogamy, clerics simultaneously secure religious endogamy and ultimately their influence and power over their followers.

Clerics have deployed kin values, codes of behavior, and principles of discipline in their relationships with sect members, thus anointing kinship with the blessings of sacred authority. (Joseph 2000: 119)

Patrilineal kin groups also have an important economic significance. In rural Lebanon, land handed down through generations is not divided up, since brothers and paternal cousins remain common property holders. Women do not formally inherit land as a rule, although they may be entitled to. The rationale here is that since the men in patrilineages remain responsible for them, leaving their land in the hands of brothers will repay the kin for protecting their women (Joseph 2000: 119).

Male kin often work together in family businesses and thus hold kin property together. In fact, the majority of economic enterprises in Lebanon are family businesses and are generally commercial constructions to keep the property of an extended family together and profitable (Hanf 1993: 80). The extended family remains a source of credit and assistance for kin members. The kin group thus finances studies, equips a doctor's practice or an engineer's office or provides the capital for a business venture (Hanf 1993: 80). Assistance of this kind to kin members has been institutionalised into so-called "family associations" that provide members with loans and other forms of financial savings and aid, networking, and political connections (Khalaf 1987a: 161-184, Joseph 2000: 120). Family associations were formed as early as the end of the nineteenth century (Khalaf 1987a: 161) but to this day have lost none of their popularity. Between 1991 and 1996, more than five hundred family associations were established and legally recognized by the Lebanese government in Beirut alone (Salem et al. 1996 cit. in Joseph 2000: 120).

As a matter of fact, it can be said in the case of Lebanon that the importance of kinship belonging has survived despite the presence of disruptive forces that could have brought about its decline. It has been argued that processes of rural-urban migration, international migration, secularisation and urbanisation would lead to individualisation and the prevalence of nuclear families. This has taken place to a certain degree. At the same time, however, we have seen kinship and family connections in Lebanon remobilised and reimagined to face precarious new situations in times of displacement, war and overall processes of globalisation.

Whereas kinship groups were previously rooted in specific villages, cities or neighbourhoods and social control and assistance for kin members took place on a daily basis in face-to-face relations, they have now managed to adapt to mobility and new situations. Rather than being seen as a potential loss of kin members, migration has been mobilised as a prosperity investment in the kin groups. It is not uncommon for family members in the village to collect money for a migrant's start, in the expectation that the latter will take on responsibility and look after the family back home later on. Indeed, the "care/control paradigm" has been effectively readapted to the new translocal circumstances. Elders and heads of families try hard to maintain control over junior members of the kin group who have migrated. New forms of communication, including (mobile) telephones, the sending and receiving of video and audio tapes and the Internet, have made it gradually more easy for family members to stay in touch and practically organise kinship groups on a translocal scale. Family members may live in very different corners of the world but most of them are committed to their translocal families.[4]

It may well be asked why migrants stick to the "kin contract", although escape from family control would be easy in faraway Africa. I would argue that the translocal kin group remains the most important support system for

Lebanese migrants, providing emotional and social as well as economic and political well-being in times of general instability. The majority of the Lebanese in Africa live in constant fear that their shops and factories will be plundered or destroyed, that they will become victims of attack or of civil wars, or indeed be expelled from the country. Thus, keeping up translocal family networks and sending remittances and goods at a time of relative prosperity can be regarded as an investment in the social support systems that might pay a dividend in times of adversity. During political crises and civil wars in African countries, South Lebanese villages are teeming with returned migrants, mainly women and children seeking shelter with their families at home. This could be observed especially during the 1990s, when civil war broke out in several West African countries. At a time when Lebanon itself was torn apart during the 1970s and 1980s, people moved in the opposite direction, fleeing to their kin in West Africa. Uncertainty is deeply inscribed in people's lives. It has made both migrants and people in Lebanon follow multiple strategies to safeguard their well-being. Keeping up family ties – even over long distances – has proved to be the most sustainable factor in securing money, shelter, work and care in times of great uncertainty and distress. In the words of Suad Joseph:

The romantic lure of the kin contract has been grounded in material realities in which kin relationalities have been, for the Lebanese, the core of social identity, economic stability, political security, and religious affiliation and the first (often last) line of security – emotionally, socially, economically, and politically. It has been the kin who care. It has been kin against whom one has had irrevocable rights and toward whom one has had religiously mandated (at times legally prescribed) moral responsibilities. (Joseph 2000: 116)

The "kin contract" becomes an ongoing subject of negotiation and contestation in the field of translocal migration. People negotiate what it actually means to care for the family back home, discuss the amount of remittances to be sent and generally try to manoeuvre between demands and possibilities.

In the village of Zrariye there is a considerable amount of rivalry. Families compete with each other over the question of who receives remittances from relatives, who belongs to the "successful migrant" group and is thus endowed with social status and can exert influence in the village and who receives no support at all from relatives. People tend to make comparisons. Some wonder why their families abroad have not sent gifts or money, leaving them with a sense of envy and disappointment that others have received more. Who gives and who does not, who gives more and who gives less, who gives to one and who gives to the other are ongoing topics of conversation whenever women and men meet. People talk about what they have received and ask others about their remittances, turning the economic situation of family members and villagers "far away" in Abidjan into a permanent subject of discussion and speculation. Someone in the village may have heard about the economic plight of a particular individual in Abidjan, for example, although the person concerned may have made efforts to conceal it from the family back home.

Pressure to send remittances can divide family members. Those who send them are spoken highly of, while others receive mere letters, tapes and more recently e-mails, despite indications by the family back home of a lack of money and other items. Thus, tension and rivalry among siblings can arise and occasionally lead to the severing of all ties with the family in Lebanon, if those concerned are not in a position to withstand the inner and outer pressure.

Imm and Abu Husayn's eldest son is someone who abandoned his family years ago without leaving a trace. His parents are seriously worried and long to see him again – before it is too late. If there was a sign of life, it came from other people. The parents are aware that Husayn divorced his Lebanese wife and moved from Abidjan to Europe, where he was seen in Paris and in London. Although one of their daughters visited him in France a few years ago, she was unable to convince him to make the trip home. During the time of the Lebanese Civil War, when contacting people at home was difficult and translocal connections were not as intense as today, Husayn was considered a successful businessman in Côte d'Ivoire. In the course of an economic crisis, however, his business declined. Imm and Abu Husayn suspect that this made it impossible for him to appear in the village. At a time when their son had money, he made no attempt to invest in the village and now he is not in a position to do so. He would be coming home empty-handed after years in migration, possibly too proud to face this reality and too afraid of confronting the village with his failure, particularly having neglected his family obligations for many years. Imm and Abu Husayn are torn between contradictory sentiments. On the one hand, they miss their son terribly and are afraid of not seeing him again before they pass away, but on the other hand, they feel angry and somewhat bitter about the fact that he "did not pay back". It could be interpreted as a sense of betrayal at his failure to fulfil the "kin contract" (cf. Joseph 2000: 116). Imm and Abu Husayn describe how they brought Husayn up, invested in his education and helped him to get to Africa. They feel that he broke faith when he failed to comply with the moral obligation of "paying back" and supporting his parents and family – especially as the eldest son. Imm and Abu Husayn are relieved that at least their other three sons send money regularly and are also pleased with their daughters, who live nearby and help with the daily chores. Nevertheless, the silence surrounding their son Husayn troubles them greatly.

On talking to migrants about how they felt, the struggle to fulfil the "kin contract" and the difficulties involved became apparent. Many of them realise that their parents and relatives sacrificed a great deal to enable them to migrate and consequently feel obliged to send money and gifts home, and to help others to migrate. If their economic circumstances in migration do not allow for this, they tend to come under pressure. This is magnified when they are reminded of their moral obligation in letters, tapes, e-mails and telephone calls. Strong translocal ties are experienced as a burden, with little hope of finding an escape from the "patriarchal kin contract". In some cases, migrants feel the strain to such a degree that they cut themselves off from their families completely. They move out of the tight Lebanese communities and try to find a new existence without the security and support of the translocal family network. It becomes extremely difficult for these people to return to the fold, as the case of Imm and Abu Husayn and their oldest son demonstrates. Bitterness, anger and frustration are sometimes all that is left on both sides.

Moving Goods

In general, Lebanese trading and business activities in West Africa are firmly fashioned along translocal Lebanese networks and social relations, as actors rely on family members and other social ties throughout the world. A small second-hand cloth retailer in Abidjan might receive his merchandise via his brother-in-law in Canada, while a Lebanese selling spare parts for cars would be linked to his family in France or Germany. In this way, global goods move along local Lebanese social networks around the world. The overlapping of social and economic networks is not a totally new phenomenon, since it was also observed during the colonial era. At that time, for instance, the Lebanese dominated the Kola trade between Côte d'Ivoire and Senegal, which was carried out on the basis of family relations. The Kola was received at intermediate stations and sent on by diverse members of the family.[5]

On a smaller and more private level, goods move along with people travelling back and forth between Lebanon and West Africa. When someone plans a visit home to Lebanon or travels to Africa, he or she is expected to inform relatives and friends of the trip. It is anticipated that the traveller will carry letters, tape-recorded messages and photographs to the family abroad as well as gifts of all shapes and sizes. On the return journey, the same traveller will be laden with goods coming from the other direction. Food specialities and ingredients for Lebanese cuisine in particular are favourite gifts that move with people: olives and olive oil, mashed wheat *(burghul)* and thyme *(za'atar)* are often sent to Africa, while migrants take back colourful patchwork trousers, African dresses, tropical fruit and cheap Atlantic fish to Lebanon. Visiting various homes throughout Lebanon, it is easy to guess where most migrants live. In villages where migration is directed to South

America, almost every home has a *mate* teapot from Argentina. The houses in Zrariye are decorated with African wood-cuts of elephants and antelopes, small pillow-cases with African motifs and various African arts and crafts, all of which are sold in African markets.

Once linked to a specific local context, these items are globalised and move along with migrants to different parts of the world in the process of migration. In Zrariye, they are then localised, re-defined and used as new markers in the process of creating difference and similarity. It is crucial to see consumer goods in this context not merely as packets of neutral utility but as symbols and signs (Featherstone 1991: 85; Lash/Urry 1994: 4). In this sense, the definition of consumption has shifted from the gratification of primary needs (food, clothing, shelter) to self-expression, giving signs and marking identity and life style.[6] Commodities are made into news and carry specific messages. Thus, African handicrafts in South Lebanese living-rooms can be understood as symbols of belonging to the "successful migrants" group and proving that one has been "there". Even more so than African items, "Western" global commodities appropriated by consumption have become boundary markers of new identities in the translocal village. Mary Douglas and Baron Isherwood have aptly put it in a nutshell by saying that "consumption patterns also have power to exclude" (Douglas/Isherwood 1996: xxi). Driving a new Mercedes around the village, buying "global products" at the "global shop", wearing expensive clothes and living in a spacious villa, all of these are an ostentatious demonstration of belonging to a specific life style with the conspicuous label "successful migrant" or village "new rich" and well suited to establishing and maintaining collective identities. "Lifestyles are something that you can identify with and use to signal that identity to others. Thus lifestyles are blueprints for the organisation of everyday life" (Gerke 1995: 12).

A short ethnographic description will give an impression of the "successful migrant life style": When the summer school holidays begin in Abidjan, hundreds of families populate the Mediterranean beaches, crowds pour into shops in the cities, towns and villages and restaurants throughout the country are packed. Those who usually live in small apartments in Abidjan move to spacious villas in Zrariye and, having saved every penny from work in Abidjan, spend it in Lebanon during their holidays. Clothes and other consumer items are much cheaper than in Africa. Migrants take their time to enjoy shopping, while shopowners eagerly await the "migrant summer".

Yussuf is a 36-year-old man from Zrariye and the most famous shopkeeper in the village. He spent several years in Abidjan but, as he explained to me, was not happy there. Back in the village, he opened a shop that he called *Yussuf's Coffee Shop*. The other small generalised shops (*dukkaneh*) in the village sell the standard variety of consumer goods from sugar, cooking oil, fruit and vegetables to cigarettes and soap. Yussuf's shop is quite different. A "global shop" in the true sense of the word, it sells popular "global products" such as *Kellogg's Cornflakes, Bahlsen* biscuits, *Kinder* surprise chocolate eggs, *Langnese* honey and *Cadbury's* chocolate. American peanut-butter, English jam, Italian spaghetti and French children's food in small glass jars all line the shelves of *Yussuf's Coffee Shop*. Various brands of ice-cream fill the freezer and a well-known poster advertises *Me and my Magnum*.

Figure 6: A "global shop" in Zrariye

While Yussuf sells a wide range of delicatessen items, 32-year-old Suad has opened a different kind of "global shop" across the road, where she sells *Moulinex* electrical appliances, jars, pots and tableware. Suad is the sister of a successful migrant, whose support enabled her to open the shop. The items in her boutique have international brand names and cost a good deal more than the stocks of pots and glasses "made in China" on sale in other shops. The décor in both stores differs notably from that of more ordinary shops. Both products and décor appeal to a specific clientele, coinciding with Yussuf's and Suad's desire to attract migrants and members of "successful migrant families" who have the necessary means to shop in high-priced global supermarkets of this kind. Expensive cars such as BMWs, Mercedes and Jeeps, one more costly than the other, are frequently seen in front of Yussuf's shop during the summer months. Women and men wearing elegant Western and modern Muslim-style clothes come to Zrariye to shop and afterwards drive away noisily at almost 100 km/h, turning the once modest village road into a dangerous highway. Some of the older villagers began to complain about people being unwilling to walk once they had a car.[7]

African nannies, brought along for the summer holidays, turn up at

Yussuf's shop to purchase biscuits and ice-cream for the Lebanese children they look after. They might have a chat in front of the shop with some of the African men who work as gardeners, chauffeurs or household employees in re-migrant households. A Sri-Lankan household employee could drop in, having been sent to buy some freshly-ground coffee, while some of the youth in the translocal village might meet at the shop for a *Coca-Cola*. Being in a position to purchase consumer goods at expensive global shops is doubtless a public demonstration of a "successful migrant", or at least of the desire to be one of "them". Those who cannot afford to shop here drop by occasionally to enjoy an ice-cream or simply to be seen in front of *Yussuf's Coffee Shop*. Although not in a position to adopt a "successful migrant" life style, these people attempt to identify with it – if only virtually or temporarily.

It can be noted that consumer durables such as cars, houses, television and video sets have become visible symbols of success and wealth. Identification as a member of a "successful migrant family" associated with a specific, consumer-oriented life style is an effort to distinguish "the new rich" from the poor, and a self-defined "modern life" from the "traditional" village way of life.

Moving Messages

The entire spectrum of communicative technologies, ranging from handwritten letters to television, allows people to get messages across to one another without a face-to-face encounter. In the age of globalisation, communication technology has not only become much more effective in reaching across space but has also introduced a new range, namely the Internet, electronic mail and satellite television. People in the translocal village of Zrariye make intensive use of the broad range of media opportunities, sending messages and information, and receiving and transforming news and ideas. In fact, the daily back-and-forth flow of spoken and written words, pictures and images exchanged by social actors living in different parts of the world but linked by lines of kinship, friendship and common village background, constitute the very basis of the translocal village. In this way, people are involved in an ongoing process of constructing and producing this permeable social unit that transgresses social arrangements formerly taken for granted. Mutual understanding of global and local events, be it a wedding in Zrariye or Princess Diana's funeral, are worked out in detail in the back-and-forth flow of mobile words and voices. Everyday experiences, once necessarily derived from a close face-to-face relationship, are now stretched out to form new "transreal" experiences. One could argue that those whose life-worlds are closely linked share "habitats of meaning" (Hannerz 1996: 22) and form a "community of sentiment" (Appadurai 1996a: 8), a group that begins to imagine and feel things together, despite the fact that they live hundreds or thousands of kilometres away from each other. In the translocal village of Zrariye people construct and reconstruct their habitats of meaning in an ongoing process relying on diverse means of communication.

Figure 7: Translocal connections: Man on the phone in Zrariye wearing African clothes

One of the most vital means of communication is the telephone. When the state communication system broke down during the war, private telephone shops mushroomed throughout the country, even in the tiniest of villages, providing international direct dial connections via satellite. There were five of them at the time of my fieldwork in Zrariye that additionally offered private lines to households. More recently, the fashionable and ubiquitous mobile phone has made its way into the villages and spread like wildfire, so that it is not uncommon today to see men walking down the streets of Zrariye, flamboyantly carrying a cellular phone. Despite "symbolic consumption", however, the majority of the village population has learned to appreciate this technical innovation as a means of rapid communication. Telephone access, be it the telephone shop or a cellular phone, allows people to keep in touch and contribute to family decision-making, as well as to participate in family events at a considerable distance. News and gossip, whether important or unimportant, circulates simultaneously in Zrariye, Abidjan, Dearborn and Berlin. In the words of one migrant: "Your relatives in Abidjan will know what you're cooking in Zrariye the same day!"

However, the telephone is an expensive means of communication and people cannot always afford to chat for hours but are inclined to use it for special events only, such as the birth of a baby, a religious celebration or in the case of sudden illness or death.

Literate and illiterate Lebanese all over the world resort to audiotapes to converse with their relatives. Taping cassettes has become a popular means of speaking personally and on one's own "colloquial" terms about events, big and small, in everyday life. It is often chosen as being the most direct way of talking to sons and daughters and confronting them with problems, wishes, expectations, criticism and social advice. Parents occasionally criticise their children for not sending enough money and report how much their neighbours recently received. Indeed, many readopt the parental role, attempting to give advice and exercise social control, although their children are way beyond the realms of their surveillance. Hearing the sound of a parent's voice in Africa, a far cry from Lebanon, can suddenly bring their authority very close again, making a tape recording an effective reminder of responsibility and a prompt for action. The familiar parental voice may induce sons[8] to sit down, record a tape and send it along with some money with the next migrant going back to Lebanon.

Figure 8: Woman in Zrariye listening to her son's voice on tape

Abu and Imm Ali, the old couple from Zrariye, have often received tapes from their children. The old woman puts a tape into the recording machine and both listen attentively to the voice of their 34-year-old son living in Abidjan. This is the beginning of a tape he sent them in May 1996:

First of all, I want to speak to my mother and my father. Hello father, hello mother. How are you, my dear parents? I hope you are in good health. I miss you a lot and hope it is peaceful in South Lebanon these days. We thought about you a lot during the Israeli air raids. Thank God nothing happened to you! I hope God gives you health and strength. I heard, dear mother, that you went to Beirut during the war. We were worried in case it was more dangerous in the southern suburbs of Beirut where you were staying. We tried to phone you but there was no one in the telephone shop. The most important thing is that you are in good health and were able to get back without any problem. I miss you a lot and hope I'll be able to come and stay with you this summer – God willing. How are you, my father? I heard that you stayed at home during the air raids. I hope you didn't suffer too much. The whole family here gathered together at the time and we thought of you and prayed for you.

The longer their son talked, the more agitated they became, until they eventually began to cry. I sat silently beside them, trying to grasp the pain and suffering migration can entail. Imm and Abu Ali have not seen their son for several years. He lost a considerable amount of money when his business failed. He now has to work hard and cannot visit them each year as he used to. Neither can he afford to phone them every week. He receives tapes and letters regularly, delivered by migrants and visitors, but he does not as yet have the means to travel between the worlds as others do.

The point I want to make here has been sometimes neglected in recent literature on transnational migration: living in transnational and translocal circuits, moving regularly between host and home country, keeping in touch by phone, sending faxes and e-mails from here to there requires considerable resources. The life that a female migrant has described as "globetrotters living between the worlds" is actually limited to a small group of high-income transmigrants. The direct flight from Abidjan to Beirut is expensive and many small-scale traders or shop-owners think twice about visiting the village with the whole family, often opting to continue working and let wives and children travel alone. Nevertheless, although people may not always have the financial means to travel, communication is not interrupted. There is always someone travelling to Lebanon who will take presents, tapes and letters. Even during the harsh war years, many migrants made the effort to come home for a visit. Since the end of the armed conflict, the number of people and entire families spending summer holidays in "their village of origin" has soared. Not only do migrants visit the village but relatives in Zrariye now travel to Abidjan to visit their relatives. In a tense economic situation, this can be a cheaper solution. The flow of people, goods and messages within the translocal village never comes to a standstill. On the contrary, the process of moving has become more rapid and efficient than ever before.

Exchanging videotapes is another effective means of up-dating the flow of information. The amateur and professional filming of wedding celebrations has become a vital element in modern Lebanese marriage ceremonies. The video cassettes are sent to relatives abroad who could not attend the ceremonies. Family members can thus virtually participate in the customary conversations about the event, asking who was there, who wore what and what kind of food was served. Women, in particular, get together to watch these documentary wedding videos, which also provides an occasion to talk about the latest news from abroad, to ask about an absent son or a newly-married daughter living in West Africa. Likewise, videos of other family events, such as a grandchild's first steps, the first birthday party or New Year's Eve in Abidjan, are filmed and videotapes exchanged.

More recently, the Internet has had a magnet effect on an increasing number of people, especially the younger generation. E-mails, voice mails and photographs are sent to friends and family via the Internet, which also provides for direct calls. Many have installed computers in their homes and Internet cafés are found throughout Lebanese cities and in many of the villages. The first Internet Café in Zrariye opened in 2002, where young people in particular meet to chat with their friends online, exchange the latest local news and finally feel close to their peers and kin so far away.

Apart from the exchange of personal information via letters, e-mails, audio- and videotapes, information transmitted through television has gradually increased in significance. Satellite television allows both South Lebanese villagers as well as migrants in Africa to witness Middle East and global events. One of the largest and most influential firms is *MBC* (*Middle East Broadcasting Corporation*), a London-based company financed by Saudi Arabia that broadcasts on a global scale. *MBC*'s potential audience includes an estimated 5,000,000 Arabic-speaking viewers across Europe and over 100 million viewers in Arab and African countries (Amin/Boyd 1994). Moreover, *Dubai TV* and a few Lebanese stations, such as *LBC* (*Lebanese Broadcasting Corporation*) and *Future TV*, went on satellite and can be received by the Lebanese in many parts of the world, including Abidjan. *Al-Jazeera*, which was set up in 1996 by the Foreign Ministry of Qatar and some former *BBC* Arab employees, is today probably the most famous Arab satellite channel and possibly one of the least censored media in the Middle East. Arabic music video clips, Mexican, Syrian and Egyptian soap operas, the news, and religious and political programmes have a huge television audience. Thus, people in Zrariye in South Lebanon and in Abidjan can simultaneously watch the same television programmes and appropriate the same information, which is then interpreted locally. These appropriated forms of information can be used as elements of new information "bricks", which, in turn, are spread throughout the translocal village via different channels. The latest peace talks in the Middle East, for example, or the Israeli air raids on South Lebanon as reported and shown on television can be addressed when migrants talk on tape. They can enquire about their relatives' personal experience in South Lebanon. By exchanging and commenting on the news, relatives, friends and neighbours are jointly involved in the shared production of what something means, thereby constructing and reconstructing the translocal village in the making.

Female Spaces – Nodal Points of Information

Whereas men were the main information carriers between Lebanon and West Africa in colonial times, women now take on a specific role in the process of passing and receiving information. When they meet as neighbours, relatives or friends in Abidjan or in Zrariye, the latest news is exchanged and discussed. These "female spaces" (cf. Lachenmann 1992) act as nodal points of information, circulating between the different migrant communities and South Lebanon. Coming together in face-to-face situations, in a specific "real" place, women absorb the latest news and transform and negotiate it according to their conceptions, norms and views of the world. If a woman has just received a phone call or listened to a tape from a son or daughter abroad, she might talk to her female neighbour or a relative living next door immediately afterwards. The fact that many Lebanese in Abidjan live in apartment buildings that are often exclusively inhabited by Lebanese contributes to the rapid spread of information. In many cases, these buildings have the appearance of Lebanese neighbourhood "islands" in African surroundings. These "new neighbourhoods" are not necessarily inhabited by close kinship groups. Still, it is quite common for someone to move in there if she or he is a relative or comes from the same village as one of the residents. Next to kinship, neighbourhood plays a very strong role in the social life of the Lebanese in Côte d'Ivoire. Where close relatives do not live in the same district or not even in Abidjan, neighbours become vital for daily social interaction, which is basically structured by physical, territorial and social proximity (Jocano cit. in Berner/Korff 1994: 8). Similar to reports on various other locations (cf., for example, Berner/Korff 1994; Werbner 1990), the Lebanese neighbourhood in Abidjan is a mainly female relation, i.e., most of the activity and interaction that makes up the neighbourhood is carried out by women. Female neighbours visit each other for a cup of sweet cardamon-laced Arab coffee or to have a chat in the courtyard where children play. Indeed, visiting neighbours, relatives and friends is a major social practice and obligation for Lebanese people, both in Zrariye and abroad. Interestingly, several women told me that visiting patterns in Abidjan are different to those in Zrariye. One 45-year-old woman who has been living in Abidjan for more than twenty years explained:

In Zrariye, people walk in and out at any time of the day. You always have to be prepared for visitors. Here in Abidjan we have more privacy. In the evening time, visitors often phone before coming and people accept that visiting is inappropriate at certain times.

Visits to female neighbours who live in the same building are often more informal than visits to relatives or friends who live further away. A female neighbour might just pop in to get some missing ingredient for cooking or to have a recipe for a Lebanese dish explained in detail. Conversations deal with a broad variety of topics and are similar to those of women in Zrariye. The price of fruit, vegetables and other foodstuffs are discussed at length and information is exchanged about where to find the cheapest tomatoes, zucchinis or eggplants. Friends and neighbours are constantly updated on the course of family events. Who married whom? What happened to the sick grandmother in the village? Did you hear that Abu Ali died? Did Leila have her baby? Indeed, life seems full of events, where the slightest change of fortune is minutely discussed. News of major events such as accidents, deaths or a scandal spreads like wildfire around the Lebanese "women's world" in Abidjan and beyond.

These "new female neighbourhoods" represent a point of reference for women in their immediate environment. Information is exchanged about practical matters such as school and health care or someone's impending trip to Lebanon. This person might be asked to deliver letters, audio or video tapes, money or presents. In addition, female neighbourhoods play a key role in the life of newcomers, who are often newly-married women from Lebanon trying to simultaneously cope with being married and having to adapt to quite different living circumstances. Several women told me that moving into an apartment building with Lebanese neighbours had been a great relief in this situation. In the absence of family members, female neighbours often give advice when problems related to marriage, pregnancy or child care arise. Although tapes, letters and telephones can help to overcome loneliness in a new environment, they cannot substitute face-to-face encounters or care shown by a neighbour or a relative.

Social differentiation processes within these female neighbourhoods generally make no distinction between second generation women and migrant "newcomers", i.e., women who arrive in Abidjan after their marriage. During my stay there, I observed and visited Mai and Jamila, two women who live in the same apartment house. Both are in their thirties and have four children. Their life-stories are quite similar, although Jamila was born and grew up in Zrariye, whereas Mai was born in Abidjan and went to a Lebanese school there until the age of fifteen. She stayed at home most afternoons helping her mother in the house and since her life revolved around her family, she rarely went out. Jamila lived a similar life in Zrariye, with the emphasis on school and home. While Mai married a migrant from Zrariye at the age of fifteen in Abidjan, Jamila got married in Zrariye at the same age and then left for Africa where she became Mai's friend and neighbour. Although they had spent their childhood and their youth in different parts of the world, these two women went through a similar experience. Both their life-worlds are comprised of their families, their children and the household. Indeed, Lebanese women's life-worlds do not necessarily alter in accordance with where they live or were brought up. I would argue that there are several different female perspectives on life, all of which are tied to a respective socio-economic, educational, political, religious and familial background. Consequently, despite initial difficulty in adapting to the African environment, a young woman newly married will in all probability encounter women from her peer group, despite having grown up in entirely different surroundings. Female neighbourhood networks are closely linked to and frequently overlap with kinship networks. Information circulating in one female neighbourhood could be spread to another via two sisters, for example, who are members of different neighbourhoods. It is thus evident that female conversations in the translocal village, i.e., in the neighbourhoods of Zrariye and the "new neighbourhoods" of Abidjan, are crucial factors in the process of constituting a translocal village-in-the-making.

Moving Social and Religious Events

Important social and religious events are celebrated both in South Lebanon and the migrant communities. If someone dies, funeral ceremonies are held in the *husayniyeh*[9] in Zrariye and in Abidjan. Despite the vast expense involved, migrants in Abidjan generally do not hesitate to send the bodies of deceased relatives home to Lebanon, where relatives can thus pay their respects for the last time. The burial site itself is probably the most potent statement on the migrant attitude to residence in Africa. Despite the fact that they may have lived in Africa all their lives, migrants have a strong desire to die in their homeland and cherish the "dream return".

Paying a condolence visit to relatives of the deceased is a social obligation for friends, neighbours and relatives in Abidjan as well as in Zrariye. Although separated by thousands of miles, people mourn in both places simultaneously and have a strong sense of connection. Time and space arrangements seem to vanish in moments of silence, while suffering becomes the dominant element linking their social worlds. Nevertheless, physical distance can be a matter for grave concern. When an elderly mother has become seriously ill, for instance, the question of whether to travel to Zrariye or not will arise. The journey could take too long to bid a last farewell, while on the other hand, the feeling of not having arrived in time causes great distress.

The death of a village member is announced by the speaker of the mosque in Zrariye. In one particular case, a woman's death was announced and funeral ceremonies called to be held in the *husayniyeh*. The villagers, however, were puzzled and began asking each other "Who is this woman?

What was her name? Who was her father?" Zaynab Z., the woman in question, was not well known in Zrariye. She was born and brought up in Abidjan like her parents before her but unlike many others had never visited the village of her ancestors. Although she had not even set foot in Lebanon, her family ties justified her membership of the village community and merited the announcement of her death and her commemoration in the village *husayniyeh*.

As mentioned earlier, the video documentation of social events has become an important means of publicising them within the translocal village. Linda Walbridge, who carried out research on the Lebanese Shi'ite community in Dearborn/USA, watched the home video of a funeral held in a Shi'ite village in Lebanon in 1990:

It was the funeral of a man who had been killed by Israelis. The emotional level was very high, with men obviously competing with one another as they pounded their chests and heads, weaving through the streets, chanting slogans as they went. (Walbridge 1997: 95)

Here, the tragic death of a young man who has become a Shi'ite martyr *(shahid)* is mourned, not only in his village of origin but also in the migrant community in Dearborn, where some of his relatives live. At the same time, the funeral was politicised and spread to the migrants through the video.

Studying Muslim burial practice in the Turkish diaspora in Berlin, Gerdien Jonker has also described the growing significance of filming and taking photographs during funerals:

The moment the washed and wrapped body is carried into the hall and the face freed to permit a last look, camcorders, cameras and polaroids are set into action. The body, the mourners, the prayer, the procession, the depth of the grave, the shovelling, are all fixed on still or moving film. (Jonker 1996: 39)

Although filming and taking photographs of these occasions falls under the general ban on pictures in Islam, living in the diaspora makes many Turkish migrants feel it to be indispensable. Jonker gives two reasons for this. The first is that when a Muslim is buried in a Christian country, the family "back home" cannot participate in the burial. In this event, photographs and films prove that the body has neither been burned nor subjected to "strange" Christian habits. The second reason is to demonstrate to the people back home that the body has been wrapped and washed correctly according to Muslim tradition (Jonker 1996: 36). Thus, as Jonker clearly points out, these photographs are not meant for the family album but seen as crucial to upholding the flow of communication. "Films and photographs are used as a bridge keeping the different parts of the family together" (Jonker 1996: 39).

Although I did not witness photographs being taken during funerals, films and photographs have become fundamental to every day life in the translocal village of Zrariye. Self-produced video tapes about Lebanese war events in April 1996 and a mass funeral in Qana after an Israeli bomb attack on a UN base, where refugees had sought shelter, found their way to Abidjan very rapidly. Family and friends came together there to relive the shocking moments. These films can strongly contribute to the West African Lebanese people's willingness to react to these events and turn feelings of helplessness into action. In the case mentioned, money, medicine as well as gifts in kind were collected for victims in Lebanon. In this way, spaces and possibilities for translocal social action have been created.

Contrary to the sadness surrounding funerals in the translocal village, marriages are happy social events. Several factors are involved in the decision of where the wedding should take place. Although the bride and groom may have grown up in Abidjan where most of their relatives live, the wedding will occasionally be held in the parents' home village and often graduate to a powerful display of the latter's migration success. In many cases, the male migrant returns to Zrariye to marry a village girl "at home" and takes her back to Abidjan as his newly-wedded wife. Sometimes a migrant will come to Zrariye only for the official engagement. Later on, his future wife travels on her own to Abidjan for the wedding and thus saves him the expense of a second trip. Regardless of where the marriage takes place, there are always some members of the family, friends or relatives unable to attend the momentous occasion. Professional or amateur filming of wedding celebrations has thus become an integral part of the festivities in the translocal village. Crucial moments such as the cutting of the cake or the wedding dance tend to be staged, as if in a theatre. Over and over again they are performed until the "stage director", often a local photographer specialising in wedding videos, is satisfied. Video tapes of the wedding are sent abroad to the relatives who were not at the ceremony. In this way, none of the family is excluded from the daily conversations about the event. While in Zrariye, I received numerous invitations to watch wedding videos. Sometimes whole families would gather to watch them, while on other occasions it was women only. Neighbours are invited and the marriage is virtually relived. Watching these videos provides the women with an opportunity to talk about the latest news from abroad. It is thus not surprising that news of relatives in Abidjan reaches Zrariye fast.

Ramadan in the Translocal Village

Ramadan, the Muslim lunar fast, carries special significance in the translocal village. Muslims all over the world are required to refrain from eating, drinking and smoking as well as from sexual relations from dawn until sunset each day of this particular month. They fast to cleanse the body, recognise God's bounty and feel kinship with the deprived, whereby travellers, children, and the sick are exempt from this obligation. Apart, of course, from those who give up after the first week, it is the regularity and prevalence of fasting that is impressive. Although it can be a tiring and difficult experience, people in the translocal village look forward to it and enjoy the opportunity for discipline and purification, as well as the shared pleasure of coming together. A Zrariye migrant in Abidjan expressed his attitude towards *ramadan* in the following words: "*Ramadan* is so good and such a joy because during this month we are all the same, both rich and poor." Notably, *ramadan* shows no signs of losing its presence in the Lebanese migrant community. On the contrary, fasting has become a key religious and social event, a public statement of religious conviction and identity. It is thus understandable in this context that more and more people who had not previously fasted in Lebanon have now begun to do so in migration. Various people in Abidjan explained to me that because of their Communist convictions they had not fasted in Lebanon and had only recently begun to do so in Abidjan. One man told me why:

I enjoy fasting here in Abidjan. It gives me a feeling of closeness that emerges when you know that others are fasting too. Then you get together with the family, with friends or other Lebanese to share food in the evening. There is a sense of real enjoyment. You cannot feel it if you do not fast.

In the evening, the breaking of the fast in Mecca is broadcast live on television. Many of the Lebanese in Africa take this as an orientation for prayer and for breaking the fast rather than adhering to local African practices. The fast is initially broken by a simple meal, followed by a more elaborate one that includes dishes served only during *ramadan*. The *iftar* or breaking of the fast usually takes place in the company of visitors, relatives, friends, neighbours or colleagues. Tea, coffee and sweets are served when people visit each other again later in the evening. These ritualised mutual visits reinforce social relations between Lebanese friends, relatives, neighbours and colleagues. Work figures predominantly in migrant lives for the rest of the year. *Ramadan*, on the other hand, provides an opportunity to focus on socialising. Some even travel to Lebanon to spend the month with relatives.

The aspect of "coming together" became an institution when a Zrariye migrant began to invite relatives and friends and other people from Zrariye to his house once a week during *ramadan*. In 1996, when I attended a few *ramadan* meetings, this particular event took place every Thursday, the night before the holy Friday *(layl al-jum'a)*. Between 30 and 50 people crowd onto the spacious terrace of the man's house. Muslim scholars are occasionally invited to give lectures on certain aspects of Islam, including the meaning of *ramadan*, after which the social part of the evening begins. Some of the women bring food and drink and there is time for discussion and small talk, as well as the latest news and gossip circulating in the translocal village. Those present the evening I was there were couples, both young and old, and numerous young unmarried men who make up a large percentage of the Lebanese community in Abidjan. In this migrant's house they experience a sense of belonging and of renewed religious orientation, which is often eclipsed in the big city of Abidjan. The end of *ramadan* is celebrated joyfully, with people taking the occasion of this meaningful holiday to telephone their relatives in Zrariye or elsewhere in the world and share their happiness.

Commemorating 'ashura Translocally

> Whosoever weeps or causes others to weep for Hoseyn will enter Paradise. (cit. in Richard 1995: 97)

The Shi'ites in Muslim countries all over the world come together annually on the first day of the Islamic lunar month *muharram* until its culmination on the tenth to commemorate and ritually reenact the murder of Prophet Muhammad's grandson, Imam Husayn, and a group of his relatives and supporters.[10] They were massacred on the Karbala plain in 680 A.D. in the month of *muharram*. Each year, the Shi'ites commemorate what for them has remained martyrdom of the greatest magnitude. For ten days, ordinary life in South Lebanon comes to a standstill, during which the focus is on mourning, ritual weeping and processions. Men, women and children are dressed in black, the men are unshaven and women wear no make-up. The entire village is decorated with black streamers. Men and women in separate groups listen to religious experts reading *ta'ziyeh*, which literally means expressions of sympathy, mourning and consolation (cf. Chelkowski 1979). The story of Husayn's death is imparted over and over again, how he and his followers were caught in an ambush set up by the Sunnite caliph Yazid and how Husayn refused to pay homage to him although defeat was certain. The *ta'ziyeh* goes on to describe how Husayn and his company were surrounded by a huge enemy force and had to remain in the Karbala desert for ten days without water. On the tenth of *muharram*, which is *'ashura*, Yazid dispatched his final order to attack. Husayn and his followers, who had refused to leave their leader, were slaughtered. Even Husayn's infant son was killed by an arrow, cradled in the arms of his father who had begged the enemy for water for the baby. Husayn, who fought to the last breath, was decapitated. Women and children were taken prisoner and led to Damascus to face the ignominy of seeing Husayn's head presented to the governor on a platter.

When these narratives are recounted during the ten days of *muharram*, what happened thirteen hundred years ago is looked on as if it were happening now. In fact, Husayn's battle has transcended history, time and space to become a vital expression of opposition, martyrdom and revolt. The annual occasion of mourning Imam Husayn, hitherto a reminder to the Shi'ites of their solitude and defeat, was to become a celebration of Shi'ite defiance in the face of injustice. In this context, the key message of the Karbala story, as formulated by Mamnoun, was able to give people renewed guidance and confidence in their daily struggle:

> The Ta'ziyeh narrative is ultimately not the story of the dispute of a man named Hussein ibn Ali with a man named Yazid ibn Mu'awiyyah, who in the month of muharram, 61 A.H., fought over the caliphate. The Ta'ziyeh narrative is the eternal story of the oppressed and the oppressor, the brave and the coward, the ascetic and the corrupt, future life and the material world, heaven and hell: the story of good and evil. (Mamnoun 1979: 161)

In Iran as well as in Lebanon, the mixing of 'ashura mourning slogans with the political was characteristic for a long time, as in the case of the Iranian Revolution (cf. Kippenberg 1981). Musa al-Sadr, a charismatic cleric who formed the *Amal* movement in Lebanon, introduced a new reading of the old tale of Karbala, transforming it into the radical politics of practice. He stripped it of its sorrow and lament and turned it into an episode of political choice and courage on the part of Imam Husayn (Ajami 1986: 143).

On the tenth day of *muharram*, ritual mourning reaches its climax. In many Shi'ite villages in South Lebanon, in Iran and in other Shi'ite areas throughout the world, Imam Husayn's martyrdom is not only recited as a narrative but also staged as a performance. The largest and most impressive passion play in Lebanon takes place annually in the South Lebanese city of Nabatiyeh. A small Iranian Shi'ite community in Nabatiyeh is said to have introduced this ritual performance at the end of the nineteenth century. It had previously been performed only in Iran (Reuter 1993: 54). Since then, the tragedy of Husayn's martyrdom has been performed in Lebanon. Actors dressed in colourful costumes, marching or riding horses and camels, depict the events that led to the final scene at Karbala. This performance was first introduced to Zrariye a few years ago and has enjoyed enormous popularity ever since, with many people involved in the play as actors, technicians or organisers. Performances take place in the afternoon, while processions of young men and boys following the voice of the cantor are held in the mornings. Followers reiterate slogans as they shout and beat their chests rhythmically with great emotional intensity. Some men deliberately cut their scalp with a knife so that blood can stream down their face.

The story of Husayn's tragic end in Karbala is deeply ingrained in the life of every Shi'ite. No matter where they move to, Husayn's drama moves with them. In Abidjan, Shi'ite migrants congregate in their *husayniyeh* to hear treading of the *ta'ziyeh* and to weep and mourn for Husayn. There are also private gatherings, where women, in particular, meet and recite the story of

Husayn's murder. Here and there people dress in black, women wear no make-up and men are unshaven. However, *muharram* rituals are not practised in the same manner as in Lebanon. Dissociated from the local, they are rediscovered in a new environment. In Abidjan and other Lebanese migrant communities, rituals take place exclusively in the mosques and *husayniyeh*. Working on the Lebanese Shi'ite in Dearborn/USA, Walbridge states that people refuse to act out their feelings in public processions. She supposes that if they did so, they would certainly risk an unpleasant encounter with the local police and possibly arouse fear and anxiety among both Sunnite Muslims and Non-Muslims (Walbridge 1997: 92). This lies in the fact that they are a migrant minority in the United States. Similarly, the Lebanese in West Africa have often experienced hostility, and in many cases have become scapegoats for economic and political crises. They therefore avoid ritual presence in public during *'ashura*.

The rituals in Zrariye are filmed and videotapes often sent to relatives in Abidjan or elsewhere, bringing the South Lebanese practice of *'ashura* into the world. They can be taken as a point of reference in negotiating the practice of this ritual in migration. Walbridge notes that there has in fact been some disagreement over how *'ashura* should be commemorated in Dearborn/USA. Some people who had seen the passion play in South Lebanon were in favour of an identical performance in the Dearborn *husayniyeh*. Others miss the processions on the streets, where men beat their chests and cut their scalps (Walbridge 1997: 92). On the other hand, watching a film of the *'ashura* rituals allows villagers to participate from a distance in ongoing negotiations of how the ritual should be performed in the future. They thus embrace an active role as members of the translocal community.

Schubel, who carried out research on Shi'ite Indians in North America, argues that *'ashura* is a crucial family ritual. He states that rituals of this kind are momentous opportunities for family members to clearly demonstrate to their children what their community stands for (Schubel 1991: 125). In South Asia, *'ashura* proved to the Shi'ite that their particular vision of Islam is true. In North America, it is an annual lesson to the younger generation that the sacred history of Shi'ism demands allegiance, even in a Non-Muslim environment that continuously competes for attention (Schubel 1991: 126).

To conclude, I argue that *'ashura* is a crucial marker of Shi'ite identity and Shi'ite life all over the world. In fact, their mourning and recounting of Husayn's tragedy brings the essential distinctions between Shi'ite and non-Muslim or Sunnite communities to the fore. Thus, *'ashura* serves as a reminder that Shi'ites are different from everyone else (Walbridge 1997: 95). The examples and descriptions of *'ashura* in migration given by Walbridge and Schubel refer to the integrative moment it entails for Shi'ite communities in the diaspora. In his case study on the Shi'ite Lebanese community in Sydney (Australia), Michael Humphrey demonstrates how conflicts between various religious-political Shi'ite groups can arise during 'ashura (Humphrey 1992: 444). Similar to my observations regarding the Amal/Hizbollah tensions during the 'ashura ceremonies in Zrariye (cf. Peleikis 1999), Humphrey reports of violent clashes between rival factions of the Lebanese Shi'ite community. The incident occurred in front of a predominantly Lebanese Shi'ite mosque in a suburb of Sydney during the celebrations to mark the beginning of muharram. The factional rivalry between pro-Amal and pro-Hizbollah groups for control of the mosque caused serious injury to six members of the congregation (Humphrey 1992: 444). This example points to existing conflicts in Lebanese migrant communities. Due to the fact that organisations and political parties have a dense network of translocal and transnational interconnections, their organisational activities unfold in the home country as well as in migration. Political and religious loyalties and activities are not left behind but move with people around the world.

Moving Organisations:
Translocal Political and Religious Affiliations

Not only Lebanese families are strongly linked translocally. Lebanese political parties, religious movements, institutions and non-governmental organisations have also looked to the Lebanese abroad as a global resource and constituency. To exemplify, I want to draw attention to the Zrariye youth club *(nadi)*, the women's organisation *El-Zahraa*, the *Islamic Centre* and the *Amal* movement. These institutions are deeply rooted in local contexts, either Lebanese or Ivoirian. At the same time, their activities and practices extend beyond the constraints of the national territories they were founded in, as they unfold translocally and transnationally.

Zrariye Youth Club
Hamzi is a member of the Zrariye Youth Club *(nadi)*. Members of the *nadi*, young men and women, meet regularly in the village, organise social and political events such as the 1996 Environment Day, when they mobilised youth to clean up their village. Hamzi currently lives in Beirut where he studies law but spends the weekends in the village. In contrast to his two brothers who live and work in Abidjan, he does not want to migrate, preferring to dedicate himself to his education. This is possible only because his brothers, who invite him to Abidjan once a year, are paying for his university studies. Significantly, Hamzi also uses his annual trip to Africa in the interests of the Youth Club. One of the Youth Club activities is to create and print a calendar to be sold as fundraising. On one of his trips to Abidjan, Hamzi took numerous calendars with him and sold them to various Zrariye migrants. The calendar is composed of photographs of Zrariye, including the

mosque, the river and other typical village scenes. The annual production of calendars of this kind by political parties and organisations is widely spread in Lebanon. Sales are frequently of a translocal nature. Migrants and visitors in both directions bring the calendars to migrant communities in Abidjan and Zrariye where they are sold to decorate private homes, shops and offices. The migrants who buy these calendars can in turn support their preferred political party or organisation. In addition, they openly demonstrate their respective support by hanging the calendars in their shops and homes.

During his stay in Abidjan, Hamzi organised a workshop with a group of Lebanese students in order to exchange ideas and evaluate plans for a possible liaison between youth in Zrariye and Zrariye migrant youth in Abidjan. The meeting turned out to be a success. Hamzi gave a lecture on the activities of the Zrariye *nadi*, while a Lebanese student from Côte d'Ivoire elaborated on the specific constraints imposed on Lebanese studying in Africa. A further meeting was planned for the following summer in Zrariye, when more of the youth as well as a number of Lebanese from Côte d'Ivoire on holidays in the village could participate.

El-Zahraa

The Lebanese Women's Organisation *El-Zahraa* (*Association Libanaise Féminine de Bienfaisance*) in Côte d'Ivoire was founded by a number of Lebanese women in 1977 as a non-political and non-religious female charity association. The expressed objective was to help the needy and the poor in their "country of adoption" and improve the friendship and mutal understanding between Ivoirians and Lebanese in Côte d'Ivoire (cf. *El-Zahraa* brochure 1993: 4). Under the ambitious leadership of Hiam Fakhreddine, who has headed the association from its foundation, *El-Zahraa* has developed into a well-known Lebanese institution in Côte d'Ivoire. Most members of *El-Zahraa* are married Muslim women from privileged backgrounds.

A small booklet printed for the eighteenth anniversary of *El-Zahraa* in 1993 lists the many projects that have been financed by the organisation. Donations in cash and kind were made regularly, for instance, to an *SOS Children's Village* in Côte d'Ivoire, to maternity hospitals in Abidjan, as well as to hospitals treating the handicapped and various other Côte d'Ivoire social and medical institutions. Several photographs in the brochure bear witness to their commitment, including Lebanese women with African children in the *SOS village* or with the handicapped. Many of these donations were given in the presence of important Ivoirian political figures and well-known personalities. Occasionally, Côte d'Ivoire ministers or the "first lady", Marie-Thérèse Houphouet Boigny, and later Henriette Konan Bédié were present at these events. The presence of these figures led to a considerable amount of public interest, with the local press giving accounts of donations provided by *El-Zahraa*. The Lebanese women were thus able to publicise their charity and at the same time found a platform to act and speak in the public domain of Côte d'Ivoire.

Pnina Werbner, who has studied a similar Pakistani women's organisation in Britain, stated that the female association *Al Masoom* represented a challenge to the established Pakistani "immigrant diasporic public sphere". According to Werbner, this has shifted from a "male dominated diasporic public sphere" to a "gendered public sphere" (Werbner 1996: 67). Werbner describes how women in *Al Masoom* have succeeded in opening up legitimate public spaces for Pakistani Muslim women, namely through popular cultural activities and humanitarian aid. In the same way, the women of *El-Zahraa* have moved into the public space and found an independent collective "Lebanese women's voice". Lebanese men are obliged to take this "voice" seriously, since they too profit from this social commitment. By publicly strengthening the friendship between the citizens of Côte d'Ivoire and the Lebanese, these women are helping to mollify popular resentment against the Lebanese in Abidjan in general.[11] This can be interpreted as a positive endeavour. However, some Lebanese women are critical of this, as the following statement from a young woman shows:

I do not want to become an active member of *El-Zahraa*. I am convinced of their work on women's issues but I do not like their practices. They always want to invite the government, the President's wife or the press. If you want to do something good you do not have to notify the press. They want to publicise what they do, which is typical of the Lebanese. They show you what they do all the time and say: "Thank you so much, Côte d'Ivoire government." They always want to show that they side with the government.

The *El-Zahraa* women have followed a similar strategy to the Pakistani *Al Masoom* women, reaching out beyond the confines of the domestic space in the Lebanese migrant community to seek recognition and legitimacy. Hence, if their activities gain acceptance in Côte d'Ivoire society and if noteworthy Ivoirian personalities appreciate their activities, even Lebanese men have to acknowledge their endeavours. They have thus positioned themselves as female social actors in the Lebanese community, creating an autonomous female public arena in the process. Apart from the assistance provided to Côte d'Ivoire organisations and projects, the *El-Zahraa* women support poor families in the Lebanese community. They help to finance a stay in hospital or pay for a flight if people do not otherwise have the means. As the president of *El-Zahraa* explained, these activities are done quietly, so that needy Lebanese are not made to feel ashamed. During the Lebanese civil war, the organisation helped orphans in Lebanon. In practice, *El-Zahraa* co-operated with women's organisations in Lebanon, first and foremost with Rabab al-Sadr and her aid programme for Lebanese orphans. As Mrs. Fakhreddine told me, *El-Zahraa* has been in contact continuously with women's organisations in Lebanon and her own personal engagement is rooted in the pre-war Lebanese women's movement.

El-Zahraa and its female members raise sizeable sums of money on a voluntary basis through a series of shows and arts and handicrafts exhibitions. It has become an annual ritual for *El-Zahraa* women to organise a big show on "Mother's Day". In 1996, this celebration was held on the 2nd June at the *Hôtel d'Ivoire* and was announced under the motto: *"Redonnez le sourire à un enfant du Liban"* (Put the smile back on a Lebanese child's face). In view of the severe Israeli bomb attack that caused a huge loss of life in South Lebanon in April 1996, half the profits of the evening was to benefit South Lebanese children, while the rest went to a maternity hospital in Côte d'Ivoire. The case in point indicates that *El-Zahraa* is intent on demonstrating its shared loyalties to both Lebanon and Côte d'Ivoire. *Fady*, a famous Lebanese singer from Côte d'Ivoire, performed at the event, which also included *Layaly el Farah*, a Lebanese folk dance group. In fact, *El-Zahraa* has supported *Layaly el Farah* in Abidjan for a long time and provided them with various opportunities to perform in public. Furthermore, *El-Zahraa* has been involved in giving extra Arabic courses to Lebanese children who are taught only French at school.

To sum up, I have shown that the *El-Zahraa* women have followed multiple approaches concerning female public engagement. While on the one hand, they have been active in humanitarian aid and forming good relationships between Lebanese and Africans in Côte d'Ivoire, they have been involved, on the other hand, in strengthening Lebanese identity by referring to translocal connections, cultural practices and language.

Islamic Centres

The *Lebanese Islamic Centre* in Abidjan opened in 1977. Similar to the *Islamic Centres* in Dakar (Senegal) and Dearborn (USA), it was not built exclusively as a mosque but was intended to meet various social, educational and spiritual needs of the Lebanese Muslim community in Côte d'Ivoire.[12] The Centre in Abidjan lacks the visual reminders characteristic of Middle Eastern mosques and is discernible from the outside only by the sign in green letters on the front of the three-storey building that reads *Centre Islamique*. On Thursday and Saturday mornings, various classrooms on the ground floor are used by *El-Zahraa* women to teach Lebanese children Arabic. When the Lebanese-Ivoirian school was established and Arabic taught parallel to French, *El-Zahraa* gave up their courses. At the moment, the rooms are being used as a *Qu'ranic* school, where children and adults are taught the basics of the *Qu'ran*. A spacious tiled staircase leads to the second floor where one large room is used as the Abidjan *husayniyeh*. The third floor of the *Islamic Centre* contains a mosque for praying and a library. The fourth floor is taken up by the private quarters of the sheikh, who lives there with his family. More than a hundred people fit into the *husayniyeh*, the largest room in the building. The front of the room is decorated with Islamic motifs and, remarkably, a huge photograph of Musa al-Sadr, a rough hint that the political orientation of the sheikh and/or the Lebanese community is close to *Amal*. Having read *"Le Liban en Côte d'Ivoire"* (1988) by Hekmat Khodr, this seems even more likely. In a short biography of the sheikh of the *Islamic Centre*, he describes how the latter grew up in South Lebanon and studied at the *Institute of Islamic Studies* founded by Musa al-Sadr. It is highly probable that the sheikh's ideological background emanates from this context. Describing the *Islamic Centre* of Dearborn (USA), Walbridge notes that it appeals to sympathisers of the *Amal* movement. Internal rivalries have led to the opening of a second centre called *The Islamic Institute of Knowledge*, which is said to be aligned with the Lebanese *Hizbollah* (Walbridge 1997: 41-86).

The *Islamic Centre* in Abidjan stands for the integration of Lebanese Shi'ites. In this context, the *husayniyeh* serves as an important meeting place for Lebanese Shi'ites in Côte d'Ivoire, where the deaths of relatives, friends, neighbours and colleagues in the translocal village are lamented. The personality of the sheikh, who is responsible for the *Islamic Centre*, is a guarantee in itself for translocal connections in the Lebanese Shi'ite community. Having grown up in Lebanon, he was educated in Iraq[13] and then nominated by the *Higher Shi'ite Council* as the sheikh in Côte d'Ivoire. Moving within the Shi'ite world, sheikhs are a strong symbol of the transnational and translocal dimension of Shi'ism.

Harakat Amal

The transnational dimension of Shi'ism comes into full play on looking at the famous Lebanese Shi'ite personality, Musa al-Sadr, the founder of the *Amal* movement. Born in 1928 in Qom, Iran, he spent the greater part of his life in Najaf, Iraq, perfecting his Arabic and carrying out religious studies at the famous Najaf Shi'ite "school" (*madrasa*). There he met the Lebanese cleric Sayyed 'Abd al-Hoseyn, the spiritual leader of Tyre at the time. Later, al-Hoseyn wrote a letter to the brilliant young Iranian cleric al-Sadr asking him to be his successor to the religious leadership of the Shi'ite community in South Lebanon. Al-Sadr accepted the ministry and arrived in Tyre in 1960, at a time of transition in Lebanon when poor Shi'ite rural areas were being opened up. During the 1960s and 1970s, rapid socio-economic modernisation, urbanisation, the spread of education and the impact of the new "Shi'ite wealth" from migration brought greater mobilisation and politicisation to the Shi'ites. In the past, they had been illiterate, confined to an agriculture in decline and dominated by a small elite of wealthy landowners. In general, the Shi'ite population had begun to challenge "the rules of the game" and to question the distribution of power and resources in the Lebanese system. Many young Shi'ite men, angered by the political establishment and acting

Figure 9: Moving organisations and clerics: Amal *and Musa al-Sadr in South Lebanon*

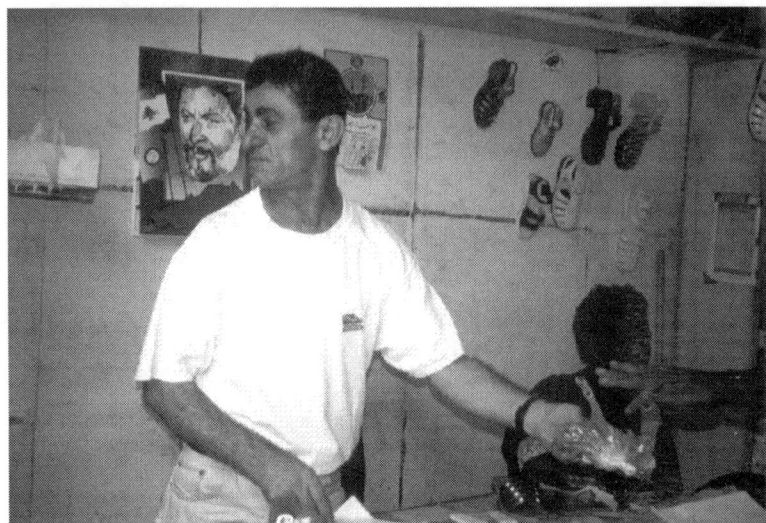

Figure 10: Amal *and Musa al-Sadr in Côte d'Ivoire (in a plastic shoe shop)*

out a new-found political consciousness, were attracted to a number of leftist political parties and movements. As the Shi'ite community became more socially mobile, the charismatic cleric and man of action, Imam Musa al-Sadr, began competing with leftist groups for Shi'ite allegiance. In 1974, he created "The Movement of the Deprived" *(harakat al-mahrumin)*, a social movement that quickly gained success. In 1975, Musa al-Sadr officially established the *Amal* movement. The literal translation of the Arabic word *Amal* is "hope" and, at the same time, it is an acronym for *afwaj al-muqawama al-lubnaniya*, meaning "Groups of the Lebanese Resistance" (Norton 1984: 162). It was formed as a Shi'ite militia and originally designed as support for the Lebanese army against Israeli incursions (Richard 1995: 130).

Musa al-Sadr and his movement had one great advantage over the Left: an authenticity essential in appealing to people whose political awareness was new and who were still tied to religion and tradition (Olmert 1987: 199). Picard argues that the Lebanese Left failed to get their message across to the people for the simple reason that they had expressed important concepts in unfamiliar terminology (Picard 1986: 168). Musa al-Sadr, in contrast, appealed to the community's own particular culture, using familiar religious terminology. Tens of thousands of Shi'ites took part in numerous mass meetings and rallies throughout Lebanon, many of which coincided with important dates in the Shi'ite religious calendar. During these rallies, al-Sadr demonstrated his ability to move people with a compelling combination of political speech and religious sermon. In brief, al-Sadr and his movement drew heavily on Shi'ite religious heritage with its symbolism, rituals, heroes and values. They attempted to reinterpret symbols and give a contemporary meaning to rituals, relating their implications to the current struggle. Thus, they used religious symbolism to legitimise political action (Nasr 1985: 14).

Al-Sadr also introduced a language that became his "trademark". It revolved around the themes of "disinheritance" and "deprivation". Al-Sadr basically stated that he was on the side of the "wretched of the earth" and was thus able to mobilise broad social support in the Shi'ite community. The language was more inclusive than the language of class conflict used by the Lebanese Left. It appealed to various groups within the Shi'ite social strata. The new intellectual elite (professionals and civil servants), the poor crisis-ridden small peasantry, rural-urban migrants and low-salaried workers in the cities became his supporters. Moreover, he appealed to the "new rich", the returned migrants who had prospered in West Africa. By the late 1960s, the impact of this new "Shi'ite wealth" had been strongly felt in the South, where migrants invested in large agricultural estates that had once belonged to the old leading families of the region. The returned migrants gained financial control over other sectors of the Lebanese economy, particularly the entertainment industry and commerce with Africa. With a few exceptions, however, the potential impact of the "new rich" Shi'ites on the national level was limited. This was partly a result of the hegemony exercised by their Sunni and Maronite counterparts over much of the industrial and commercial sectors (Halawi 1992: 75). Furthermore, the old system of clan politics excluded them from the political and social elite in Lebanon. Faced with these obstacles, the "new rich" Shi'ites pushed for change and like Musa al-Sadr, questioned traditional feudal structures. They made ideal partners for the Shi'ite cleric, as Ajami stresses: "Like him, they were searching for a place in the country, some middle course between feudalism *(al-iqta)* and extremism *(al-tatruf)*" (Ajami 1986: 84).

Musa al-Sadr did not deliver diatribes on the illegitimacy of wealth but stressed that contributions were needed. He assured them that wealth was a blessing *(nima)* and should be converted into political and social power. Al-Sadr appealed to the "new rich" and their embittered recognition that money had not brought social and political power in the old system. Imam Musa, as they called him later, not only addressed returned migrants but travelled to West Africa, including Nigeria, Ghana, Sierra Leone and Senegal. Significantly, he was the first political and religious personality in Lebanon to realise that Shi'ite migrants in West Africa might be a consequential support group. He gathered the Lebanese migrant communities around him in Africa and gave passionate political and religious talks. Although most of these people were neither pious nor endowed with religious learning, al-Sadr's religious terminology and his inclusion of Shi'ite culture and history appealed to them. His dynamic speeches, which made use of his rhetorical and charismatic abilities, gave them a strong awareness of belonging to the Shi'ite community, with its traditions, history and culture. This occurred at a time when they were struggling to redefine their identity as Lebanese in West Africa. As many of them had left their country for economic reasons, they appreciated al-Sadr's social commitment to setting up institutions and charities. When asked for financial support, they were ready to give assistance. He had something important to offer in return: "He gave voice to their own vague resentments and claims" (Ajami 1986: 99). Their sentiments were directed against the old political system with which they could no longer identify. Aptly, he gave them the opportunity to become an integral part of and identify with a new Lebanese Shi'ite movement that was not tied exclusively to a specific place in Lebanon but relied on new emerging religious identities developed translocally "at home" as well as among the migrant communities "abroad".

Whereas the pre-war years were marked by Musa al-Sadr's impressive mobilisation of the Shi'ite population, the civil war signalled the decline of his influence. During the war, Shi'ite recruits were also attracted by other militias, with more of them carrying arms under their banners than under those of Sadr's movement. As Norton pointed out, the war ruined Imam Musa's prospects, since he was not a man of war: His weapons were words and symbols, lost in the loud din of war. His efforts to stem the bloodshed – ranging from a public fast to meetings without end – had no effect upon the furious fighting. Sadr seemed to be eclipsed by the violence that engulfed Lebanon. Ironically, it was his disappearance in 1978 that helped to redeem the promise of his earlier political efforts (Norton 1987: 208).

Musa al-Sadr arrived in Libya on August 25, 1978 to visit Libya's ruler, al-Qaddafi, but vanished under mysterious circumstances. There is a general belief that the latter was responsible for al-Sadr's disappearance. While Musa al-Sadr's fate still remains a mystery, it took on immense symbolic significance in the *Amal* movement, where he was elevated to the rank of a Shi'ite martyr. Shi'ite doctrine proclaims that the twelfth Imam, who vanished in 873-874, will return at some future date (Ajami 1986: 21). The mystification of Musa al-Sadr was complete and his faithful followers left to console themselves with his picture, while awaiting the return of the Hidden Imam *(al-imam al-gha'ib)*. In fact, the "absent Imam" became a symbol for further political mobilisation of the masses. Today, almost twenty years after his enigmatic disappearance, his picture still hangs in public and private spheres throughout South Lebanon, as well as in migrant homes. The 31st August is celebrated as the commemoration of Musa al-Sadr's disappearance. Organised by *Amal* in Nabatiye, it has become an important political-religious event. Days or even weeks later, *Amal* supporters in Abidjan can watch a video of the event or listen to an audio cassette as they too commemorate the 31st August.

As shown above, Musa al-Sadr not only addressed Shi'ites in South

Lebanon but realised that he could reach their relatives in the migrant communities all over the world. By doing so, he became a pioneer in the creation of a translocal Shi'ite identity that linked Shi'ites and *Amal* activists all over the globe. Nowadays, this has become common practice and local religious leaders engage in intensive travelling. They are thus able to take care of the followers who are not confined to Lebanese national territory but live in various migrant communities in all corners of the earth. In this context, local *Amal* or *Hizbollah* sheikhs and clerics travel to Abidjan and other West African countries, as well as to Europe and the United States of America, giving lectures and sermons and engaging in political discussions.

This chapter outlined how, in the course of migration, a local village population transgressed boundaries formerly taken for granted and thus developed into an emergent translocal village-in-the-making. Instead of pursuing the idea that social relations are framed by a container such as the nation state or a locality, I argue that the translocal village-in-the-making should not be taken as a fixed, stable or bounded reality but as the result of the practices of its social actors. Religious events such as *ramadan* and *'ashura*, important life-cycle occasions (births, marriages, deaths) and business activities, all of which encourage the maintenance of social ties across space should not go unmentioned here. Although people who consider themselves members of the same village no longer necessarily live in the same place, they are nevertheless able to produce new deterritorialised forms of proximity and virtual face-to-face relations. By making use of recent communication technology developments that help to transcend and reduce time and space constraints and availing of the rapid feedback of communication channels, people achieve some of the efficiency of face-to-face interaction.

5. Gendering the Translocal Village

> Diaspora women are caught between patriarchies, ambiguous pasts, and futures. They connect and disconnect, forget and remember, in complex, strategic ways. (Clifford 1994: 314)

Gendered Mobilities

The following chapter is a contribution to the question of how translocal migration is gendered. Focusing on the specific experiences and agencies of men and women moving between South Lebanon and West Africa and vice versa, I would like to shed some light on how gender relations have been negotiated and changed in the dynamic processes of producing translocal social fields. Does the making of a translocal village tend to sustain gender hierarchies and inequalities or does it hold the potential for women to manoeuvre in new spaces? How is the making of a translocal village gendered and how are gender relations constituted translocally? Gender constructs are not fixed and unalterably given in society. On the contrary, they are subject to constant negotiation as are constructs of place. How these processes are intertwined and mutually constituted in a translocal arena will be outlined in the following.

Analysing the continuous movement between Zrariye and Abidjan with a gender-conscious gaze, it is obvious that men and women have quite different experiences in the process of migration. Most men leave for Africa for the first time as young single men looking for better job opportunities. During the sixteen years of civil war in Lebanon, many of them fled the country as war refugees. In a troublesome economic era in Lebanon, unmarried men are often the main breadwinners for their families back home. Many see migration as an opportunity to earn more money, enabling them to support their families and still have some left for their personal use. In addition, it allows them to save the money required to get married. The overall deterioration of the Lebanese economy presents a bitter challenge to young men of marriageable age. Faced with job insecurity and the high cost of living, many have to postpone marriage (Khudr 1997: 17). Khudr states that in present-day Lebanon most young men who marry either belong to very wealthy families in a position to support their sons or they are migrants and can afford the steadily increasing marriage expenses (dowry, marriage festivities) (Khudr 1997: 17).

Migration is an escape from war and economic crisis for many young men, and an opportunity to avoid immediate social control and the modesty of village life. The transnational move from Zrariye to Abidjan is at the same time a global rural-urban flow. African cities represent newly-found freedom, either in the form of bars, discotheques, alcohol or the first sexual experiences with African girl-friends or prostitutes. One Zrariyen woman told me: "A lot of Lebanese men go to prostitutes. They have money, own houses and want to buy women as well". Now that the trafficking of women has entered the global arena, the prostitutes are no longer exclusively West African but also come from Morocco. More recently, they have been brought from Eastern European countries to Abidjan, which has a reputation for being the "prostitution capital". Sexual freedom and income opportunities are equally relevant options for young men and may account for continued migration despite a decline in the chances of finding a well-paid job in Abidjan. For male adolescents living in fairly poor circumstances in South Lebanon, "Abidjan" still has the semblance of being the end of the rainbow, the land of "unlimited" possibilities. Interestingly, migration has virtually become a *rite de passage* in the minds of the male village youth. They see it as the turning-point from "innocent" boys to men of experience. Alia, a 25-year-old woman from Zrariye, gave me her view of this male *rite de passage*:

You know, Lebanese men are twenty years old or younger when they go to Africa. They have never had a love affair or a sexual relationship before. Then they travel to Africa and meet girls willing to have sexual relationships with them. They won't find this here because life is much more sheltered. In Africa they have sexual relationships without any protection. They are so careless and they know nothing. So, when most of them come back to Zrariye, the only thing they talk about is their sex life. They feel much far superior to us girls and boys who stayed in the village, which is horrible.

The above is an indication that young men are able to move more freely in Abidjan and seek adventure. Although this attitude is not openly accepted in the Lebanese community, it is silently tolerated, especially as many young men are alone in Abidjan, removed from the direct control of their close family. A dangerous "side-effect" of these male activities was the spread of the HIV virus among the male migrant group, making them a potential risk to their current or future wives in Lebanon. The Lebanese state reacted to this and introduced a compulsory premarital medical examination (Abul-Husn 1994: 14). However, male mobility has not been restricted and it can be concluded that young men's freedom of movement generally increases with migration. They are single, have a monthly income and can move about in the city of Abidjan to their heart's content.

Contrary to men, the mobility of women in Abidjan is subject to constraints. 25-year-old Mariam has been living in Abidjan for a few years. She arrived shortly after her marriage and in the meantime has two children. Comparing her life now and then, she confessed:

Life in Zrariye is better. A woman can walk through the streets at night alone. No one has to be afraid of thieves or murderers. In Zrariye, I worked as a telephone operator and came back from work at 11 o'clock at night. No one worried about me and I wasn't afraid either. Here in Abidjan we are constantly afraid. Women move around more freely in the villages and visit each other more often. In Abidjan, people are more restricted to the house or their work. My husband works all day long and only comes home late in the evening. I miss my family, which I used to visit very often. The friends and relatives I have here in Abidjan live a good distance away and I can't afford a taxi every time I want to visit them.

Mariam points to the isolation she faces in such a large city, where the Lebanese do not always live in the same neighbourhood and where work has become the predominant feature in people's lives. Relatives and neighbours visit each other less frequently than they would in the village and, as the extended family pattern begins to show signs of disintegration, the overall shift from extended family households to nuclear families is visible everywhere. Whereas many young couples in Zrariye are forced by economic circumstances to live with the husband's family, the concept of privacy has gained significance in the Lebanese community in Abidjan. In some instances, women in Abidjan judge this development positively, stating that they are happy to have more "privacy". Others, in contrast, acknowledge that they miss the close contact with their kin group. Unlike Mariam, Zaynab prefers conjugal life in Abidjan:

I prefer to live alone with my husband. In the beginning, we lived with my parents-in-law in the same house. Then my husband migrated and for a whole year I was on my own with his parents, who always tried to interfere in my son's education. I was relieved when my husband sent me the air ticket. After that we began life on our own in Abidjan. We live a more sheltered life here and don't have visitors coming and going at any time of the day. They usually phone before they come. I am more at ease here and feel less controlled.

The primary objective of most Lebanese in Abidjan is "to work and save money". Middle-class women are not prepared to spend a lot of money on taxis to visit friends and relatives living in a different neighbourhood and are often not in a position to do so. Therefore, women who do not work for a regular wage are more likely to be at home alone. Their spatial mobility is even more restricted than in the village and close contact to female neighbours only arises when they live in apartment buildings inhabited by other Lebanese.

The prevailing element of fear of Africans, which is particularly pronounced among girls and women, puts a further constraint on their movements. It is evident that mobility constraints hamper young girls in Abidjan more than in Zrariye. Many families are concerned about their children, fearing the "bad influence" of African youth. A mother of three young girls (2, 9 and 13 years) puts it as follows:

> The children are only allowed to go to school and play in the house. We have to be more careful here than in the village. We can't let them play outside or be with the Africans.

The village presents quite a different picture. Even small children can play outside during the day or wander around and explore the village. Older girls regularly go for walks on Zrariye's main street or go shopping. 23-year-old Dunia, who is single, was born in Abidjan and lived there until five years ago when her father made the decision to return to Lebanon and live in the village. Asked about her life in Abidjan and Zrariye, she replied:

> I personally have more freedom in Zrariye. Here, I can go wherever I want to and my father doesn't say a word. In Abidjan he was much stricter and I was not allowed to go out alone. Here, no one cares when I go out!

Fear of being attacked by Africans can, on the one hand, be explained as a response to the "unknown" and the "foreign", and as a racist reaction towards Africans. On the other hand, Lebanese in several African countries have had to face violent attacks deliberately aimed at them and their property. Their fear is more understandable from this point of view.

To conclude, it can be said that migration does not necessarily entail greater freedom or introduce more opportunities for women. On the contrary, after close social observation of the villagers, it becomes apparent that girls and women can often move more freely in the village than in the city of Abidjan. This is notably so in families where the parents have only recently migrated to Africa. In such cases, the city tends to evoke a sense of the unknown, coupled with anxiety about male harassment and violence. Even in families that have been in Abidjan for a long time and whose daughters were born there, parents are often afraid that rumours of their daughters' behaviour and interaction with Africans could spread around the translocal village. Moreover, female mobility can be restricted as a result of the economic circumstances of husbands or fathers. The legitimation to stay in Abidjan is first and foremost to earn money and attempt to save it, thus expensive transportation fees to visit female friends or relatives are not always approved of.

These examples confirm that the meaning of South Lebanese migration to Côte d'Ivoire is not the same for women as it is for men. Indeed, male migration and female migration provoke quite different reactions from the social environment in Zrariye and Abidjan. In general, men's movement to Abidjan and their mobility within the city is accepted more and controlled less than that of women. If men keep to the "kin contract" and send remittances regularly, the family at home or in Abidjan is far more likely to accept men's freedom of movement or even their escapades. On the other hand, if a man stops sending money, the family back home will almost inevitably try to exert social control and pressurise him in Abidjan. This can include criticism of his life-style, about which they may have heard from other people in the translocal village.

Despite women having migrated thousands of kilometres from Zrariye to Abidjan, they may experience social control and restriction of movement as more extreme than "at home" in the village. Women who migrate to Abidjan on their own are compelled to stay with a close family, so that their behaviour and mobility tend to be more curtailed than at home. To migrate alone as an unmarried woman is in itself to question the norm of remaining a father's responsibility. Women in Abidjan thus feel obliged to be on their best behaviour if rumours in the translocal village are to be avoided. It seems that young women – married or unmarried – can move around more easily in the village and South Lebanon in general. Some of them work in nearby cities and are able to move around on their own. As a rule, these movements and activities are less questioned and controlled.

Renegotiating Marriage Practices in the Translocal Village

Despite the fact that life in Africa is not entirely easy for Lebanese women and can entail confinement, most girls from Zrariye dream of marrying a rich Lebanese man from Côte d'Ivoire. When the dream comes true and the young women travel to Abidjan, they frequently have to adapt to difficult and unexpected realities. Similarly, most of today's young male migrants have notions too of marrying a Lebanese girl, preferably from the same village. Although they may have had relationships with African women, the translocal family expects them to marry a Lebanese. For a young man in Abidjan, "home" becomes essentially a female place. It is where his mother is left behind and where he chooses his future wife. The wife, a man's imagined "home", ideally moves with him later to Africa where she remakes a Lebanese home by cooking Lebanese dishes, decorating the house with Lebanese/Muslim objects and raising the children in the Lebanese and Muslim tradition. Marrying Lebanese women from the same patriclan and/or the same village has in fact been a key factor in the making of the translocal village, drawing people, families and patriclans closer to each other in the process, despite the spatial separation between Lebanon and West Africa.

Local and patriclan endogamy has always been a cherished norm in Lebanon but the first migrants who left for Africa at the beginning of the twentieth century were not able to live up to normative expectations. They were too poor to return to Lebanon to look for a bride or even to pay her fare, should a relative at home have found one for them. It was only when travel between West Africa and Lebanon became cheaper and communication technologies made it possible to keep in touch regularly that migrants were in a position to remobilise the value of the village and patriclan endogamy, and to cherish them anew.

It was once quite common, especially for poor small-scale traders living in the hinterland villages and small towns of Guinea, Sierra Leone and Senegal, to marry African women (van der Laan 1975: 251; Khuri 1968: 92). The parents of the bride and the elders in the community normally approved of these marriages. Van der Laan states that there must have been at least a few hundred mixed marriages in Sierra Leone, many of which were successful (van der Laan 1975: 251). A "successful" marriage generally meant that the Lebanese husband identified with the African family and the ethnic group he married into. He learned the language and was aware of the cultural obligations, took the decision to settle in his wife's village and gave up his plan to retire to Lebanon.

In other cases, a marriage broke down when the husband decided to move away from the village and his wife and children refused to go with him. In Sierra Leone, many Lebanese withdrew from the villages in the 1950s and moved to Freetown. Mixed marriages tended to fail, not alone through the refusal of women to follow their husbands but because African-Lebanese marriages were frowned on in the cities (van der Laan 1975: 252). Another reason for divorce was the sudden arrival of a Lebanese wife. More often than not, a Lebanese man's relatives in Lebanon would decide that he was to marry a Lebanese girl. Some marriages were prearranged long in advance (van der Laan 1975: 252). Thus, entire Lebanese family groups in Africa could rise to put pressure on African-Lebanese couples. Men were urged to remarry Lebanese girls. A Lebanese married to an African usually remains an outsider in the Lebanese community. He is said to have abandoned what was perceived as the initial purpose of emigration, i.e., to earn money and return to Lebanon. Thus, any ties that would oblige an emigrant to settle in Africa, such as marriage to an African, are strongly opposed and punished with social rejection as well as exclusion from important economic networks. Being married to a Lebanese woman, on the other hand, means attachment to a broad network of social relations that can engender business advantages.

In present day Côte d'Ivoire, African-Lebanese marriages are rare and most of the Lebanese born in West Africa marry within the Lebanese community or choose a wife in Lebanon. In the same vein, many of the migrants return to the village after a few years in Abidjan "on the look-out" for a future bride. Indeed, parents are often involved in the hunt for a potential marriage partner in their sons' absence. Thus, the engagement is frequently announced during a young man's one-month visit home, while the marriage generally takes place on a second visit one year later. Interestingly, migration has changed the "marriage procedures". In the past, an engagement was an informal agreement between the respective families of the bride and groom. Today, especially if the groom is a migrant, an official engagement entails the writing and signing of the marriage contract (*katab al-kitab*, literally: to write [sign] the book) in front of a local sheikh or an urban religious court. The chief component of the marriage contract is the *mahr* (dowry). It consists of a sum of money or its equivalent, which the bridegroom is obliged to present to the bride. The *mahr* becomes the exclusive property of the bride after marriage and in many cases she is free to dispose of it as she wishes. Divided into two portions, the "prompt" portion of the *mahr* is paid on the occasion of marriage, while the "deferred" portion is payable only if a divorce arises. Although husband and wife are legally married after signing the contract, they are socially accepted as having a sexual relationship only when the marriage festivities are over and the bride has moved into her husband's house. Someone explained to me that "Most people, particularly the girls' parents, want the marriage contract to be signed before the official wedding ceremony because it obliges the future husband to keep his promise", which specifically refers to migration. Young men come and go and occasionally make marriage promises. However, they might not show up a year later, leaving the girl and her family waiting in vain. On the other hand, the official engagement that represents a legal marriage contract has given rise to new social problems. If men or women change their minds and no longer want to marry, the procedure is the same as if they had indeed got married. Although sexual relations may not have taken place and the couple not seen each other during the official engagement period, the marriage contract was signed and thus a legal divorce required. The following incident was related to me:

> I know the case of one woman who got engaged by signing a marriage contract. During the two-year engagement period, the husband became more closely affiliated with the *Hizbollah* and wanted his future wife to wear the veil. In the end, the woman refused to marry him but the husband wouldn't let her go. The family had to fight to get the divorce legalised and pay a lot of money, although the couple had not even lived together. Then he finally gave in!

The case above exemplifies how social norms and legal practices are renegotiated when new social challenges like migration question procedures hitherto taken for granted. The new practice of legally treating an engagement as the marriage contract itself has made it more difficult for young men and women to cancel an engagement. Thus, these legal readaptations reinforce social relationships set up within the translocal village between a male migrant living and working in Abidjan and a bride living at home in Zrariye. They transcend distance and compel people to uphold their decision despite spatial separation and wait until enough money has been raised to cover the marriage celebrations.

Women's Diversity: Deciphering Translocal Female Identities

> Just as Western feminists make a political statement when they choose between overalls and shoulder-padded suits, so too do Arab women, often with more dire consequences. (Bulbeck 1998: 33)

When I visited Zrariye for the first time in 1993, I was amazed by the different styles of women's clothes in this Shi'ite village. Walking with curiosity through the village, I passed a woman wearing a mini-skirt, a skin-tight body, high-heel shoes and flashy make-up, while on the other side of the road a woman passed by wearing the typical black, cloak-like, Iranian-style *chador*. She had black gloves on and thick black socks despite the summer heat of the day. Only her eyes, nose and mouth were uncovered. A little later, I went into a "telephone shop", where I was confronted by a young woman wearing a colourful silk headscarf pinned under her chin, a long-sleeved blouse and a long skirt. While I was waiting for a connection, I noticed an elderly woman, who was talking loudly on the phone to some relative in Abidjan, wearing a large white scarf loosely wrapped around her head. When I left the shop, I met a woman who was dressed just like me in jeans, T-shirt and tennis-shoes. I was very puzzled by these total contradictions in dress and wondered what they were all about.

Do they represent lives that are lived differently? Are they expressions of political and/or religious beliefs and identities? What elements in women's backgrounds and experience are responsible for their distinct type of dress and specific life-styles? In what way does migration and life in an African environment influence how women live?

I will pursue these issues by focusing on the lives of several women. Amira, Rima, Zaynab, Neyla, Sanaa, Alia, Randa and Hind are women from the translocal village of Zrariye and come from diverse family, generational, educational, political and economic backgrounds. Some of them share the experience of migration and remigration, while others have never left Lebanon but lived through years of civil war, Israeli occupation and finally the post-war period. I chose these life stories as typical for a great number of South Lebanese women, in an attempt to point out their differences, struggles and common interests. In the age of globalisation, of translocal and transnational migration, these women are obliged to redefine and reconstruct their local identities. Migration has led to the much cited quest for identity, particularly for those who find themselves abroad, but also for those who remain behind and find their local life-worlds transported to new settings and practiced in novel and occasionally disturbing ways. Old habits, life-styles, norms and values have to be renegotiated in the context of new surroundings and challenges. Similarly, local female identities have to be redefined in globalised contexts. Women struggle, for example, for "true" translocal female identities and go through negotiation processes that are not limited to the village in Lebanon or a specific migrant community, but transcend national and geographic boundaries and unfold translocally. In this sense, it is no longer possible to differentiate between the social worlds of "migrants", on the one hand, and "people left behind", on the other – the translocal village in-the-making is the social arena for negotiation processes. A case in point is the ongoing struggle for the meaning of appropriate religious practices. I argue that women in the translocal village, in Zrariye, in Abidjan and elsewhere, take up these controversial discussions by making distinctive and demonstrative statements about their political-religious, kinship and gender identities. Specific life-styles and modes of dress are employed to signify a point of view or political affiliation. These modern dress styles exposed in the translocal village, whether "modern Muslim" or "Western", differ greatly from the traditional local dress in South Lebanon.

The trend in the Middle East and in Lebanese migrant communities all over the world up to the Iranian Revolution of 1979 was the abandonment of any form of veiling by the younger generation. However, in areas such as South Lebanon, women have long since practiced only a limited form of veiling, particularly manifest in the peasant population. Adopting a key role in agricultural production, women used to work in baggy breeches, long shirts and wear thin scarves tied at the nape of the neck over which they often wore a big straw hat as protection from the sun. This was in fact the most practical and convenient form of dress for working on the land. It would be impossible for these women to appear in the fields dressed in the long coats now worn by "modern Muslim women".

Not many women opt to dress in this fashion, presumably due to its "peasant" look. It has become a symbol of the backward and the "traditional", with which most of the women in Zrariye or Abidjan no longer want to be identified. The latter prefer "modern" clothes that represent competing female identities in the translocal village. In the following I will illustrate this clash of visual signifiers by presenting different female identity "types", such as "modern Muslim women" and "Westernised women", whereby these so-called "types" should not be taken as fixed, static or closed entities. On the contrary, in presenting these life stories, I will be voicing the complexities, ambiguities and conflicts that make up the lives of South Lebanese women.

Translocal "Modern Muslim Women"

Amira's Rite de Passage from a "Westernised" to a "Modern Muslim Woman"

The term *rite de passage* is a classical anthropological denomination to describe rituals that accompany changes of place, state, social position and age. Many *rites de passage* take place as a result of a personal crisis, in the transition from one stage of the life-cycle to the next as in birth, puberty, marriage or death. I want to suggest here that the social phenomena of the so-called "new veiling" described for various Muslim countries can be understood in Amira's life as a *rite de passage*. I was told by several women that a specific event in their life-cycle was chosen for the "veiling" step. It could be marriage, the birth of the first child or a religious event such as *ramadan*, all of which further a decision that has gradually matured.

I met Amira for the first time in the summer of 1995 in Zrariye, where she spent a three-month holiday at the house of her parents. Her permanent residence is in Abidjan. Thirty-year-old Amira grew up in Zrariye, where she passed her *baccalaureate* and began studying at a Beirut university. She broke off her studies two years later to marry Muhammad, whom she had known for many years. At that time, Muhammad had already been living in Abidjan for several years where he owned a plastic shoe factory. Amira followed him to Africa and stayed at home to look after the household. Amira and Muhammad are very concerned that they have not had any children in their seven years of marriage.

When I first encountered Amira in Zrariye during her summer holiday, she asked me to go to the beach with her. She drove her father's Mercedes and was accompanied by her three sisters and their children. Amira, like her sisters, was dressed in shorts and a T-shirt and wore her long black hair in plaits.

She invited me to visit her at her home in Abidjan, which I did during my two-month stay in Côte d'Ivoire. On my first visit she was dressed in the same kind of clothes she wore in Zrariye. When I came to visit her again a few days later – it was the first day of *ramadan* – I got a surprise when she opened the door: She had swapped her T-shirt and shorts for a long skirt, a long-sleeved blouse and a colourful scarf that hid her hair. She laughed when she saw the astonished look on my face and began to talk:

I have been thinking about wearing the scarf for a long time. Now I am very sure about it. This year I decided that on the first day of *ramadan*, which is today, I would put on the scarf and wear it forever. It is very bad if you put it on and then take it off later. My sister did that. She lives here in Abidjan and used to wear the veil. Then she went to Lebanon for a holiday and my other sisters and her friends, none of whom wear a scarf, laughed at her. It happened when they went for a picnic one day. She was laughing and joking, and all of a sudden she took it off her head and wrapped it around her hips and began to dance! That's not good. It is forbidden (*haram*). You have to be sure about your decision. If you are not sure you shouldn't wear it. But I am certain about my decision and very happy about it. I did not know much about Islam before. My parents are not very religious, you know. They pray and they fast but they don't really know how to do it properly. They do it out of tradition. I began to read and went to seminars held by a sheikh here in Abidjan. He is an intellectual and explained Islam to me. It is a Muslim woman's religious duty to wear the scarf, which doesn't mean that she has no rights. She is allowed to drive a car and work outside the home. To do anything.

I wanted to know what her husband thought of her decision. She replied:

He said it is my decision. He is neither in favour of nor against it. I know some Lebanese men who force their wives to wear the veil. These women are veiled because of their husbands, others again want to wear the scarf but their husbands don't let them. Most of the women I know do what their husbands want because they want to avoid an argument.

That evening, the first of Amira's visual alteration, I was still at their house when Muhammad came home from work. He was speechless when he saw his wife in her new outfit. He even seemed a little disturbed, hurrying away to take a shower without saying a word. Later, I went with Amira and her husband to have dinner at her sister's house. Two unveiled sisters welcomed her, hugged her and congratulated her: "*Mabruk* (congratulations)!" Muhammad said very little during the evening, apart from a few snide remarks to his wife: "You look like Imm Hassan in Zrariye – the ugliest woman in the village!" Muhammad was in a bad mood for a week and he complained to me:

It's as if she were another woman. She looks totally different and I don't like it. But I can't tell her to take it off because I am a Muslim as well!

He teased her constantly about her new official attire. Obviously annoyed, she finally asked him: "Do you want me to take it off? God will punish you in the end!" Muhammad could not help laughing and said: "Oh, God is going to punish me for so many things anyhow!" Nevertheless, Amira continued to wear her scarf in public and Muhammad had to get used to it. In describing her changed attire, Amira declared that she didn't know much about Islam as a result of her parents' ignorance. She explained:

My mother has always worn the scarf. She wore it out of tradition, whereas I wear it out of conviction!

Amira is keen to detach herself from the "tradition" she associates with a specific local practice and a lukewarm attitude towards religion. In contrast to her mother, who wore the scarf out of habit, she emphasises her deliberate personal choice in wearing the scarf, which emerged from intense religious studies. She has begun to read the *Qur'an* and attends religious lessons given by Shi'ite sheikhs at the *Islamic Centre* in Abidjan.

In fact, the *Islamic Centre* has existed for the last ten years and serves as a *husayniyeh* (a religious gathering place especially used for funeral rituals) and a religious school. Its teachings have influenced both women and men, and contributed to a distinct Shi'ite religious attitude and life-style in Abidjan. Amira claimed that: "Wearing the scarf is a question of priority for women in Islam. It is a religious duty!" She holds the opinion that it is the personal decision of each individual woman to wear the scarf or not. However, she considers herself closer to the path of God and superior to her girl-friends and sisters who do not wear a scarf. Although she still meets her unveiled friends, she is now closer to her veiled friends, who helped her with the practical problems in her "new life". They showed her how to fix the scarf, gave advice about the kind of clothes she should wear and lent her the religious books they discuss. Within the last few years, her life has centered more and more around religion. In fact, Amira has a good deal of free time and currently devotes herself to religious studies. She has no children. Two household employees relieve her of most household tasks and her husband opposes the idea of her working outside the home:

I used to spend my time shopping and talking about the latest fashion. I have always prayed and fasted; little by little I have learnt more about Islam and spent more time on religious studies. I feel much happier now!

It is quite poignant that Amira took her decision independently, without explicitly asking her husband for his point of view:

From time to time I talked to Muhammad about the scarf. He has never been either totally opposed to it or in favour of it. That's why I thought he had left the decision to me.

He was nevertheless perturbed and unable to cope when he saw his wife in her new outfit for the first time. Leading a religious life gives Amira a new orientation. She is very unhappy that they haven't had any children yet. Some people I talked to interpret her veiling as a way of pleasing God. A 35-year-old woman from Zrariye told me:

When I heard that Amira had put on the scarf, I first thought her husband wanted her to do so. If it was not his idea, then I suggest the following explanation: Amira and Muhammad have a number of problems. I mean, first of all economically. His business is not going well and they have no children. I can imagine that Amira believes if she puts on the scarf, *Allah* will see it, be merciful to her and give her a child!

In fact, several people told me that childless women often put on the scarf as a sign of faithfulness towards *Allah*. Others do so after a severe illness. They hope that *Allah* will see their religious submission and help them to recover.

A young woman who has worn the scarf from the age of twelve shared the following with me:

Some women are afraid of the final judgment and that they might go to hell. When they are young they don't think of death, that's why many don't care. As soon as they get older, they are afraid and ask God to forgive them. Last year in Zrariye, for instance, a young woman died in a car accident. She was wearing a mini-skirt and a sleeveless top. People said, "Oh, the poor thing. *Allah* will judge her and she'll be sent to hell."

Amira's decision to change her style of dress and present herself as a modest "modern Muslim" is by no means an exception but a general tendency, both in Lebanon, and in the Muslim Lebanese communities of Abidjan, Dearborn/USA and Europe.

Up until the Iranian Revolution of 1979, the younger generation in the Middle East and in the Lebanese migrant communities had set a trend to abandon all types of veiling. The removal of the veil was considered to be an unmistakable sign of women's emancipation and modernisation.[1] I saw photographs of Lebanese weddings in Abidjan at the end of the 1960s, where nearly all the women, including the bride, wore the sleeveless mini-dresses that were fashionable in Europe at the time. Those who wore the scarf tied it at the nape of the neck, exposing plenty of hair. The bride in the picture was the woman who showed me the photographs, explaining that they were attracted by this new fashion and the idea of wearing it:

We wore mini-dresses but this did not question our religious beliefs! We considered ourselves Muslim women. We prayed and fasted.

Similarly, Helen Watson cites a 70-year-old woman who talked about her youth and the "new veiling" in Egypt:

It wasn't that *hijab* [veil] and modesty were unimportant, it was just that girls were not so serious about it, meaning that we took modesty for granted and did not associate a certain style of dress with the actual modesty of the person underneath the clothes. [...] A woman's modest conduct is more important than what she wears. (Watson 1994: 150)

Several older women, all of whom wore the fine white gossamer scarf, expressed the same opinion, declaring that women's overall behaviour is more important than how they dress and how covered they are. This view does not imply their indiscriminate tolerance of young women wearing mini-skirts, either then or now. However, they accept women in jeans and do not think every woman should wear an Iranian-style *chador*.

Much has been written recently about the "new veiling"[2]. The number of books about women behind, beyond or beneath the veil may give the impression, "that Muslim women's main activity and contribution to society is being in a 'state of veil'" (Watson 1994: 141). In Western discourse, the "veil" has often been used as the most visible symbol of women's oppression. In contrast, Muslim writers are among those who have suggested a more positive position on the "veil" (*hijab*) and have emphasised the liberating potential and personal advantages of public anonymity. It is crucial to stress that speaking of the "veil" is misleading, given the diverse styles of female dress found in the Muslim world in general and specifically in the Lebanese context.

Considering Amira's latest outfit, I will argue that in the process of making translocal social fields, dress plays a valuable role in the reconstruction and renegotiation of female identities. A change in dress publicly symbolises a woman's altered identity and manifests group inclusion and exclusion at the same time by modifying and supplementing the body. I would thus like to analyse the role of dress in the context of identification and maintain that distinct modes of dress can be interpreted as an index of status, individual as well as kinship and confessional identity. Referring to Lebanon, Jean Said Makdisi states:

If it is impossible to tell a man's political beliefs from his clothing, it is relatively easier to tell a woman's. Militiamen all look alike [...]. Their wives and daughters, on the other hand, do not look alike. From the bikini to the *chador* lies a range of clothing that bespeaks a parallel range of beliefs and action. And yet, while perhaps nothing has created as much passion as the sight of the *chador* on the streets of Beirut or the bikini on the beaches, nothing is as easily misunderstood or as prone to simplistic interpretation as these items of clothing. (Makdisi 1990: 144)

Following Makdisi's argument, I want to stress that it is virtually impossible to draw a simplistic line between "veiled and unveiled". The wide range of clothing styles manifest in the "modern Muslim" group of women can represent very different identities and reveal diverse political, confessional and religious loyalties and backgrounds. Moreover, each woman is an individual creative actor, whose identity, perspective on life and agency cannot be mirrored exclusively in her mode of dress. Dress in this sense should not be analysed independently but seen in the context of overall identification processes. Nevertheless, I assert that to a certain degree specific "styles" can be put in correlation to "identity types".

When Amira was once asked "Who are you wearing the scarf for, *Amal* or *Hizbollah?*", she answered "I am wearing it for *Allah!*" She does not belong to a political party nor is her step politically inspired, she merely stresses over and over again that "It was a personal religious decision!". Many women have distinct perceptions about this and apart from signalling modesty, their dress code can be considered an explicit statement of religious and political commitment. One example is Rima, who represents the "modern Muslim woman" with a political affiliation.

Rima: "Everyone in my Family supports Amal"

I first met 22-year-old Rima, who is unmarried, in the Zrariye "telephone shop". She works there as an operator in the afternoons and works as a local school teacher in the mornings. While waiting for a connection in the telephone shop, I used to chat with her. I later visited her at home, where she lives with her mother, father and two sisters. Three brothers and two other sisters live in Abidjan. When I asked her to tell me about her life, she began by explaining that it had been deeply affected by war, with which her childhood and youth had coincided:

I was born in 1973 and the war started a short time after, so that my childhood was part of the horrific war years. I will never forget the day the Israelis came to our house at night and took my brother Ahmad. I was ten years old at the time.

Her eyes filled with tears at the mention of her brother, who had been sent to an Israeli prison camp in Ansar[3] and later killed.

They came several times and always at night. It was so frightening! They came, shouted and levelled their guns at us. Each time they were looking for our brothers, Muhammad, Ali and Ahmad, who were all in the resistance (*muqawamah*).[4] Once they even found Muhammad and put him into prison in Ansar. He survived and was released later, thank God. When they came and took Muhammad, we went to our neighbour's house. A few hours later, they bombed our home. The whole house was destroyed and we lost everything. Life was very difficult then. Are we not living in our own country? We are Lebanese living in Lebanon. We are only defending ourselves. But they call our men terrorists although they are defending our country. We are poor and Israel is rich. It has the United States on its side, which is why the whole world believes we are terrorists. Many young men and women fought in the resistance – and many of them died. I was too young. Everyone in our family supports *Amal*. That's how I got to know about it. My other sisters and I were sent for several years to a summer school organised by *Amal*, where they taught us about religion and about Musa al-Sadr. They also taught us how to dress and how to wear the scarf.

Rima's childhood and her youth concurred with the Lebanese war years. She recalls those terrible years and cannot dispel the memory of the day the Israeli soldiers took her brother, who was subsequently killed. Like many other girls, she was politicised through her brothers who supported the Shi'ite *Amal* movement. Musa al-Sadr, the founder of *Amal*, mobilised a very huge social support within the Shi'ite community, particularly young men. In several cases, parents were mobilised by their children. This was evident in a discussion with an elderly woman: "My children were in *Amal*. They went to war against Israel. I saw that they were doing something valuable and it made me support them and the movement."

Rima had covered her hair since she was ten years old:

My mother told me how to cover my hair. I was very proud to do so because I looked more like my mother and more adult with a scarf. Religion has always been important at home and my parents taught me how to pray, how to fast and how to wear the scarf.

Rima's veiling was not a self-assured decision made as an adult (in comparison to Amira) but came from a childhood socio-religious habit. At the summer camps later on, she acquired the typical method of covering the hair, identified in the translocal context as being associated with *Amal*. Her parents and brothers, who were themselves *Amal* supporters, furthered her interest in becoming a member. As a result, Rima participates in local *Amal* female group meetings in post-war Lebanon and works as a teacher at *Amal* summer camps.

Rima stands for a group of women who grew up in a family context, where the local practice of Islam, e.g., reading the *Qur'an*, praying, fasting and adhering to an explicit moral dress code played a considerable role in the organisation of everyday life. Therefore, becoming an *Amal* woman meant in certain respects following moral and religious principles and norms that had already influenced her since childhood. At the same time, her orientation towards the political-religious movement implies a distinct deviation from her mother's generation, life-world and daily activities. Whereas the latter's life was defined by household tasks, taking care of the children and working in the fields, the new political-religious Islamist movements such as *Amal* and *Hizbollah*, provide new opportunities for female social and political activities. Rima's affiliation with *Amal* legitimises her social and political engagement outside the private sphere.

In the course of telling her life story, Rima repeatedly stressed her interest in studying, education and work, and her express disinterest in household tasks:

I went to high school and completed my *baccalaureate*. I was certainly a very good student and liked studying, so I wanted to go on to university. I attended university in Saida, which is a branch of Beirut University. Unfortunately, you can only study something like literature or languages in Saida and I was more interested in natural sciences. My family does not have the means to pay university and accommodation fees in Beirut and even the daily trips to Saida became very expensive. That's why I had to quit studying and begin working again as a teacher. I work in the telephone shop in the afternoons.

Education is the most important thing in the world for Rima. She does not question marriage and, indeed, hopes to marry one day and have children. At the moment, however, education provides her with the ability to "think differently" and consider new openings. In this sense, Rima's vision of life differs considerably from that of her mother:

I don't like household work at all and I'm very pleased that my other sister likes doing it. I prefer to be out all day, either at school or in the telephone shop. I prefer to work instead of sitting at home.

Several women in the *Amal* movement have served as outstanding examples to the younger generation of women. Rima told me that she was personally motivated by Rabab al-Sadr, who ist the sister of the famous *Amal* leader Musa al-Sadr. She runs a vocational institute in Tyre that was originally founded by her brother and provides vocational training for orphans in Lebanon. Motivated by her, Rima works on a voluntary basis in *Amal* summer camps and teaches young girls religion and modest modes of behaviour.

Even Musa al-Sadr tried to reinterpret the role of women in Lebanese society by making references to Shi'ite history, to its symbolism, rituals and heroes. In his speeches, he glorified Fatima al-Zahra, the daughter of the Prophet Muhammad, as "the woman that Islam wants women to be". She carried within her that "special knowledge" of religion (*'ilm*) (Al-Sadr cit. in Halawi 1992: 179). Further, he celebrated the central position of Fatima's daughter Sayyida Zaynab, who witnessed the murder of her brother Husayn and lived to tell Muslims of the tragedy inflicted at Karbala. "The woman at Karbala complemented the man's role and his struggle. Islam needs women of this kind" (Al-Sadr cited in Halawi 1992: 179).

By publicly calling upon the vitality of women from the Prophet's family, he openly acknowledged the presence women have had in the history of Islam. This has motivated women to take over important responsibilities.

Prior to the war, Lebanon was the sole Arab country with an independent women's organisation not affiliated to a political party. The women's movement was predominantly centred in the cities, where educated and quite Western-oriented women were organised.

Musa al-Sadr and the *Amal* women addressed a different group of women, namely the poor Shi'ite women of Southern Lebanon and the Bekaa. In the course of the Lebanese wars, women became political activists, with largely unmarried women[5] either openly or secretly joining political parties and the resistance movement against Israel. In Zrariye the story of Yassar

Mroué and how this courageous young woman in her early twenties, carried out several operations against the Israelis before they killed her is often told. Today, her photograph hangs next to the other (male) Zrariye war martyrs in the village *husayniyeh*. She is highly esteemed in the village and people speak of her with great respect. This shows that women's active involvement in the resistance has been accepted – although not without ambivalence.[6] Regardless of whether they were politically organised or not, many South Lebanese women became active agents in the resistance against Israel. Some poured oil on Israeli soldiers, others fought Israeli occupation with sticks and stones or stood unarmed in front of Israeli military vehicles. Another woman told me that she secretly carried weapons in the food baskets she took to the fields and delivered them to the resistance fighters hiding there. She told me that she did so without her husband's knowledge, saying: "He would have been too worried!"

For Rima, identifying with the *Amal* movement can be interpreted as maintaining continuity in the family and not radically breaking with her background. The sentence "Everyone in my family supports *Amal*" symbolises Rima's loyalty towards her family, which was also evident when I visited her at home. She was having breakfast with her mother and two sisters when I came. The younger sister was wearing the same colourful scarf as Rima, while her older sister Fatima was uncovered. In a conversation about different modes of dress, Rima's mother told me the following story:

If you have a young tree and don't give it water or don't give it something to help it stand upright, if you don't look after it carefully, it will always lean to one side and never straighten up. In the same manner, a small child won't obey if you don't look after it carefully. A young child is like a flexible young tree.
I am sharing this example with you because I want to tell you about the differences between my daughter Rima and her older sister Fatima. I tried everything with Fatima, but she wouldn't listen to me. She has never wanted to do what I wanted. Rima, in contrast, wears a scarf and dresses modestly. Fatima never wanted to cover her hair. I tried to force her but she always took the scarf off as a young girl. She is 33 years old and still not married.

The mother feels that her parenting has failed with the eldest daughter. This is because the latter does not dress according to her mother's expectations and neither prays nor fasts. She is not married and lives a fairly "independent" life as a working woman. Being the mother of a 33-year-old "girl" implies having failed to marry her off. For the mother, Fatima personifies her failure to have looked after her daughter sufficiently. Rima, on the other hand, who dresses and behaves in accordance with her mother's values, is a "well-trained" daughter. Her mother believes she will soon find a good husband. Rima's professional ambitions and political activism as an *Amal* member is accepted, especially since her father and brothers openly support the movement. Thus, Rima is seen as being a loyal family member who embraces their political commitment. It is important to understand in this context that families in Zrariye are often affiliated to a specific political or religious party or movement. Countless people from the Zorkot patriclan support the *Amal* movement, while some of the Mroué family support *Hizbollah*. Another fraction of the Mroué family supports the *Communist* party. I observed old rivalries among the patriclans from the village being acted out under the new banner of antagonistic, political affiliations. It is, therefore, of great relevance for a father if his daughter is affiliated to a different political-religious party than he himself supports, an affiliation that could be openly or symbolically expressed in the style of dress. Both the political interest of the father and the "honour" of the entire family and patriclan are at stake. Rima has been loyal to her family. Simultaneously, as shown above, orientation towards *Amal* has provided her with a new "space to manoeuvre" and provoked an unmistakable breach with the so-called "traditional" world of her mother.

Amira, whose life was discussed earlier, chose a different path to distance herself from the world of her mother. She criticised her mother for her incorrect practice of Islam. By turning towards Islam and altering her style of dress from that of a "Westernised woman" to a "modern Muslim woman", she has detached herself from the "easy-going" attitude of her parents.

When Rima spoke to me, her hair was covered with a colourful silk scarf. Her chin and forehead were uncovered and she was wearing jeans and a long-sleeved blouse. When I mentioned my amazement at seeing so many radically different styles of dress worn by the women in Zrariye, she said:

> We *Amal* women are like that. We wear jeans, long skirts, long-sleeved blouses and colourful scarves. We are different to *Hizbollah* women, many of whom cover their chins and foreheads as well. Only the eyes, nose and mouth are not covered. They don't wear trousers like we do but only long dark coats or the black Iranian-style *chador*.

Rima does not attempt to clarify that the way she dresses is individual taste or style, but links it conspicuously to being an *Amal* woman. Her clothes serves as a visible marker of association with *Amal* as opposed to *Hizbollah* women. In an attempt to distinguish the contexts of these different female groups in the village, I will relate what I observed during the 1996 *'ashura* procession in Zrariye.

The next time I saw Rima was at the procession. She was with a large group of women that comprised an *Amal* group. Walking behind the men's *Amal* faction, they were waving green flags bearing the *Amal* emblem and shouting the names of Musa al-Sadr and Nabih Berri. The latter is the present leader of the *Amal* movement and President of the Lebanese Parliament. In fact, the religious *'ashura* march has become a political event where women

Figure 11: Contesting female identities: Amal *women during an 'ashura procession*

Figure 12: Hizbollah *women during an 'ashura procession*

demonstrate their political affiliations. Behind the *Amal* block, the *Hizbollah* men were followed by *Hizbollah* women waving *Hizbollah* flags and shouting their support for the *Hizbollah* and Khomeini. The *Hizbollah* women were dressed in black coats and scarves or wore the Iranian-style *chador*. Although both religious and political parties are Shi'ite movements that stress their Shi'ite Muslim background, each strongly disapproves of the other. Antagonisms were played out blatantly during this *'ashura* procession, as Rima shared with me later:

We *Amal* women walked in front of the *Hizbollah* men and women. *Amal* is larger and more important than *Hizbollah* in Zrariye. That's why we always walk in front of them. That day, the men from *Hizbollah* wanted to walk in front of *Amal*. They began shouting at each other. Everyone got so furious and *Hizbollah* women began to pull at our scarves. We responded by pulling theirs. This was a real fight between them and us! Later the sheikhs came and stopped the fight. In the end we won and continued to walk in front of the *Hizbollah*. We are more important than they are!

The above is an example of the sharp conflict between the two opposing parties. *Amal* women are intent on distinguishing themselves from the *Hizbollah* in general and from *Hizbollah* women in particular. Women's dress serves as an identity marker through which they can publicly demonstrate their adherence to a religious-political group. Thus, by including those who share the same identity, as expressed by their apparel, and excluding those who do not, a specific female "we-group" (cf. Elwert 1989) is constructed.

Zaynab: "My Family and I are with the Hizbollah!"

I will now introduce Zaynab, a *Hizbollah* supporter. I will strengthen my argument outlined above by suggesting that the propensity of women for these movements can be partly explained by loyalty to the family; their own desire to become actors in the political arena and their personal concern to "live differently" to their mothers and the older generation.

I met Zaynab on one of my extensive walks through the village. She was dressed in a long black coat and, immediately struck by her lively open expression, I wondered who she was. We introduced each other and she later invited me to visit her at home. I went there the next morning. Her elderly mother, Imm Ridda, was wearing a long dress with a big white gossamer scarf, which was the "typical" fashion for older South Lebanese women. Noticing how I looked at the framed photograph of a young man, she explained "That is my son. He died in the resistance five years ago in the Taklima-Tuffah area!" I knew that the *Hizbollah*[7] was particularly active in that area and thought her son had probably been with them. The photograph was decorated with artificial flowers and hung next to a picture of the Iranian leader Khomeini and Lebanon's highest *Hizbollah* cleric Fadlallah. These symbols reinforced my assumptions about the religious-political orientation of the family. Zaynab's mother, Imm Ridda, then invited me to join her for a visit to her neighbour, the sheikh's wife. I was curious to meet her. Sheikh Muhammad is known in the village as the *"Hizbollah* sheikh", while a second sheikh is referred to as the *"Amal* sheikh".[8] I was told that sheikh Muhammad is from the Mroué patriclan and later noticed that most of the people living in his neighbourhood are also Mroué and support the *Hizbollah*. This strengthened my awareness of the relationship between family background, residence and political-religious affiliation.

In the course of my conversation with Imm Ridda, the sheikh's wife and two other female visitors, Zaynab came into the room with a girl-friend, who happened to be the daughter of one of the visitors, both laughing and talking in loud voices. Both girls, 18 and 19 years old, wore black coats and dark headscarves that covered their chins and eyebrows. They were in fact more covered than Imm Ridda and her neighbours. The moment they entered the room, the girls took over the discussion, even interrupting their mothers in an attempt to convey their point of view about the "real Islam" and an appropriate Islamic way of life. I was astonished by their behaviour. I had previously been accustomed to a certain degree of respect towards the older generation and to parents in particular. They are perceived as an authority and, as a rule, it is not permissible to interrupt them or contradict their position. Zaynab and her friend surprised me with their over-confident behaviour and somewhat patronising attitude towards their mothers. I had the impression they felt religiously superior[9] and had the desire to educate their mothers, whom they described in various discussions with me as "traditional and slightly backward". They acknowledge the fact that their mothers supported *Hizbollah*, as did their fathers and brothers, but considered themselves more qualified on the practice of Islam. Zaynab explained her affiliation to the *Hizbollah*:

Many people are afraid of *Hizbollah*. No, *Hizbollah* is not frightening. It convinces people to dress and live their lives in an Islamic manner. It is when people know nothing about the *Hizbollah* that they are afraid. They simply think members of the *Hizbollah* are terrorists – as the Israelis say – but they are not. Israel bombed our villages and cities. Are we not supposed to defend ourselves? *Hizbollah* is defence. Before they existed, people did not know much about Islam. But then *Hizbollah* built their own institutions, such as schools and hospitals, and introduced their own radio and television stations. That's how they instruct people!

Gendering the Translocal Village | 143

Figure 13: "Traditional" women

Figure 14: "Westernised" women

Figure 15: "Modern Muslim women"

Zaynab and other young village women, who are quite often relatives or from the same patriclan or neighbourhood, form the female *Hizbollah* group in the village. They come together to read and discuss the *Qu'ran* or to celebrate Muslim holidays such as Prophet Muhammad's birthday.

During one of the commemoration ceremonies in the local *husayniyeh* at *'ashura* events in Zrariye in 1996, I noticed young *Hizbollah* women forming a circle in front of the *husayniyeh* and publicly contesting the ritual being taken for granted. Whereas most village women were listening to a reading of the *Qu'ran* by a woman inside the *husayniyeh*, these young women outside the building performed their own ritual, using their own words and *Hizbollah* slogans. They visually distinguished themselves from the rest of the women through their clothes and their performance. They were simultaneously questioning the course of the *'ashura* ritual, hitherto taken for granted, and the authority of older women.

Zaynab has just finished her *baccalaureate* and has notions of going to Beirut to study at the Arabic University. She hopes to stay with relatives who live in the southern suburbs there and passionately wants to become an active member of the *Hizbollah* women's organisation. The southern suburbs of Beirut were developed predominantly during the war. Commonly referred to as the "misery belt", it is the largest constituency of the *Hizbollah* and their biggest stronghold. *Hizbollah* activists built up an effective network of social institutions during the war, such as hospitals, schools, and kindergartens, all of which provided assistance at various levels to poor migrants and war refugees from the Shi'ite South and the Bekaa (cf. Jaber 1997: 145-168). It was here that *Hizbollah* found the followers, both men and women, who were prepared to work in the interests of the "true" Islam. Many women became active as teachers, nurses, doctors and lawyers in these institutions or in the *Hizbollah* women's organisations.[10] Zaynab told me of her frequent visits to relatives in *Haje Sillum* (one of the southern suburbs). On one occasion, her aunts took her to a meeting of the *Hizbollah* women's organisation, where she was so impressed by the female activists that she felt a strong urge to become "one of them."

Similar to Rima, Zaynab is another young woman interested in studying and participating in activities in the public sphere. Generally speaking, *Amal* and *Hizbollah* have provided women with new female public spaces. Within the confines of these Islamist movements, women can legitimately study, work and act politically and publicly without relinquishing their modesty and dignity. In this context, *Amal* and *Hizbollah* exhibit a certain degree of flexibility in their position on women and, as a rule, encourage women's education as a means of producing more informed mothers. Coincidentally, they provide possibilities for women to engage in public activities. In this context, the stories of the early Islamic heroines close to the Prophet Muhammad serve as historical prototypes for female public engagement and activity. Those particularly celebrated are Fatima al-Zahra, the Prophet's daughter and mother of two Imams, Hassan and Husayn, and her daughter Zaynab, who saved her nephew's life in the battle of Karbala:

[...] it was she who lifted her brother's mutilated body, presented it to God and said: "Oh God! Accept from us this sacrifice." And it was Zaynab who went with the caravan of prisoners to Kufa and ... spread the news of the battle from the heart of the desert to the capitals of the Muslim world, from Kufa to Hums to Hama to Aleppo to Ba'labak and then to Damascus. (Halawi 1992: 180)

In referring to these figures from the early Muslim period, female activists in Islamist movements are making use of the glowing examples of great Muslim women in history. Moreover, El-Bizri quotes *Hizbollah* women who stated that Khomeini had exhorted Iranian women to leave the house and become active in the Islamic Revolution. To the Lebanese *Hizbollah* women, these Iranian women often serve as a worthy example of being both politically active and engaged in the spread of the "true" Islam (el-Bizri 1995: 73-77).

Rima and Zaynab can pursue their own interests and become involved outside the house because their parents support them. Similar to the majority of working women who are politically active, they are young and unmarried. El-Bizri quotes a *Hizbollah* woman who criticises the fact that *Hizbollah* men are still on the look-out for housewives to raise the children. This particular *Hizbollah* woman, Jamila, claimed that she would rather remain single than give up her work and her political engagement. Another *Hizbollah* woman,

Asma, who is married with several children and works in *Hizbollah*, demands that "the oriental man" change his ways and take over half the household work, so that women can be both politically active and at the same time have a family: *"ce qui doit changer c'est l'homme oriental"* (*Hizbollah* woman in El-Bizri 1995: 51). Interestingly, I heard this opinion from people ranging from "modern Muslims to Westernised women", demonstrating that various young Lebanese women who live in Lebanon or abroad are searching for new life perspectives beyond the options of housewife and small-scale farmer.

To sum up my observations and interpretations regarding the two Zrariye women, Rima and Zaynab, it can be concluded that both of them have remained loyal to their family and their patriclan. Both became interested in the *Amal* and *Hizbollah* movements through their families, more precisely through their brothers' active involvement in military action and resistance. Their parents support the overall political and religious convictions of their children, although they themselves are not active. Equally, both movements have created "new female spaces" for women's public engagement, thus opening up alternative life perspectives for women beyond the "traditionally" prescribed models hitherto taken for granted. Both the Islamist movements and the women themselves are notably "modern" in this sense and by no means backward or "traditionally" aligned. Women make their own choice to support these Islamic movements that bring forth new "manoeuvring spaces" in the social arena of the translocal village in-the-making.

Moving Modern Muslim Women

In the following I will outline that the various identification processes, whether *Hizbollah* or *Amal*, are not limited to the South Lebanese villages. Contrary to conventional discussions on migrant identities, "female village identity" cannot be placed in opposition to "female migrant identity". Neither is it correct to say that the "modern Muslim woman" is a South Lebanese phenomenon and that "the Westernised woman" prevails in francophone Côte d'Ivoire. In the era of globalisation, previously assumed identity concepts of Lebanese women in Abidjan and Zrariye are being questioned and need to be redefined. From this perspective, the translocal village is the social arena where negotiation processes take place. Discussion and contestation of a "genuine" local female identity are thus not restricted to village life in Lebanon or a specific migrant community but transgress national and geographic boundaries and unfold translocally. Women in both locations take up these controversial discussions and make convincing statements about their religious, political and gender identities. Specific life-styles and modes of dress are "employed" by political movements and by women themselves as visible signifiers of their point of view and conviction, and to demonstrate their adherence to a specific female "we-group", political association or party.

The black *hijab*, the garment that represents *Hizbollah*, can be seen in

Lebanon as the expression of a specifically localised political belief. Considerably, it carries the same meaning in the Lebanese community in Côte d'Ivoire, as it does in other Lebanese migrant communities. Linda Walbridge, who carried out anthropological field work in the Lebanese Shi'ite migrant community of Dearborn (USA), describes a similar range of Lebanese female attire in an American environment (Walbridge 1997). The message transported by the Iranian-style *chador* is the same for the Lebanese worldwide and is evident in the dress code of women with a Lebanese background living in South Lebanon, Abidjan, Dearborn, Sydney or Berlin. These women are making a clear statement about their religious and political commitment and are universally identified with *Hizbollah*. I argue that the specific forms and statements manifested in localised clothing have been globalised and transported all over the world. In this sense, both *Amal* and *Hizbollah* women constitute "translocal we-groups" that not only encompass the women living in a specific South Lebanese village but include migrants, who are linked to each other by family networks and customs.

To illustrate this argument, I would like to draw on the case of Rima, whose three brothers and two sisters live in Abidjan. One of them is her 36-year-old sister Neyla, who married a migrant fifteen years ago and has been living in Abidjan ever since. I visited Neyla shortly after my arrival in Côte d'Ivoire and brought letters and tapes from her family in Lebanon. She was delighted to hear from her family and was not at all surprised to receive the letters through me. In fact, the news of my presence in Zrariye was well-known among the Zrariye migrants in Abidjan, and many were aware that I was coming to visit. Rima talked to Neyla on tape and told her about the discussions we had. Neyla was dressed similarly to her sister Rima in Zrariye. She wore a colourful headscarf, a long-sleeved blouse and a long skirt. In the Lebanese translocal context, it was easy to identify her association with *Amal*.

When I entered Neyla's apartment, my gaze immediately fell on a framed photograph hanging on the wall. I remembered seeing the same picture in their parent's house in Zrariye. It showed Rima's and Neyla's brother, Ahmad, who became a martyr (*shahid*) during the war. Next to his picture was a large sketch of Musa al-Sadr. "I like drawing!" Neyla commented and continued: "I have been drawing ever since I was a child. I drew this on the day Musa al-Sadr's disappearance is commemorated!"

On this first meeting we had an ordinary conversation. Neyla told me that she had spent the previous evening with her husband at the *Hôtel Ivoire*, a favourite meeting place for Lebanese in Côte d'Ivoire and a traditional venue for Lebanese marriages and political events. On that particular evening, the famous Rabab al-Sadr had given a reception. Neyla shared with me:

Rabab al-Sadr is an influential personality in charge of an important social organisation that helps orphans in South Lebanon. She showed slides, outlined the situation of orphans in Lebanon and described the work of the organisation. Numerous Lebanese were invited to the event, where dinner was also served. Not everyone was invited, of course, but lots of important people within the community, and especially *Amal* members. My husband and I are involved in *Amal*, that's why we were invited.

Neyla went on to tell me that fund-raising had been the overall aim of the evening:

She came to Abidjan to request the help of the Lebanese people here. Many are better off than the Lebanese at home. That's why people and organisations have lately been coming to ask for support for their social work.

Rabab al-Sadr's brother, Musa al-Sadr, was one of the first political and religious figures in Lebanon to realise that the Shi'ite migrants in West Africa had the potential to become substantial advocates, which indeed they did. He travelled to several West African countries, gave religious and political speeches and talked about his movement. He thus gave them a voice to identify with the new Lebanese Shi'ite movement that was not bound exclusively to a specific place but developed translocally. Women and men got involved in the movement – in Lebanon and in West Africa – and became its advocates. Migrants closely followed the events in Lebanon during the war. Many felt guilty when they saw the daily reports on television and thought that they should be with their tormented relatives. The only thing they could do was to help financially, which in fact many did. The flow of information showed no sign of interruption during the war years and the new war refugees were frequently carriers of the latest news and information. During the war, many young men were sent to West Africa by their parents, as Rima confirmed in the case of her brother:

Muhammad fought for *Amal*. My parents forced him to travel to Abidjan. He did not want to. He refused. However, they were afraid, as they had already lost one son and didn't want to lose another. That's why they sent him away!

Muhammad, who was sent to Abidjan against his will, sought political activity and became involved in fund-raising in the migrant community. Visits by *Amal* representatives have not ceased since then, not even after the war when the militia was converted into a political party. These days, Shi'ite political leaders direct their message to the migrant communities with a request to support the country's strenuous reconstruction process and to re-invest in the Lebanese economy. Interestingly, the present *Amal* leader, Nabih Berri, who was born in Sierra Leone, came to Abidjan in 1996. On another occasion, his wife, Randa Berri, visited Côte d'Ivoire and I was told that she invited the Lebanese in Abidjan to a "Lebanese cultural evening", where a film and slides of famous archaeological sites in Baalbek, Saida and Sour were shown in the course of the evening. Since many of the second and third-generation Lebanese born in Abidjan have never been to Lebanon, this media show served to inform them about their "homeland" and stimulate their interest in visiting the country. "Cultural evenings" can be interpreted as a method of attracting migrants and their extended families to Lebanon, as they are considered valuable potential in a social, economic and political sense for the process of reconstruction and reconciliation.

Using the case of Rima and her sister Neyla, who both grew up with a distinct political affiliation although living in two different places, I demonstrated that commitment to the political-religious movement grows translocally and that convictions are revealed in the designated life-style and the specific values adhered to. They express a distinct localised identity that can be referred to as "the modern Muslim woman", one that is lived and expressed translocally. Thus, women's political involvement contributes to the making of a translocal village and gives it its specific gendered, in this case female characteristic.

Translocal "Westernised Women"

Sanaa in Zrariye: "We are with the Communist Party"

Sanaa is a 34-year-old Lebanese woman, who was born and brought up in Zrariye. She is the youngest of ten children and the only one who did not migrate. Her brothers and sisters are spread all over the world, including West Africa, Europe and the United States. She married Ahmad three years ago and now has two children. Talking about her life, she soon touches on her relationship with Ahmad:

My love for Ahmad is a long story. I fell in love with him at school. But he did not know that I loved him and I didn't realise that he loved me, either. Ahmad was very active in the *Communist Party* and I admired his political commitment. The *Communists* were keen to fight the old sectarian system and create a new secular Lebanon. I was very enthusiastic about the idea because I saw the people in my village suffering and I wanted this to change, too.

Sanaa refers to the political development in Lebanon that began at the end of the 1960s and early 1970s when left-wing secular parties such as the Lebanese *Communist Party (al-hizb al-shuyu'i)* emerged throughout Lebanon and enjoyed significant recruitment success. For the South Lebanese who had suffered under the *zu'ama* for a long time, there was an obvious appeal to party slogans that pledged equality, improvement of health and social services, housing and better employment conditions. Thus, quite a large number of mainly young Shi'ites joined the Lebanese *Communist Party*, rebelling against "tradition" and the given social structure. The link between the situation of the Shi'ites and *Communist* rhetoric becomes apparent in the following commentary written by a political observer in the Lebanese newspaper *Al-Nahar*, 18th March 1974:

The Shi'ite are the proletariat of the earth; the class the most subdued in appearance and the most revolutionary at heart. The revolt of the Shi'ite masses could become a revolt in the name of all communities. (cit. in Picard 1986: 164)

The main objective of the South Lebanese in aligning themselves to the new left-wing parties was first and foremost the desire to overcome the confessional system and move towards secularism and socialism. After the rise of the Shi'ite *Amal* movement, the secularist left wing lost many of its supporters. Although *Amal* and the Left were concerned with similar problems and demands, the *Communists* tended to express key concepts in unfamiliar terminology. Musa al-Sadr, on the other hand, was a Shi'ite cleric with the ability to exploit references to Shi'ite history for legitimate change.

Today, young men and women in the village with a left-wing orientation still sympathise with the *Communist Party*, since an alternative left-wing party has not emerged. However, supporting the *Communist Party* in the Lebanese context does not necessarily mean being an atheist. Their vision of a socialist system differs from those of former East European countries and is primarily concerned with detachment from local religious movements and parties such as *Amal* and *Hizbollah*. Above all, it entails a secular conviction.

Women who openly support the *Lebanese Communist Party* are frequently the wives or daughters of *Communist* men and dress in Western-style clothes. They wear jeans and T-shirts, fashionable skirts and blouses, and some wear mini-skirts and sleeveless blouses. All of them are unveiled, which for them is a public statement on their aversion to the religion domination of their lifestyles. At the same time, they do not consider themselves atheists. Some deny that Islam demands wearing the scarf and consider Muslim values such as honesty more crucial than covering their hair. Others are convinced they know the demands of Islam but either do not care or claim they will probably wear the veil when they grow older. Many of them pray and fast, whereas others admit to being Muslim but not to practicing their religion.

Sanaa does not question Islam but is opposed to a confessional political system and religious-political movements. She feels wonderful wearing mini-skirts and sleeveless blouses and loves buying fashionable new clothes. I got the impression that she was even proud of wearing them. Her husband considers himself a *Communist* and is not bothered by how she dresses. She acknowledges a sense of freedom in wearing a mini-skirt and letting everyone see her beautiful long, curly hair: "I can wear whatever I like and whatever I consider beautiful. It makes me feel free. I do not have to cover my body with ugly loose clothes."

She feels superior to "modern Muslim women". Similar to several other "Westernised women", Sanaa does not think that women cover their hair voluntarily or choose to wear a *hijab*. She told me:

> They might say they do it of their own free will but I don't believe it. They do it because of their fathers or their husbands. Generally, I believe that the veil is a symbol of women's oppression.

I frequently observed women from both groups, the "Westernised women" and the "modern Muslim women", attempting to demonstrate their superiority *vis-à-vis* the "other". Let me illustrate this with the following empirical observations:

I once accompanied Sanaa to a "modern Muslim woman" called Fatin, who lives with her family in Abidjan and only spends the summer holidays in the village. Sanaa specialises in beauty-products from a well-known French company and her favourite customers are migrant women. On that particular day, Sanaa was dressed in a skin-tight body and tight-fitting jeans. Fatin, in comparison, wore loose clothes in the "modern Muslim" style. Sanaa began to advise her on the advantages of the assorted creams and body lotions. The message Sanaa was attempting to transmit soon became apparent. "Look at me, I did not migrate, my husband is not rich but I am free to be beautiful and do my work. I do not have to cover my head like you do because of your husband. Buy some of my creams and you will at least be a little more beautiful." After the meeting, I asked Sanaa if she pursued this strategy consciously. She laughed and said:

> Look, I am a business woman. You have your work and I have mine. I want to earn some money with my beauty products. The veiled women have a strong desire to be beautiful and as migrant women they have the means to buy!

On the other hand, "modern Muslim women" repeatedly told me: "We are further on our way to God". They believe that they are the better Muslims because they are dressed modestly and only show off their beauty to their husbands. God will acknowledge this. Thus they are better off than "Westernised women". I conclude that both groups of women are actively involved in constructing differences and look for arguments that make them feel superior to the "other". At the same time, there is considerable competition among the women with regard to their attractiveness. Strangely enough, women more or less agree on what "beautiful" entails, namely feminine Westernised clothes and long hair. Whereas "Westernised women" feel free to show their beauty, "modern Muslim women" are only prepared to reveal it to their husbands or in the confines of an exclusively female group. Sanaa told me about one specific experience:

Once a group of friends and I were invited to a woman's birthday party. She wears a scarf. We decided to wear modest clothes. I'm talking about long trousers and long-sleeved blouses, nothing that could really shock them. But you know what, when we arrived at the party we were shocked! This was a female party and the women who were normally veiled in public were all dressed in mini-skirts and sexy clothes. We were so amazed!

During this female birthday party, the "modern Muslim women" were able to expose their "beauty" and thus compete with the other women. Whereas different life-styles and modes of dress are used in public to construct difference and imply superiority, women make use of a similar code in the "female world" to compete with other women and enjoy the feeling of physical well-being.

In the above case, I portrayed Sanaa from Zrariye as a "Westernised woman". It is essential to stress that, although influenced by "Western" ideas on women's emancipation, Sanaa's aims and values – and those of other Westernised women – are not in themselves West European. In practice, they use their knowledge of West European gender relations to redefine their own local identities. Although their clothes are Western-style, they nevertheless express a particularly localised form of taste. As outlined above, I argue that these specific identification and distinction processes are not limited to Lebanon or a specific migrant community. They are globalised and are of significance in Lebanese communities all over the world, despite very distinct local variations. Consequently, what I identified as the "Westernised woman" could be living in Zrariye, in Abidjan, in Dearborn or in Berlin. On a trans-local level they stand in contrast to and in competition with "modern Muslim women".

Marriage and Education as Identity Markers

> In the dream, I used to fly without a plane. My body would rise in the air, and I would fly over the roofs of houses, the top of trees, and the oceans [...]. My grandmother would say: "Flying in dreams means success and you will marry an emir or a prince." I would yell into her face: "I hate the king and I hate marriage."
> (Nawal El Saadawi cit. in Malti-Douglas 1995: 182)

Up to now I have presented political, religious and family affiliations as important markers in the process of creating competing female identities in the translocal village. In giving the examples of Alia, Randa and Hind, I want to touch on the topics of marriage and education as further factors in female identification processes. As outlined for the portrayal of political affiliations, it similarly cannot be assumed that women in South Lebanon marry earlier than their sisters raised in migration. In both Zrariye and Abidjan there are women who marry at an early age and those who opt for education first and marriage at a later date.

Several articles in *Al-Raida* (Winter 1997), a journal published by the *Institute for Women's Studies in the Arab World* in Beirut (IWSAW) describe and discuss altering marriage patterns in Lebanon presented in a recent quantitative survey. The most striking finding is the increase in the proportion of unmarried women in the age group between 20 and 39, as well as a general delay in the marital age of women.

Analysing this data, Adele Khudr states that the single most important determinant in the age of marriage is education. Access to education seems to have a tremendous impact on women's perception of themselves, on gendered identities and on their expectations of social mobility. There is a prevailing idea that marriage will hamper a woman's ability to pursue her education, and hence marriage is delayed until a later age (Khudr 1997: 17). Similar to Khudr, I put forward the argument that for the women involved in my case study, the age of marriage is a crucial identity marker that very often gives information on how certain women lead their lives.

Alia: Struggling against Gender Expectations

27-year-old Alia, a "Westernised woman", is the oldest of four children and came to Abidjan at the age of eight when her parents left Zrariye and set up a plastic shoe business in Côte d'Ivoire. Like her two brothers and one sister, she was sent to the French international school in Abidjan where she received her *baccaleaurate*. "My parents consider education as very valuable and they made no difference between us girls and our brothers. At least during primary and secondary education", she explained. But when Alia expressed her wish to study medicine, her parents tried to intervene.

They consider medicine to be a "male profession" and too tiring for a woman. It takes too much time. They think a woman who works as a doctor will eventually be the same as a man and not have time for a family. They wanted me to study biology or pharmacy instead. But I insisted that I only wanted to study medicine, so they gave in.

After tiring night shifts at the hospital, she sometimes asks herself: "What kind of profession did I choose?" But then she smiled and continued:

Anyway, I don't regret my choice. I am happy with my life. There are women who think, oh, the poor dear, she has to work because she's not married. They can't imagine that it was my choice and that I prefer to work very hard rather than sit at home!

She continued to tell me about her parents and what they think of her:

My parents are rather traditional. In one way they are proud of me. Proud that I am going to be a doctor. On the other hand, it is very important for them that I get married and have children. In fact, I am a big problem for them! I am 27 years old and not married yet. Some people think I am going to stop working when I find a husband, but there is no question about that for me! I am not fifteen anymore. Even when I was fifteen I didn't want to marry and have a husband who gives orders and dominates me. I saw what men promised young girls. That they would live like princesses and the like. Ah, I didn't believe this, I would never give up my freedom for marriage! The older I get, the more self-confident I have become and the more difficult!

I asked her what she meant by difficult: "We know what we want. We don't give in easily. We open our mouths. We are not the obedient calm women, people and especially men think about. That's why *they* consider us difficult!" When she talks of "we" she means educated women in general and her friends in particular:

For educated women it is especially difficult to find a husband. Men in our society are afraid of educated women. They think we might dominate them because women know more. I often talk with my fellow students about the question of whether it is possible to marry, have children and continue a career. We repeatedly have to accept the sad result that we have to decide between family and job!

Still, Alia hopes to marry and continue her career since she also sees limitations in her life as a single woman:

I am 27 years old and I want to have a husband and children. Here in our society women need men. It is not easy if you are on your own. If I want to go out in the evening to a restaurant or a cinema, I need a man to accompany me. It's always a question of who will come with me. I live with my uncle since my parents went back to

Figure 16: Working in a telephone shop in Zrariye

Figure 17: Woman at Abidjan University

Lebanon. This was really a bit of freedom for me. Still, I can't live on my own. I live at my uncle's and I can't invite people to his house. My sister lives nearby but I can't meet people there because her husband does not accept this. All this makes my private life difficult.

Alia's education has changed her needs and expectations. She is self-assured and makes her own decisions in life. Still, she confronts the value systems and expectations of translocal Lebanese society that make marriage, motherhood and home-making a priority for women. As a single woman she participates in public life via her professional career and at the same time faces the problem of being accepted in social circles. She indicated that she would only be accepted at public events with a husband at her side. Moreover, it is not possible for her to live on her own and be completely independent. Alia explains:

Marriage and children have regained some value for me, although I used to think it was not at all my aim in life. Now, I want to be married, I want to have children. I nevertheless want to lead a different life to the girls who get married at the age of fifteen.

Acknowledging that society would not give her space to participate as a fully independent single woman and be accepted, Alia attributes new value to marriage and family life. However, she does not want to lead a "traditional" family life but redefines the "roles" within a family framework she conceives as possible. She needs a broad-minded husband whose education is equivalent to hers, and a degree of independence in marriage equal to that enjoyed by a husband, i.e., the right to work outside the home, freedom to spend money as desired and the right to share in family-planning decisions. In short, Alia refuses to give up her freedom in the context of marriage and therefore abstains from it.

Living in Abidjan away from the village in Lebanon does not necessarily mean increased freedom for women, as one might expect. Comparatively, Alia states that there are not many unmarried Lebanese women in Abidjan and even less who study:

Parents with money send their children abroad to study, either to France, the United States or nowadays to Lebanon. The others prefer to marry their daughters off here. This is slightly different in Lebanon, where many unmarried women study, work and even live on their own in Beirut.

Alia feels more of an "outsider" in Abidjan and does not identify easily with the large group of intellectual single women as she might have done in Lebanon. Young unmarried girls and women are essentially a minority in the Lebanese community of Abidjan and are usually second or third generation descendents. However, the regular influx of young unmarried men to the community puts the number of young single women in perspective, making it infinitely smaller than that of young unmarried men. In Lebanon statistics tell a different story. The percentage of unmarried women has increased dramatically over the past twenty-five years (Khudr 1997: 16)[11]. This is partly due to the loss of young men during the war years and the continuing departure of even more young men in search of job opportunities. The rise in the number of unmarried women in Lebanon is coupled with an increase in the level of the education for women and their participation in the labour force. The drastic changes that have taken place in the Lebanese economy as a result of the war have forced women to join the labour market to ensure a decent standard of living for themselves and their families. As Mona Khalaf states, this has helped to focus on the appropriateness of the education women receive (Khalaf, M. 1995: 15).

The fact that more and more women in Lebanon are unmarried and engaged in wage labour combined with the fact that many of them remain unmarried throughout their lives, could lead to a major upheaval in the socially constructed image of women in Lebanese society – single women may in time become socially more acceptable. Gender relations hitherto taken for granted may be questioned and renegotiated from the vantage point of single women.

Many unmarried women in Zrariye are actively engaged in income earning. They work as teachers, telephone operators, hairdressers, saleswomen, seamstresses, small-scale business women or agricultural labourers in citrus plantations and tobacco fields, depending on their education and abilities. These working women aim at becoming economically independent and do not want to rely on their fathers or brothers for economic survival. Many single women admitted that lodging and being under their father's control was a major issue for them. They have become economically self-sufficient and self-aware, are in control of their own lives and make their own decisions about who to meet, where to go etc. Since girls and unmarried women are placed under their family's authority, few are allowed to live on their own. Pertinently, their behaviour guarantees the "family honour", which is upheld as long as all unmarried women in the family are concerned with "safe-guarding their sexual organs" (Ismail 1996: 42). Thus, unmarried women are supposed to remain virgin and devote their lives to work or to ailing parents.

Compared to socially accepted thinking, Shi'ite Muslim tradition and practice recognises the institution of temporary marriage (*mut'a*). *Mut'a* can be best translated as "enjoyment" or "pleasure" and is understood to be a contract whereby a man and an unmarried woman (young woman, widow, divorcee) decide on the length of the marriage and the amount of money to be paid beforehand. This contract takes place solely between the parties involved and does not require the presence of a religious figure or witnesses, and does not need to be registered (Sfeir 1997: 18)[12]. Consequently, from a pure Muslim-Shi'ite[13] point of view, it would be legitimate for an unmarried woman, whether a young girl, a divorcee or a widow, to have a sexual relationship. Myriam Sfeir cites an interview she carried out with Ayatollah Al-Sayyed Muhammed Hussein Fadlallah who is the leading Shi'ite cleric in Lebanon. He told her that some religious personalities of the Shi'ite-'*ulama* (Islamic religious scholars) believe that "virgin" women should not be allowed to contract this type of marriage as it brings social shame on them, although from a religious point of view it is both legitimate and acceptable. These '*ulama* maintain that "a virgin" should obtain the approval of her father before entering a temporary marriage. However, Al-Sayyed Fadlallah disagrees with this position, arguing that, if a "virgin" is an adult and capable of managing her own money, she should not have to acquire her father's permission (Sfeir 1997: 20). At the same time, he states that because of the Eastern way of thinking and the high value attached to "virginity", *mut'a* marriage could put women in a dilemma and affect their lives negatively:

Given that our society is still very conservative, Al-Sayyed affirms that Eastern women should protect themselves from its wrath. They should not be contented with what religion proclaims as legitimate or illegitimate, for many things acceptable to religious law are unacceptable to society. A woman should protect herself from the injustices of society. (Sfeir 1997: 20)

Thus, although there are no religious restrictions on "virgin" women who desire to contract a temporary marriage, society demands that a woman must be a "virgin" at the time of her first permanent marriage. Shahla Haeri, who wrote a book about temporary marriage in Shi'ite Iran, notes that in both Iran and Lebanon, temporary marriage is a marginal institution with a stigma and is associated with conflicting moral values. She states that educated urban middle-class Iranian women, and some men, perceive temporary marriage as legalised prostitution[14], whereas more religiously inclined Iranians, particularly the clerics, view it as a divinely sanctioned and "rewarded" activity, preferable to "decadent" Western-style promiscuity and free love (Haeri 1993: 107).

The women in Zrariye told me of the rumours circulating about unmarried women who are said to be involved in temporary marriage. Regardless of whether they are rumours or reality, temporary marriage always takes place in secret and a temporarily married couple does not appear in public. Thus, social order does not accept this religious institution, since it challenges the rules that sanction the association of the sexes. Haeri, who carried out intensive ethnographic research on temporary marriage, states that the institution is alive and well among the lower socio-economic strata in Iranian society. Women who contract temporary marriages tend to be primarily young divorced women from a lower-class background, but also include middle-class women (Haeri 1993: 107).

Contrary to the popular image of Muslim Iranian women, research reveals that temporarily married women are not only aware of their own needs and their sexual appeal to men (which they enjoy) but that they also frequently initiate the relationship (Haeri 1993: 107). Introducing several female life stories, Haeri acknowledges that women see their female sexuality independently and view temporary marriage as an alternative to permanent marriage and living together. She concludes that temporary marriage is, at least theoretically, no longer primarily a male erotic discourse or a male prerogative but that women are actively involved and make use of it in their own interests (Haeri 1993: 107). Fundamentally, temporary marriage can be a choice for widowed or divorced women or for women who have clarified for themselves that they do not want to get married 'permanently'. It might thus be the personal decision of an unmarried woman, frequently stigmatised as an "old maid", who chooses temporary marriage in preference to live as a single woman.

Since the issue of female "virginity" is consequential, it can seriously compromise a woman's chances of marriage. This is paramount for the understanding why unmarried girls abstain from pre-marital relationships. There is also the case of young women who have pre-marital sex and try to have their hymen restored before marriage, as has been reported for Egypt and Lebanon (cf. Werner for Egypt 1997: 179). On the other hand, one of the easiest ways to safeguard a girl's "virginity" is to marry her off at a young age. Therefore, many village girls in South Lebanon and in migration marry at a young age. The fear that a girl could lose her "virginity" or become "an old maid", urges many parents of 14 and 15-year-old girls to accept marriage offers. Girls, themselves raised to think that marriage is the optimum, are well aware of the fear of becoming an "old maid" and may accept marriage at this young age without being sure about their future husbands.

Randa: A Woman who married early

Randa is sixteen years old. She was born and brought up in Abidjan and came to Zrariye to marry Muhammad, who also grew up in Abidjan. Two years earlier, she had been introduced to her husband-to-be and got engaged, after which she left school and stayed at home. We met at her aunt's home a few days before her wedding in Zrariye. In the context of the wedding, I asked her how she had met her fiancé.

Well, I hardly knew anything about him. One day he came to my father and asked to have me. My father talked to him and agreed to the marriage. Then my uncle came and spoke to me about Muhammad. He said he was a good guy, that he came from our family clan and that his father is rich. Then I met Muhammad and agreed. Two years ago we got engaged here in Zrariye.

I asked her how often she had met her fiancé in Abidjan and whether they had gone out together. She replied, "No, we don't go out together. He comes to visit me at my parents house. That is what you do when you are engaged!" She told me later that her future husband is fifteen years older than she is and commented on the age difference in the following manner: "It is good thing if the husband is older than the wife because women get older more quickly than men!"

The wedding was a huge event in the village. The families of the bride and groom, both "successful" migrant families in Abidjan, took the opportunity of celebrating their wealth and influence. I met Randa in Abidjan six months later. She was five months pregnant and was wearing a scarf, which was not the case when I met her first. She said she did not really like the scarf, "but you know, I am a married woman now. I am going to be a mother. It is a religious duty". After a pause, she continued quietly, "and my husband is a religious man, he likes the scarf".

Later I talked to Leila, a neighbour of Randa's parents and the mother of two unmarried young women. She shared her point of view with me as follows:

I don't think it is right for girls to marry so young. It is the parents' fault. There are still many Lebanese parents, both in Lebanon and here in Abidjan, who think it is best to marry a girl off as young as possible. They tell their daughters at a very early age that the best thing of all is to marry, have children and stay at home. They put no emphasis on a girl's education. The most important thing for these parents is that their daughters "make a good match" and marry a man with lots of money and a big house. Someone who can offer their daughters everything, a villa in Abidjan, a Mercedes, jewellery, two house maids, clothes, furniture, and travel. If a man can provide this, they will marry their daughter off, even if the man is much, much older. I do not agree with this. I went to secondary school and dreamed of studying. I didn't have the chance either because my parents wanted me to marry. I want my daughters to do what they want, to study or to get married. It is their decision. Many parents want to shed responsibility for their daughters, that's why they marry them off. Nowadays girls want to go out to discotheques and the like. Parents worry about their daughters. On the other hand, sometimes parents forbid their daughters to dress the way they want to. They force them, for example, to wear a headscarf. The daughters then think that if they get married, they will have some freedom. Well, that's the problem. The husband could be worse than the parents!

I noted an enormous discrepancy between women who married at a young age and women who married in their late 20s, early 30s or remained single.

Women who marry early generally do not have educational resources to articulate their own problems and struggle for change. Older women are frequently more self-aware and able to formulate their point of view and fight for it. In discussions with couples and non-married women, young wives rarely made their point of view clear or took their space in discussion but tended to reproduce the image of correct female behaviour. This generally emphasises not taking too much space in the form of "don't speak too loud", "be reserved", "don't argue too much". In contrast to this, women who were unmarried often engaged in discussion and were not afraid to contradict a man's argument.

Let me now present another opinion on the question of early marriage, formulated by 23-year-old Hind.

Hind: The Fear of Becoming an "Old Girl"

Born in Abidjan, Hind came to Zrariye with her parents at the age of ten. When I asked her about her family, she replied: "I have a sister who is 18 years old. She is married in Abidjan and has two children. That's young, isn't it?" I nodded and answered: "Yes, but a lot of Lebanese women marry when they are very young, don't they? Do you think about getting married?" This question sparked off a lively discussion during which Hind made her outlook very clear:

Ah, no, I don't want to marry early. When I am twenty-seven I will probably start to think about marriage. My parents are not like others who forbid things. No, no, they trust me and I can do what I want. I have to take responsibility for my actions. My sister grew up in Africa like me. She was young when we came back and she didn't want to study. She wanted to stop school and get married. She loved her fiancé and they married very young. If I meet someone, I will go out with him for a year, maybe two years. If we get on very well for a few years, I will think of marriage. There are not many girls who think like me. Girls here think it is not good for a woman to work. They think of getting married and starting a family. That's their life. But this concept is wavering at the moment. Women want to work. Today you have more choice. I am now 23 years old. If I fall in love with someone right now, I have the freedom to get to know him. I am not forced to marry him immediately. Here, people marry although they don't have the chance to get to know each other beforehand. That's it. However, if there is some degree of freedom, you can meet the person you love, you can sit together, you can talk, you can go out. I think you can choose better then. But here, do you know what people say when a girl is about 25 years old and not married? They say "old girl"! "Old girl" means that someone who is 25 years old is almost too old to marry! That's crazy. In Europe, someone who is about forty and can't have children anymore might be called an "old maid". Here they think that when someone is 25 years old, it's over. That's what frightens girls! But any girl or woman can marry at any age if she meets the man she loves. What's the problem? Here, girls of eighteen think: "Oh, I will be twenty in two years". If a man comes and asks her to marry him, even if he is 45 years old, they will only think: "I don't want to become an 'old girl'!" I am 23 years old, for instance, I could have got married nearly ten years ago. They will soon start calling me an "old girl". But I haven't seen anything of life yet. I am still very young, aren't I? People here exclaim: "She is 23 years old and isn't married yet!" They ask: "Why are you not married yet? Is there something wrong with you? Are you sick? You are going to be an 'old girl'." It's over! People think like this. That's it!

Hind got very excited when she was expressing her opinion and made her long statement without a break. She was obviously involved in the process of redefining her personal identity as a woman. Like many other young women in the village, she challenges old images and conceptions of what "being a woman" means. She questions early marriage and favours free choice of the marriage partner as opposed to arranged marriages. She believes women should have the choice to work, become intellectually and economically independent and thus be self-confident enough to decide on the person they want to marry or not to marry at all. One could argue, on the one hand, that this is a Western concept of women's identity that she has learned and adapted as a result of French-based education, global media and the Western life-style promoted in Lebanon. Nevertheless, her concepts and ideas are strongly embedded in local Lebanese and South Lebanon Shi'ite Muslim practice and thinking. Thus, for example, the concept of pre-marital "virginity" is relevant to her, as she indicated: "There are limits to pre-marriage friendship between a girl and a boy". Myriam Sfeir, who carried out a study called "Hymenophobia: Virginity and Family Honour in Lebanon" (1996), stated that "virginity" is one of the constituting components of identity for Lebanese women themselves: "Virginity is not merely perceived as a physical reality but also as a social and psychological factor that involves a woman's definition of her social identity" (Sfeir 1997: 5).

In her thesis, Sfeir expresses how young women are made to understand from a very young age that those who dare to deviate from sexual norms have to pay a very high price. Thus, the commonly views on virginity remain a major issue for women in Lebanese society today.

Women's Differences – Women's Shared Struggles

> We were flying high, far from the kitchens of our mothers, and far from the embroidery work destined for our trousseaus. (Sharara 1978: 7)

The aim of this chapter was to present a complex picture of women's lives as I encountered them in the translocal village of Zrariye. I learned that women, in particular, are placed in diverse, often competing patrilineal kinship groups that provide them with protection but also exert control over them. Nowadays, these kinship groups are no longer merely present in the village but are constituted translocally. Belonging to one of the main patrilineal village families defines women's identities as daughters, wives and mothers. Kinship endogamy is still the cherished norm that allows the kin group to maintain "control" over women with the aim of reserving women exclusively for the men of the confessional or family group. In the words of Accad: "Each of the group's laws, rites, practices, and psychological and sexual pressures aims at keeping their women exclusively for the men of their community" (Accad 1990: 29). Thus, much of the kin group's "honour" rests on the behaviour of its women. Moreover, social constructs of "an ideal woman" (Papanek 1994) are used to mark their specific group identity (Moghadam 1994; Yuval-Davis 1996). As shown earlier, women now have their own methods of expressing their group belonging, which include fashion and lifestyle. Women in the translocal village express their sympathy with *Hizbollah* by, for example, wearing the Iranian-style *chador*, while quite a different "outfit" is linked to the *Amal* movement. Since adherence to *Hizbollah* or *Amal* is often intertwined with kinship belonging, women are not only symbol-carriers of these movements but mark the boundaries between different kin groups. Thus, the patrilineal kinship and confessional system divides women according to their family and religious belonging.

Although women have largely embraced kinship, they have also negotiated, manipulated and struggled both within and against the kinship system. In depicting various female life-stories, I have tried to show how women manoeuvre kinship and confessional norms and expectations within the translocal village. Despite their differences and diverse kinship and political-religious loyalties, I found a variety of common concerns. Although the *Hizbollah* and the *Communists* may seem miles apart, their women share similar problems and desires. One such issue is the interest in education, a profession, public commitment and a family. In their attempts to combine these domains, women encounter a variety of problems common to all of them. As more and more women strive for improved education and the development of professional plans, the social expectations of being "a good wife, mother, housekeeper and kinship member" nevertheless continue to rest on their shoulders. In opposition, Randa Abul-Husn illustrates her vision of Lebanese gender relations as the rejection of equating women with "the private":

With proper allocation of gender resources in the family, women and men can share the responsibilities assigned to the family/private and those assigned to the society/public. The idea is to move away from either male or female worlds. Women's entry into the public world must be countered by a similar entry by men into the private/family. (Abul-Husn 1993: 8)

While many women would highly appreciate rotation of this kind, for the moment they believe it to be an illusion. Thus, I contend that women who appear to be quite different frequently carry out a similar struggle. However, patriarchal pressure from their kin and confessional groups weighs heavily on them and divides rather than unites them in challenging male hegemony.

6. Beyond Translocality

> Lebanon can be saved *because* it is mixed, hybrid, composite: its history is the history of hybridity, mixture, tolerance. (Edward Said in Khalaf 1993: 13)

Cosmopolitans and Translocals

Not all Zrariye migrants are translocals. For a variety of reasons, some people sever ties with the families they leave behind. While some do so because they lack even the minimal resources to fulfil their obligations to relatives at home, others may abandon their connections because they experience the translocal village as socially too dominant, restricted and closed. Others again may have moved to the United States or Europe, where they try to live an "American" or "European" way of life and get away from their backgrounds.

In the following, I would like to portray the life of Salwa, a Zrariye woman who moved out of the translocal village to get away from gender norms and control and to follow her professional and political aims. She has not cut herself off completely from her family and relatives in Zrariye and Abidjan, but she has managed to move out of the translocal circuits.

Hannerz's specific distinction between "cosmopolitans" and "locals" and Pnina Werbner's imaginative metaphors expanding on his ideas were of invaluable assistance in grasping the difference between Salwa's situation and that of other women (Hannerz 1996: 102-111; Werbner 1997: 10-11). In his article "Cosmopolitans and Locals in World Culture", Hannerz sketches the experience of Nigerian market women, who travel between Lagos and London. They board London-bound planes wearing loose-fitting gowns that enable them to travel with dried fish tied to their thighs and upper arms. On their return, they carry similarly concealed bundles of frozen fish fingers and dried milk. Although they move through the world, on no account can they be defined as cosmopolitans, since their shopping trips rarely go beyond the horizon of urban Nigerian culture. They simply integrate items of some distant provenance into a fundamentally local culture and are thus locals moving around the world (Hannerz 1996: 103). As distinct from the locals, Hannerz comes to grips with cosmopolitanism as follows:

A more genuine cosmopolitanism is first of all an orientation, a willingness to engage with the Other. It entails an intellectual and aesthetic openness toward divergent cultural experiences, a search for contrasts rather than uniformity [...]. At the same time, however, cosmopolitanism can be a matter of competence, and competence of both a generalized and a more specialized kind. There is the aspect of a state of readiness, a personal ability to make one's way into other cultures, through listening, looking, intuiting, and reflecting. And there is cultural competence in a stricter sense of the term, a built-up skill in manoeuvring more or less expertly with a particular system of meanings. (Hannerz 1996: 103)

Hannerz's main argument is that, in contrast to locals, cosmopolitans are more willing to become involved with the other and are concerned with achieving competence in cultures that are initially alien. Salwa, the young woman whose life-story I will elaborate on, has acquired this ability to become involved with the other and constructed her own unique perspective from a collection of experiences within very different cultural contexts. Unlike cosmopolitans in general and Salwa in particular, the majority of South Lebanese migrants living in Abidjan tend to be "locals", or in my definition, "translocals". This means that they travel in the world regularly but are at the same time deeply anchored in translocal Lebanese social networks that stand for specific translocal cultural practices and habits.

Pnina Werbner uses the zoological metaphor "gorgeous butterflies in the greenhouse of global culture" to describe cosmopolitans, in contrast to translocals, who are characterised as "transnational bees and ants who build new hives and nests in foreign lands" (Werbner 1997: 12).

"Transnationals are people who move, often in great swarms, in order to create collective "homes" around them wherever they happen to land" (Werbner 1997: 12). Werbner admits that her zoological metaphor breaks down here, as transnationals do not simply replicate culture in migration:

Like cosmopolitans, transnationals are also cultural hybrids, but their hybridity is unconscious, organic and collectively negotiated in practice. Like cosmopolitans they think globally, but their loyalties are anchored in translocal social networks and cultural diasporas rather than the global ecumene. Most translocals have to contend with incredible social and economic hardships, and they draw on culturally constituted resources of sociality and mutual aid for survival. (Werbner 1997: 12)

The majority of Zrariye migrants living in Abidjan are translocals, whose life-worlds have expanded throughout the world. They do not replicate "home" but are involved in reconstructing "home" on the basis of their involvements and exchange with Zrariyens in Lebanon. For them translocal ties constitute an important economic, political, social and emotional resource in times of mobility. Salwa, in contrast, chose a different path, looking for economic, political, intellectual and emotional security in various social contexts beyond translocal connections. It can be said that her personal home lies in a more cosmopolitan social sphere, described by Jonathan Friedman as follows:

The global, cultural hybrid, elite sphere is occupied by individuals who share a very different kind of experience of the world, connected to international politics, academia, the media and arts. Their careers are thoroughly cosmopolitan. (Friedman 1997: 84)

Friedman elaborates that these cosmopolitans are defined first and foremost in cultural terms, "in terms of the combination of differences, often quite reflexively" (Friedman 1997: 84). Salwa thoughtfully reflects and analyses the different multiple elements that make up her cosmopolitan thinking and identity.

Salwa: Making a Home of her Own

I met Salwa for the first time at the beginning of my field work in the summer of 1995. Someone told her there was a German anthropologist in the village interested in Lebanese migration. As soon as we met, we immediately got involved in a discussion about our common topic: Lebanese migration. Salwa, who was born and brought up in Abidjan, was 25-year-old at the time. She received a Master's degree in history from Abidjan University, was simultaneously involved in a Ph.D. project and worked as a history teacher at a French international school in Abidjan. That summer she was staying in Zrariye, her father's village of origin, for the second time in her life. In the course of our discussions, she told me about her plan to move to Lebanon to work and finish her Ph.D. in Beirut. I visited her again during my stay in Abidjan in 1996 and from 1997 onwards, I have met her regularly in Lebanon or Europe.

When I asked Salwa to tell me her life-story in August 1995, she began by talking about her childhood. However, she quickly switched to a discussion of migrant identity from a personal perspective:

I have always asked myself when I first felt conscious about the fact that I was a migrant child. It is a difficult question and I can't answer it properly. But I remember, in fact, that I never felt strange in Côte d'Ivoire. You see, inside, I have never felt a stranger in Côte d'Ivoire. Nowadays, I think it's a chance for me. It's a chance to feel at home in both Côte d'Ivoire and Lebanon. You know, I visited Lebanon for the first time in my life when I was 20 years old and I didn't feel like a stranger there either.
Let me tell you, I learnt at a very early stage in my life that I am not a Lebanese, but an Arab. My father is a great Arab nationalist, you know. When I was a child, my father always asked me – actually, it's one of my oldest memories – he always asked me: "What are you?" And I had to answer: "I am an Arab". I was not supposed to say I am a Lebanese but an Arab. Arab identity is very important to my father. Arab identity is even more important to him than Lebanese identity. He thinks being a Lebanese is very limited, but being Arab is much stronger, much bigger, much more noble, you see.
Well, I became conscious of being an Arab very early. And even today, when someone in Côte d'Ivoire asks me "Where are you from? What is your nationality?", I immediate-

ly answer that I am an Arab. I don't say I am Lebanese. This is how the idea of "being an Arab" left its mark on me. I was very conscious of being Lebanese during the civil war. I was four years old when the war started in 1975 and the only thing I heard about Lebanon was war. I was very upset by it because I realised that this was my father's country, this was my country. I was upset by the pictures I saw on television. I always have to remember the time when I was a teenager, around 13 years old. I thought a lot about the war in Lebanon then. It was in the 1980s, when Israel invaded the South and Zrariye. At the time, everyone from Zrariye gathered here in Abidjan. Many people lost their relatives during the war. It had a huge effect on me. People suffered a great deal because they were far away from their tortured country and they felt like traitors. I felt like that myself. At the same time, I felt strongly attached to Lebanon and the pictures of war reinforced this.

Thinking back, I realise it was a time of change. I changed a lot, for example, in relation to religion. Up to the age of thirteen or fourteen, I believed in religion. Later I started to question religion, something that was related to the war in Lebanon. At that time I was very influenced by literature, in fact it has always been like that. I need literature, poetry, theatre and novels as a source of life. At that time I was reading Simone de Beauvoir, whose books had a great impact on me. She influenced French culture enormously. Her books helped me to understand who I am.

I went through a crisis when I was thirteen. I can't think of a better word than crisis. I think I went through a long phase of adolescence, not in the physical sense, but mentally. It was the usual period of revolt that everyone goes through, revolt against the established order, against parents, against society. One specific point in this crisis was the struggle for my cultural identity, being an immigrant child. I was living in different worlds. I was in the Arab world because of family and education, especially transmitted through my father. My father is the only one in my family who really has an Arabic background. My mother was born in Africa. She received a French education and passed it on to us. You see, I experienced Arabic culture from my father, French culture through school and personally adapted several elements of African culture as a result of my daily life there. I love Africa very, very much and I can't bear to see it suffer, it makes me suffer, too.

At the beginning I had the feeling I couldn't solve this conflict between the different cultural elements inside of me. I think all immigrant children have the same cultural conflict. It was very difficult for me to overcome it. I had the impression that there were walls dividing these different cultures; between the image my father gave me and the image I was given at school. School and home taught me different values and I felt sandwiched between these cultures and wondered which one I should choose. I want to give you an example of what comes up when I think about my identity. If I am asked: "What is your mother tongue?" I answer "French". French is literally my mother tongue because it was the first language I spoke and the language my mother taught me. Equally, I can say Arabic is my father tongue because I learnt it from my father. The word "father tongue" doesn't exist in French but I like to use it because Arabic is really my father's language. Furthermore, it is not only the language but the entire culture, the values that come with a language. All in all, my perception of Arabic culture and Lebanon in general is largely influenced by my father. You see, the French culture my mother gave us symbolises confidence and tenderness to me. She symbolises confidence and I feel very close to her. We are both women and have much in common. I have a different relationship towards my father and the values he conveys. They are from another world. The values are stricter – discipline and the like. There was in a way a conflict between the two cultures represented by my parents. The values I absorbed were sometimes contradictory. My father's values are centred very much around religion, whereas in school I learnt to appreciate the value of secularism.

Salwa's life-story shows that she incorporates Lebanese, African and European cultural elements, conveyed to her by her parents, through school and from her African environment. She describes the painful process of coping with these disparate components of herself.

Salwa's father represents her Lebanese and Arabic cultural and religious background. Born and brought up in Zrariye, he migrated to Abidjan at the age of twenty-five. He worked for many years in a plastics factory owned by a relative. He recently began running his own plastics firm. He spoke Arabic to his children but they soon began to answer him in French, which they learned from their mother and at school. He encouraged his children to attend Arabic lessons after school, which where given by a member of the Lebanese women's organisation, *Al-Zahraa*[1]. There, Salwa learnt the basics of reading and writing Arabic.

Salwa's mother, Zaynab, was born in Abidjan in 1950. Her parents also came from Zrariye but her father migrated to Africa in 1937. Zaynab's mother followed him in the late 1940s. She went to a French school in Abidjan, which was still under French colonial rule at the time, and received her *baccalaureate* at a French college. When she told me her personal life-story, she talked a great deal about her youth and the pleasant years she spent at school. She would like to have continued her studies, she said, but her father would not allow it, preferring to marry her off instead. She spoke of her early marriage years:

I had four children in six years. I did nothing except have children and look after them. I just wanted to take care of them and give them a good education. I deeply regret that I couldn't go on with my studies. That's why I want to give my daughters what I didn't have!

Her husband did not allow her to work outside the house. She countered this by giving private French lessons at home, an occupation she still enjoys very much. French is also the language she uses in communicating with her children. Salwa told me that her mother used to sing French children's songs to them and later they sang French *chansons* together. Mother and daughters still enjoy discussing French literature, art and music. Teaching the French language and culture to other women as well as to her own children can probably be interpreted as Zaynab's personal method of struggling with the patriarchal gender ideology that restricted her personal interests and prospects in life. As a second-generation Lebanese woman, Salwa's mother has had to cope with multiple realities and identities. Married to a migrant who grew up in Lebanon, she continued to behave according to the values and traditions she was taught in her parents' house. She speaks Arabic with her husband, prepares Lebanese meals and moves within the Lebanese community with all its rules and obligations. Equally, the French language and culture have become a symbol of another identity she has not been able to pursue but hopes her daughters will achieve. Although Salwa's father is portrayed as a rather "traditional" man, he did not hinder his daughters from studying and working outside the house and encouraged them in pursuing their careers.

Salwa reflects her personal development as a second-generation Lebanese who was born and brought up in Africa. Puberty brought up the question of "who am I?", "Am I Lebanese, French, or African?" She points out that she does not want to have a particular national identity because of its exclusive character and the dangers nationalism and confessionalism can entail, and does not want to choose between her various identities. She is Lebanese, French and African, and she is a Shi'ite Muslim by birth, a woman, a daughter, a teacher and a historian.

In her book "Cartographies of Diaspora" (1996), Avtar Brah, who is of Indian descent and grew up in Uganda, describes a similar personal experience. Once she was asked: "Do you see yourself as African or Indian?" The question first struck her as somewhat absurd: "Could he not see that I was both?" (Brah 1996: 2). Of course it was not possible to *see* that she felt both:

I could not just "be". I had to *name an identity*, no matter that this naming rendered invisible all the other identities – of gender, caste, religion, linguistic group, generation.... (Brah 1996: 3)

Salwa's life-narrative vividly illustrates that hers are not closed entities either. There is no primordial feeling of belonging, nothing eternally given or inherited. She does not see herself as a passive product of this miscellany of external and contradictory influences, but is actively involved in constructing her identities in a complex field of social interaction. She stated that she wants to be recognised first and foremost as a "human being" but acknowledges that she will be always identified by different categories. In one of our ongoing discussions she talked of the following:

Who am I? When I'm at university, I show my student card. When I'm at school, I show my teacher's card. When I'm in the Lebanese community, I show my Lebanese card – but not always, (*she smiles*) because there are times when I want to show my French "education card" to the Lebanese and demonstrate that I'm not completely one of them. When I'm with French friends, I show my "French culture" card. Being able to choose a specific so-called identity card, whether it's national, religious or professional, is – for me – a symbol of liberty! I am free to choose who I want to be!

Salwa's case illustrates that identity is situational. At school, she defines herself as a teacher. When she goes to university she prefers to be identified as a student. When she is with the Lebanese, she shows her "Lebanese card". She also declares that she sometimes simply refuses to show her "Lebaneseness", thus demonstrating that identity involves quite a number of strategies. Speaking French in a group of "Lebanese" in Abidjan, she refuses to be "one of them", thereby excluding herself from a specific group. In other circumstances she may act as one of them, as a "Lebanese", detaching herself from her African surroundings.

Schlee and Werner suggest grasping identities as "pluritactical constructs" (1996: 14). In the given circumstances, social actors strategically include or exclude others by referring to elements that involve sameness or difference. These elements change according to the situation and are dependent on an inclusive or exclusive strategy of argumentation. For instance, dialectical variations within a language may not be addressed if an inclusive strategy is to be embraced, whereas in another situation, the concept of two very different languages is constructed to exclude a specific group of people (Schlee/Werner 1996: 14).

At the end of the quotation above, Salwa evokes the image of being totally free to choose whatever she wants, according to the specific situation. In various discussions I had with her, it nevertheless became apparent that her so-called "freedom" is also restricted. Specifically, even if she perceives herself as a student on entering Abidjan University, it could happen that her African fellow students see her primarily as a "white Lebanese" and exclude her from student groups.

Taking up the identity of an educated woman may, moreover, confront the gender images constructed within the Lebanese community and especially within her close family. During my stay in Abidjan, Salwa explained:

Our father was very strict and traditional. He believed that it was not good for Muslim girls to go out to the cinema or to a disco. My sister and I never challenged this. We pursued a different strategy. We concentrated on our studies and soon realised that studying was the only chance to overcome the restrictions we were confronted with. We sacrificed our free time to study, while our girl-friends went out and got married young. We didn't want to marry early. We didn't believe what men told our girl-friends about

"You are going to live like a princess..." and all that stuff. We didn't want that. Our father never tried to marry us off, I mean he and especially our mother supported our studies. That was very helpful. Now, I am planning to travel to Lebanon, to migrate to the country my father comes from. I know that this may be a way to overcome the family restrictions I am confronted with here. For example, I can't live on my own here because my father would get upset. You see, I have finished my studies. I have a very well-paid job as a history teacher at the French school, I'm economically independent but still can't do what I want because I am my father's daughter. I want to go on studying and do my Ph.D. in Lebanon. I don't think my father will object to that.

In the end, Salwa did not take a confrontational course with her father or her Lebanese Muslim background but manoeuvred between choices and barriers. Her wish to travel to Beirut, to work in a research institute and write her thesis not only derived from the desire to further her career, but was a well-formulated strategy to escape her father's control.

I met Salwa for the third time a year later, in February 1997, when she had moved to Lebanon. She pursued her goal and came to Beirut in the summer of 1996, where she took up teaching at the French Cultural Institute and worked on her Ph.D. at a research centre. I asked her about the first few months in Lebanon on her own:

Everyone believed that my father would not let me go on my own, because you know how strict he was with me in Abidjan. But I know him better and I believed that he would trust me. He didn't say anything. Here I am in Beirut, fully responsible for myself! It was great. It was a great, great pleasure for me. Nevertheless, it was awfully difficult at the beginning. I think I must have been in a kind of transition phase. I really found out what it means to migrate, to leave your own place of residence and move to another. I used to dream at night. I would wake up and not know where I was, in Abidjan or Beirut. At first I didn't know where to stay. That was difficult. I searched for a room in a student hostel. I had heard of this hostel here for girls run by Christian nuns. I tried everything to get in because I liked the rooms. But the nuns said no, although I knew that there were free rooms. This was the first time in my life I felt I was being discriminated against because of my religion. I was very upset about it. But I wanted this room and I tried again and again and finally they gave it to me. Adapting was not easy. I was very unhappy at first and I remember just sitting in my room, being so lonely. I didn't want to go out. Then I said to myself, what are you doing? Everyone goes out and you wanted this freedom. You wanted to be on your own. Now I have friends. I have my job. I visit my grandparents in Zrariye regularly and pick up the letters migrants bring from my family. I am also in close contact with my sister through e-mail, which is great. I enjoy life in Beirut after all.

In conclusion, Salwa managed to come to terms with her new life alone in Beirut. Although she has relatives in Beirut, she preferred to stay in a girls' hostel and later moved into an apartment of her own. This is quite unusual for a single woman, who – even in Beirut – is expected to live with her family or at least under the auspices of a male relative. It was Salwa's aim, however, to move completely away from family and confessionalist "control". She decided that the best strategy would be to find an apartment in a Christian-dominated area of Beirut. She explained that in Muslim areas, people would find a woman living on her own even more strange and try to "include" her in their families and neighbourhood networks, which in turn would also involve elements of social control. Thus, in order not to fall into the trap of "new" social control, she chose to move into a "non-Muslim" neighbourhood that offers her more freedom of uncontrolled movement. Still, Salwa keeps in touch with her family and relatives in Zrariye and Abidjan on a regular basis. She visits her old grandfather and aunt in the village and sends letters and, more recently, e-mails to her parents in Abidjan. These "arrangements" allow her to live a fairly unrestricted life in Beirut, earning her own money and moving around socially without having to ask for permission.

She became quite nervous when she heard that her parents had finally decided to move back to Lebanon. She was afraid that when they moved to Beirut, they would expect her to return to the fold and live under their roof again. However, her parents decided to move back to the village, so that Salwa's living arrangements were not endangered. She tries to visit her parents more often since their return to Lebanon, which can be difficult to organise due to her work load and political activism. Living in Beirut gives her the opportunity to detach herself from the translocal circuit and become part of a more cosmopolitan, intellectual "we-group". Her most important point of reference now is her professional identity as a historian, social scientist and political activist. She managed to complete her Ph.D. thesis and took up lecturing at St. Joseph University in Beirut. It is quite unique for a Shi'ite woman to lecture at the French-speaking St. Joseph University, since it is run by Jesuit priests and has traditionally attracted first and foremost students and teachers from (Maronite) Christian backgrounds.[2] As a French-educated Shi'ite woman, Salwa represents a challenge to many of the stereotypes. This is in fact her aim and she has succeeded in achieving it in different contexts. During her summer holidays, for example, she volunteered as a French teacher for a summer youth camp in Zrariye. She explains:

I decided to teach these students French at summer camp, not because I wanted them to learn French grammar but because I wanted to discuss important issues with them on post-war Lebanon. The school system suffered during the war. Children went to school one day, the next day they stayed at home. The State no longer had any control over education programmes and all kinds of private schools began to emerge. In Maronite schools, children only learnt about Lebanon's Christian history, for example, and in Muslim schools, they were taught Arab history. I believe that education has a crucial role to play in post-war Lebanon. Teachers must enable children to liberate themselves from the social milieu they come from and not reproduce it along confessional lines. At least this is my belief as a teacher.

Salwa explains that she has difficulty in accepting and living the Lebanese confessional system (*ta'ifiyeh*) deeply inscribed in all spheres of Lebanese public and private life, as well as in its education programmes. Her discontent with the political system motivated her to become an activist in a Lebanese human rights organisation. In contrast to many Lebanese groups and organisations constituted along kinship and confessional lines, some of these secular human rights groups primarily attempt to be "transconfessional" and "transfamily" and thus unite people from different confessional and family backgrounds.[3]

When I met Salwa in Beirut in 1998, she was busy working with other political activists on a campaign for optional civil marriage.

It is difficult to get used to the idea that confessional belonging is such an important factor in Lebanese society. I genuinely believe in secularism and that's what I work for. We need a common family law that includes all Lebanese without exception.

Being active in these groups, being in contact and exchange and enjoying friendship with Lebanese of different confessional, family and local backgrounds and jointly working in political campaigns and workshops partly provides Salwa with a new "home" and new identity. It provides her with different networks, resources and possibilities beyond the restrictive kinship and confessionalist connections in the "translocal village".

Blurring or Reproducing Transnational Kinship and Confessionalist Boundaries?

Lebanese citizens do not share a common legal culture that regulates family matters. All issues of personal status, marriage, divorce, inheritance or child custody fall under the authority of the eighteen legally recognised confessional groups, with fifteen family codes authorised by the state. This means that women in particular face very different personal status laws depending on their confession. Greek Orthodox, Shi'ite and Sunni women, for example, can get a divorce, whereas Catholic women (as well as men) are excluded from this option. Muslim women may have to face a marriage with co-wives, Christian women do not. Each confessional group has very different inheritance laws that conjure up difficulties for couples of mixed religious backgrounds, especially for women. Women who marry out of their confessional community may not pass their own religious heritages on to their children.

This right is reserved for men (Joseph 2000: 131). Mixed couples who do not wish to convert and have a religious marriage, have no other choice but to marry outside the country, for example in nearby Cyprus.[4]

Fifteen different legal cultures condition the experiences of Lebanese citizens around kinship issues. Which legal code applies to any particular citizen has been determined by descent, designed by "birth group" – by kin affiliation, by religous descent designed through the patrilineal line. (Joseph 2000: 130)

Joseph shows that the basis of these legal confessionalist practices lies in the "quasi" natural "belief" and ideology of belonging to patrilineal lineage groups into which individuals are born and through which they "inherit" their religion (Joseph 2000). However, these "beliefs" are in fact "civic myths", used to fortify group boundaries and create a politics of "inclusion" and "exclusion", of "we" and "them" (Joseph 2000: 107). "Civic myths" of extended kinship and confessional pluralism are actually kept alive and redefined in the interests of extended families who thereby secure their political power and influence. Elite families have been prominent in national politics for generations, with deputies inheriting seats from their fathers or other close kin. Furthermore, male heads of extended kin groups form powerful alliances with male religious leaders and establish the basis of control over junior men, women and children within these kinship and confessional groups.

These so-called "civic myths" have been extremely mobile, too. In the era of globalisation and transnational migration, they expand translocally and transnationally and are renegotiated and relived in Lebanon itself, as well as in Lebanese transnational migrant communities worldwide. In the case of Zrariye, I have shown how patriarchal kinship networks expand translocally and maintain control of their members, especially of women. Indeed, modern global communication technologies have made it possible for kinship control to be exercised more efficiently than ever before from a distance. By endeavouring to establish marriages between young men and women from the same village, for example, or better still, within the same patrilineal families, these translocal kinship groups are "effectivly" reproduced beyond distances. Thus, kinship endogamy and tight control over girls and women, which includes preventing the latter from "marrying out", is an effective strategy for reconstituting kinship groups over generations and distances. Furthermore, not only are the latter reproduced over distance but the political system of confessionalism and its concomitant identities are transnationally redefined.

Muslim sheikhs and Christian clerics move between Lebanon and places of migration to remobilise people's religious and political-confessional identities. Although Lebanese migrants living in West Africa, Europe or the States may have obtained citizenship in their countries of residence, many have also kept their Lebanese passports and citizenship. They consider themselves – and are considered – as Lebanese citizens. Some may come back home to vote, which frequently implies support for the "kin group candidate". Others remigrate and settle down in Lebanon again, where the men eventually become the "chosen representative" of their kin group, in other words a modern *za'im* (patron), and can pursue a career as a local or national politician.[5] As I have shown elsewhere, these translocal returned migrants/politicians do not necessarily come home with new political ideas beyond the confessionalist system. On the contrary, many of them are deeply involved in local confessionalist and clientelistic practices, although in the guise of new forms mediated by their migration experiences (cf. Peleikis 2001a).

Thus, I put forward the idea that in the era of globalisation, transnational migration and mobility in general, local, confessionalist and national identification politics and practices are no longer confined to this tiny country in the Middle East, but involve the Lebanese abroad and are linked by translocal and transnational kinship and confessional groups and political-religious movements. Following Nina Glick Schiller and Georges Fouron, it could probably be argued that Lebanon has effectively developed into a transnational nation state, in which "long-distance nationalism" binds together migrants, their descendants, and those who have remained in their homeland (Glick Schiller/ Fouron 2001a: 20). For the case of Lebanon, it may be even more appropriate to speak of processes of "long-distance confessionalism", as nationalist identities and ideologies are strongly confessionalised. These processes could, at worst, lead to a further reconfessionalisation, radicalisation and fragmentation of the Lebanese social landscape. However, they are being actively challenged by both women and men in the ongoing struggle with (trans-)local and (trans-)national kinship and confessionalist practices, in an attempt to change them or at least create space to manoeuvre.

As I have shown, women's translocal lives are influenced, restricted and controlled by patriarchal kinship norms and practices. At the same time, they themselves have largely embraced kinship and live up to expectations as daughters, mothers and wives in extended families that supply both care and control. In this context, women have "paid a price", namely the acceptance of the patriarchal structures of authority (Joseph 2000: 136). Still, women have also manipulated and contested extended kinship in various ways. Many have chosen the path to political-religious groups. Despite the fact that this mainly occurs with the approval of their fathers, who often support the same groups, they offer spaces for manoeuvre and the construction of "female we-groups" with opportunities for work and other activities. The adherence to these political-(religious) groups, in the case of Zrariye to *Amal, Hizbollah* or the *Communist Party*, links them translocally and transnationally to members of identical groups abroad. As a result, women in the translocal village can share communication, identities and social practices with their fellow *Amal*,

Hizbollah friends and relatives "abroad" with greater ease than they can overcome differences with other women in their own dwelling place. This implies that genuine boundaries between Lebanese women with diverse kinship and confessional backgrounds are less likely to be broken down. On the contrary, they are reinforced in a translocal context. In this way, women may even contribute to the reproduction of kinship and confessional boundaries within transnational Lebanon.

In an attempt to escape from the tightly-knit "translocal circuits", other women (as well as men) have chosen individual strategies or political activism to express, quietly or boldly, their opposition to the Lebanese confessionalist system and the persistent hierarchical dominance of family and religious leaders. In becoming activists in human rights organisations and demonstrating, for instance, for civil marriage, women express their desire to break out from patriarchal family and confessional institutions, which, although providing a certain amount of security, limit their rights and possibilities.

The construct of human rights is historically linked to the concept of the individualised citizen, one that some scholars and activists have been at odds with. On the other hand, it has provided many Lebanese activists with a legal, normative and political framework within which creative renegotiation of old patriarchal kinship and confessionalist concepts can be initiated. Questioning societal structures by locally appropriating "global discourses" on topics such as human rights has the potential to destabilise the hegemony of constructs hitherto taken for granted and, in doing so, permits social actors to experiment with alternative forms of relationship in translocal and transnational Lebanese social fields.

Notes

Preface

1 Between 1998 and 1999, I worked on the project "Gender, Locality and Confessionalism: Changing Local Identities in Multi-Confessional Villages in Lebanon" and in this context carried out several months of anthropological fieldwork in the village of Joun/Mount Lebanon. Between 2000 and 2002, I worked on the project "Translocal Actors: Vision and Practice of Social Change in Lebanon". Both projects were funded by the German Research Council *(DFG)*.

Chapter 1

1 On the production of locality and translocality, cf., for example, Luig 1999; de Jong 1999; Sökefeld 1999.
2 Although empirical studies and theories on "place" and "landscape" have in the past been neglected in anthropological literature, they have recently received more careful attention (cf., for instance, Hirsch/O'Hanlon 1995; Rodman 1992; Bender 1993; Bender/Winer 2001; Tilley 1994; Low/Lawrence-Zúñiga 2003; Luig/von Oppen 1997a/b; Feld/Basso 1996.
3 Cf., for example, Smith/Guarnizo 1998; Al-Ali/Koser 2002; Pries 1999, 2001; Glick Schiller/Fouron 2001a; Levitt 2001; Bryceson/Vourela 2002; Westwood/Phizacklea 2000; Portes/Guarnizo/Landolt 1999.
4 Cf. http://www.transcomm.ox.ac.uk/ and Al-Ali/Koser (2002).
5 Cf. Peleikis 2001a-c.
6 Cf. Glick Schiller and Fouron (2001a), who raised this question in a similar manner, and Clifford (1994: 314).

Chapter 2

1 See Häusermann Fábos (2000) and Gearing (1995) who reflect openly on their experience of being married to a person from their research community.
2 Despite my arguments about the potential for insight that I see in "blurring the boundaries", for example through erotic subjectivity, I do not claim that it automatically provides an insight. As Don Kulick has stated: "We are all only too aware that sex can be, and regularly is, used to

thwart understanding, quash challenge, and fortify hierarchies of gender, class, and race" (Kulick 1995: 23).
3   On "situated knowledges", cf. Haraway (1988).

Chapter 3

1   There are numerous spellings of the Arabic name, the most common of which are Zrarié, Zrariye, Zrariyé and Zrariyeh.
2   Zrariye is situated ca. 35 km southeast of Saida, 15 km northeast of Sour and 11 km east of Nabatiye.
3   When a woman gets married, she transfers her place of registration from her father's to her husband's locality.
4   Almost 700,000 Lebanese (about a third of the current population) were displaced during the Lebanese civil war (cf. Khalaf 1993: 94).
5   On the making of landscape cf., for example Luig/von Oppen 1997 a/b.
6   On the production of locality and translocality through rituals cf., for example, Luig 1999, de Jong 1999.
7   3D Stickers Technoprint Lebanon, http://www.3dstickers.com/plan1.htm, website visited 12.11.2002.
8   Fayrouz must be seen in connection with the Rahbani brothers, Asi and Mansur al-Rahbani, who wrote the major part of her repertoire and composed the music. *Jisr al-qamar* (Bridge of the Moon, 1962), *al-layl wa-l-qandil* (The Night and the Lantern, 1963), *bayya' al-khawatim* (Rings for Sale, 1964) are some of the plays with strong reference to Lebanese village life.
9   Allusions to a "Mount Lebanon village" evoke images of mountains, red tile-roofed houses, cold snowy winters, pleasant summers, wine orchards and silk production (common up to the end of the nineteenth century in that region). The population of Mount Lebanon is traditionally Maronite and Druze.
10 Racy, Ali Jihad (1996): "Legacy of a Star" (text on the Lebanese singer Fayrouz) published on the Internet at http://almashriq.hiof.no/lebanon/700/780/fairuz/legend/music.html, website visited, 12.11.2002.
11 Zaatari, Zeina (2001) Homepage, http://www.lebwa.org/life/fayrouz.php, visited 23.04.2003.
12 Cf., for example, Gibran Khalil Gibran (1919) *al-mawakib* (the processions).
13 Cf. Hobsbawm/Ranger (1983), who show how popular traditions and folklore are put to use in national ideologies.
14 Joun, H&C Promotion Husni Hammoud (1999) http://joun.leb.net, visited 23.04.2003.

15 Cf. for example: http://joun.leb.net/; http://www.kounine.com/ kounine1.htm; http://www.ainabmunicipality.gov.lb/ainab/village.html; http://www.kalamoun.com/; http://www.achkout.com/guest.htm; http://ankoun.8k.com/; http://www.meziara.org/english/; http://www.angelfire.com/on/tannourine/frames.html; http://www.mobmas.com/; http://www.chhime.com/.
16 Kalamoun (2002) http://www.kalamoun.com/, visited 23.04.2003.
17 Yazbeck, Rabih A., a 23-year-old villager from Tannourine, Lebanon (1999) http://www.angelfire.com/on/tannourine/frames.html, visited 24.04.03.
18 Joun, H&C Promotion Husni Hammoud (1999) http://joun.leb.net, visited 23.04.2003.
19 Joun, H&C Promotion Husni Hammoud (1999) http://joun.leb.net, visited 23.04.2003.
20 Cf., for example: http://www.qana.net/, http://www.future.com.lb/qana/; http://web.cyberia.net.lb/qana/, http://tyros.leb.net/qana/; http://almashriq.hiof.no/lebanon/300/350/355/april-war/qana/; http://www.saida.org.lb/qanasowe.htm, http://qana.lebinfo.org/;
21 City of Saida, http://www.saida.org.lb/qanasowe.htm, visited 23.04.03.
22 Future TV Network, http://www.future.com.lb/qana/, visited 23.04.03.
23 "Imm and Abu Ali" literally means mother and father of Ali. Parents are frequently referred to in association with their first born son.
24 The South of Lebanon has been known for centuries as *Jabal 'Amil* and describes the geographical area between the Awali River (near Saida) in the north and Galilee in the south.
25 In 1861 the Mount Lebanon region was granted formal autonomy within the Ottoman Empire and placed under a Christian governor who was directly responsible to the Ottoman Sultan in Constantinople (Salibi 1991: 219).
26 For a detailed discussion of the patron-client system in the Lebanese context, cf. Johnson 1977; 1986, Gilsenan 1977.
27 Typical of many others, I chose Leila's migrant story to depict general elements of South Lebanese migration to West Africa.
28 Lebanon experienced an intellectual and literary awakening during the second half of the nineteenth century. National and foreign schools and universities were established and education became more accessible (Khalaf 1987b: 27).
29 Africa's interior did not have the best reputation towards the end of the nineteenth century. Its inhabitants were often described as savages and its rulers as cruel and despotic. During the first two decades of the twentieth century, many Lebanese were deterred by the myth surrounding the forbidding interior (van der Laan 1992: 537).

30 In contrast, French traders considered it demeaning for their wives and children to be in this position and therefore hired clerks and vendors (Cruise O'Brien 1975: 100).
31 This argument has been outlined in detail by Evers/Schrader 1994; cf. also Evers 1990.
32 For a theoretical and empirical discussion of contemporary trading minorities, see especially the studies of Bielefeld researchers who worked on trading minorities in Southeast Asia: Buchholt 1992; Buchholt/Menkhoff 1994; Buchholt/Mai 1992; Evers 1990; Evers 1994. Cf. also Bonacich 1973. For a depiction of an ancient trading diaspora, cf. Haarmann (1998), who elaborates on traders in Ghadames (Libya) in the nineteenth century. On trading diasporas from a historical perspective, cf. also Curtin (1984).
33 The Lebanese in Côte d'Ivoire still cling to the idea that their presence there is merely temporary. Even second and third generation Lebanese speak of "returning to the village". "Abidjan is for working, Zrariye is for living!" is a popular phrase.
34 The enforced exodus of the Indians from Uganda in 1972 springs to mind. In many West African countries, Lebanese have become scapegoats for economic and political crises. Their shops have been targets of window-smashing and plundering on many occasions. Numerous examples of this occurred during the political upheavals in Liberia in 1996, in Sierra Leone in May 1997 and in Kongo-Brazzaville (the former Zaire) in June 1997.
35 Whereas only a small number women were involved in the first migration phase, the second phase gradually developed into a family project.
36 There are two basic types of shoes: those made exclusively from primary materials and those that are made partly or fully from recycled material, e.g., old shoes.
37 If a certain plastic shoe model is selling particularly well, the machines run day and night and workers are divided into three shifts. One machine can thus produce approximately 2000 shoes in 24 hours.
38 Côte d'Ivoire is still in possession of a relatively good infrastructure: electricity, water, industrial space and good roads. In comparison to other West African countries, this infrastructure and the political environment were found to be more favourable for investment.

Chapter 4

1. I saw these slogans on MEA (Middle Eastern Airlines) posters at their Beirut office in 1999. The first was a caption under the picture of a little girl, while the second was underneath the picture of a man standing in front of a wedding cake.
2. Writing about the Lebanese in North America, Elsa Marston Harik mentions exceptional cases of women who migrated alone to the United States. Some of them played a very important role in the economic life of the immigrant community, working as peddlers, as factory workers or employees (Marston Harik 1987: 62).
3. In the age of globalisation and different family laws, it has become more common for wives to be addressed as "Madame" followed by her husband's family name. In official documents, however, she retains the name of her patrilineage.
4. On the importance of Lebanese kin relations in migration cf., for example, Jabbra/Jabbra (2001); van der Laan (1975: 234-244), Khuri (1965).
5. I am grateful to Salma Kojok, CERMOC (Beirut), for this information.
6. In their influential work "The World of Goods" [1979] (1996), Douglas and Isherwood have shown that consumption is always both a cultural and an economic process.
7. For a stimulating portrayal of "The Dynamics of Culture: The Car", see Miller (1994: 236-245), who analyses the various cultural meanings embodied by cars in Trinidad.
8. Sons are basically expected to support their parents. Daughters are not generally asked but many daughters do help their parents, frequently more than their brothers.
9. The *husayniyeh* is a Shi'ite assembly hall where mourning rituals for the deceased take place. During *'ashura*, mourning ceremonies are held there in memory of Imam Husayn.
10. For a general discussion on *'ashura* in Shi'ite Islam, cf., for example, Ayoub (1978), Chelkowski (1979), Duda (1934), Hooglund (1981), Ende (1978), Kippenberg (1981). Regarding *'ashura* in Lebanon, see González-Quijano (1987), Al-Haidari (1977), Maatouk (1974), Peters (1956), Reuter (1993). On the practice of *'ashura* in Shi'ite migrant communities, cf. Humphrey (1992), Schubel (1991), Thaiss (1994), Walbridge (1997).
11. It is common practice among the Lebanese in West Africa to make a number of financial contributions to "buy" their security there (Bigo 1992).
12. On the *Islamic Centre* in Dearborn (USA), cf. Walbridge (1995: 337-34; 1997: 41-53).

13 All Lebanese Shi'ite clerics are educated in the great Shi'ite "schools" of theology in Iraq and Iran (Najaf, Qom, Mashhad).

Chapter 5

1 In the early twentieth century, rulers in countries like Turkey, who wanted to be seen as modernisers, went as far as prohibiting the wearing of "the veil" (Papanek 1994: 48).
2 Cf., for example, MacLeod (1992), Hessini (1994), Werner (1995, 1996, 1997), Zuhur (1992).
3 After the 1982 Israeli invasion, over 5,000 Lebanese civilians in the south of Lebanon were imprisoned in a camp near the village of Ansar (Fisk 1992: 655).
4 A term used to refer to the various resistance groups (including *Amal*, *Hizbollah* and the *Communists*) fighting Israeli presence in South Lebanon.
5 Describing women's activism in the Palestinian Resistance Movement, Julie Peteet also points to the fact that mainly unmarried women were mobilised and that they left the Resistance Movement after marriage (Peteet 1991: 133).
6 For a comparative discussion on women in the Palestinian Resistance Movements, cf. Abdo (1994), Kazi (1987), Peteet (1991), Sayigh (1993).
7 *Hizbollah* literally means "the Party of God", whose foundation was clearly linked to the triumph of the Islamic revolution in Iran and to Israel's invasion of southern Lebanon in 1992. For more details, cf. Deeb (1988), Hamzeh (1993), Jaber (1997), Ranstorp (1997), Rosiny (1996).
8 Sheikhs do not necessarily need a political affiliation but in contemporary Lebanon, many of them are quite openly affiliated to political parties and movements.
9 On this point, see Werner (1997: 205-211).
10 Cf. Dalal el-Bizri's study on women in the Hizbollah (1995) and Klaes (1999).
11 According to the "National Commission for Women" the percentage of unmarried women in the age group 25-29 has increased from 25.4 % to 46.6 %; in the age group 30-34 from 14.1 % to 30.4 % and in the age group 35-39 % from 9.7 % to 20.9 % (cit. in Khudr 1997: 16).
12 For a detailed discussion of *mut'a* (temporary marriage), see Haeri (1989), (1993) and Sfeir (1997).
13 In contrast to the Shi'ite, who consider this marriage to be legitimate, the Sunni Muslims agree that *mut'a* existed at the time of the Prophet but say that it is forbidden today (Sfeir 1997: 18).

14 A Shi'ite Muslim man is allowed to hold several temporary marriage contracts simultaneously, in addition to the four permanent wives legally allowed to all Muslim men. A woman, however, is not permitted to marry more than one man at a time, either temporarily or permanently (Haeri 1993: 105).

Chapter 6

1 There was no Lebanese school in Abidjan when Salwa and her siblings were of school-going age. This changed in the 1980s. Today there are two Lebanese schools where Arabic is taught as a first language by Lebanese teachers.
2 A large number of private schools and universities, many of which have an explicit or implicit confessional background, exist in Lebanon. Their eduction programmes, language and goals are often very different and reproduce the making of confessional groups.
3 Kinship and confessional belonging structures Lebanese society so profoundly that elements can even be found in the very groups intent on overcoming it programatically.
4 On the "Civil Marriage Debate" in Lebanon cf., for example, Traboulsi 1998; El-Cheikh 1998-1999; Welke 2001.
5 Since places on an election list can be "inherited", a "successful migrant" has a good chance of being nominated.

Bibliography

Abdo, Nahla (1994) "Nationalism and Feminism: Palestinian Women and the Intifada – No going back?" In Valentine Moghadam (ed.) *Gender and National Identity. Women and Politics in Muslim Societies*. London: Zed Books, pp. 148-170.

Abul-Husn, Randa (1993) "Familism!" *Al-Raida. The Quarterly Journal of the Institute for Women's Studies in the Middle East* (Beirut) 10/63, pp. 6-8.

— (1994) "Women and HIV/AIDS. A Heterosexual Disease in Lebanon and the Middle East". *Al-Raida. The Quarterly Journal of the Institute for Women's Studies in the Middle East* (Beirut) 11/67, pp. 14-17.

Accad, Evelyne (1990) *Sexuality and War. Literary Masks of the Middle East*. New York, London: New York University Press.

Ajami, Fouad (1986) *The Vanished Imam. Musa al Sadr and the Shia of Lebanon*. Ithaca, London: Cornell University Press.

Al-Ali, Nadje (2002) "Loss of Status or New Opportunities? Gender Relations and Transnational Ties among Bosnian Refugees". In Deborah Bryceson/ Ulla Vuorela (eds.) *The Transnational Family. New European Frontiers and Global Networks*. Oxford, New York: Berg, pp. 83-102.

Al-Ali, Nadje/Koser, Khalid (eds.) (2002) *New Approaches to Migration? Transnational Communities and the Transformation of Home*. London, New York: Routledge.

Albrow, Martin (1997) "Travelling Beyond Local Cultures. Socioscapes in a Global City". In John Eade (ed.) *Living the Global City. Globalization as a Local Process*. London, New York: Routledge, pp. 37-55.

Al-Haidari, Ibrahim (1977) "Die Ta'ziya. Das Schiitische Passionsspiel im Libanon". In Wolfgang Voigt (ed.) *19. Deutscher Orientalistentag, Vorträge. ZDMG, Supplement III/1*. Wiesbaden: Franz Steiner Verlag, pp. 430-437.

Amery, Hussein A./Anderson, William P. (1995) "International Migration and Remittances to a Lebanese Village". *The Canadian Geographer* 39/1, pp. 46-58.

Amin, Hussein/Boyd, Douglas (1994) "The Development of Direct Broadcast Television to and within the Middle East". *Journal of South Asian and Middle Eastern Studies* 18/2, pp. 37-50.

Appadurai, Arjun (1988) "Putting Hierarchy in Its Place". *Cultural Anthropology* 3/1, pp. 36-49.

— (1991) "Global Ethnoscapes. Notes and Queries for a Transnational Anthropology". In Richard Fox (ed.) *Recapturing Anthropology. Working in the Present*. Santa Fe, New Mexico: School of American Research Press, pp. 191-210.

— (1995) "The Production of Locality". In Richard Fardon (ed.) *Counterworks. Managing the Diversity of Knowledge*. London, New York: Routledge, pp. 204-225.
— (1996a) *Modernity at Large. Cultural Dimensions of Globalization*. Minneapolis, London: University of Minnesota Press.
— (1996b) "Sovereignty Without Territoriality: Notes for a Postnational Geography". In Patricia Yaeger (ed.) *The Geography of Identity*. Ann Arbor: The University of Michigan Press, pp. 40-58.
Ardener, Shirley (ed.) (1993) *Women and Space: Ground Rules and Social Maps*. Oxford: Berg.
Assmann, Aleida (2001) "Three Memory Anchors. Affect, Symbol, Trauma". In Angelika Neuwirth/Andreas Pflitsch (eds.) *Crisis and Memory in Islamic Societies. Proceedings of the third Summer Academy of the Working Group Modernity and Islam held at the Orient Institute of the German Oriental Society in Beirut*. Beirut: Ergon Verlag, Würzburg, in Kommission, pp. 43-58.
Ayoub, Mahmoud (1978) *Redemptive Suffering in Islam: A Study of the Devotional Aspects of 'Ashura in Twelver Shi'ism*. The Hague: Mouton.
Basch, Linda/Glick Schiller, Nina/Szanton Blanc, Christina (1994) *Nations Unbound. Transnational Projects, Postcolonial Predicaments and Deterritorialized Nation-States*. New York: Gordon, Breach.
Bender, Barbara (ed.) (1993) *Landscape. Politics and Perspectives*. Providence, Oxford: Berg.
Bender, Barbara/Winer, Margot (eds.) (2001) *Contested Landscapes. Movement, Exile and Place*. Oxford, New York: Berg.
Berger, Peter L./Luckmann, Peter (1966) *The Social Construction of Reality: A Treatise in the Sociology of Knowledge*. Garden City, New York: Doubleday.
Berghe, Pierre L. van der (1975) "Asian Africans Before and After Independence". *Kroniek van Afrika* 3/6, pp. 197-205.
Berner, Erhard/Korff, Rüdiger (1994) *Globalization and Local Resistance: The Creation of Localities in Mania and Bangkok*. Working Paper 205, Sociology of Development Research Center, University of Bielefeld.
Bertaux, Daniel (ed.) (1981) *Biography and Society. The Life History Approach in the Social Sciences*. London: Sage.
Bertaux, Daniel/Kohli, Martin (1984) "The Life Story Approach. A Continental View". *Annual Review of Sociology* 10, pp. 215-37.
Bierwirth, Christian (1994) *Like Fish in the Sea: The Lebanese Diaspora in Cote d'Ivoire, ca. 1925-1990*. Ph.D. thesis, University of Wisconsin-Madison.
— (1999) "The Lebanese Communities of Cote d'Ivoire". *African Affairs. The Journal of the Royal African Society* 98/390, pp. 79-99.
Bigo, Didier (1992) "The Lebanese Community in the Ivory Coast: a Non-Native Network at the Heart of Power?" In Albert Hourani/Nadim Shehadi (eds.) *The Lebanese in the World. A Century of Emigration*. London:

The Centre of Lebanese Studies in association with I.B. Tauris, pp. 509-530.
Bonacich, Edna (1973) "A Theory of Middlemen Minorities". *American Sociological Review* 38, pp. 583-594.
Boumedouha, Said (1992) "Change and Continuity in the Relationship of the Lebanese in West Africa". In Albert Hourani/Nadim Shehadi (eds.) *Lebanese in the World. A Century of Emigration*. London: The Centre for Lebanese Studies in association with I.B. Tauris, pp. 549-564.
Bourdieu, Pierre (1973) "The Berber House". In Mary Douglas (ed.) *Rules and Meanings*. Harmondsworth: Penguin Books, pp. 98-110.
Brah, Avtar (1996) *Cartographies of Diaspora. Contesting Identities*. London, New York: Routledge.
Brennan, T./Cooney, E. W./Pollins, H. (1954) *Social Change in South-West Wales*. London: Watts & Co.
Bruner, Edward M. (1986) "Experience and its Expressions". In Victor W. Turner/Edward M. Bruner (eds.) *The Anthropology of Experience*. Urbana: University of Illinois Press.
Bryceson, Deborah/Vuorela, Ulla (eds.) (2002) *The Transnational Family. New European Frontiers and Global Networks*. Oxford, New York: Berg.
Buchholt, Helmut (1992) "Der niemals endende Konflikt? Händlerminoritäten in Südostasien". *Sociologus* 42/2, pp. 132-156.
Buchholt, Helmut/Mai, Ulrich (1992) "Marktagenten und Prügelknaben: Die gesellschaftliche Rolle von Händlerminoritäten in der Dritten Welt". *Die Erde* 123, pp. 309-320.
Buchholt, Helmut/Menkhoff, Thomas (1994) "Huaqiao, der heute kommt und morgen bleibt. Die Soziale Rolle der Nanyang-Chinesen am Beispiel Indonesiens". *Asien. Deutsche Zeitschrift für Politik, Wirtschaft und Kultur* 51, pp. 25-38.
Bulbeck, Chilla (1998) *Re-Orienting Western Feminisms. Women's Diversity in a Postcolonial World*. Cambridge: Cambridge University Press.
Caplan, Pat (1993) "Learning Gender: Fieldwork in a Tanzanian coastal Village, 1965-85". In Diane Bell/Pat Caplan/Wazir Jahan Karim (eds.) *Gendered Fields. Women, Men & Ethnography*. London, New York: Routledge, pp. 168-181.
Casey, Edward S. (1996) "How to Get from Space to Place in a Fairly Short Stretch of Time: Phenomenological Prolegomena". In Steven Feld/Keith H. Basso (eds.) *Senses of Place*. Santa Fe, New Mexico: School of American Research Press, pp. 13-52.
Chelkowski, Peter (1979) "Ta'ziyeh: Indigenous Avant-Garde Theatre of Iran". In Peter Chelkowski (ed.) *Ta'ziyeh. Ritual and Drama in Iran*. New York: New York University Press, pp. 1-11.

Clifford, James (1992) "Traveling Cultures". In Lawrence Grossberg/Cary Nelson/Paula Treichler (eds.) *Cultural Studies*. London, New York: Routledge, pp. 96-116.
— (1994) "Diasporas". *Cultural Anthropology* 3/3, pp. 302-338.
Clifford, James/Marcus, George E. (1986) *Writing Culture: The Poetics and Politics of Ethnography*. Berkeley: University of California Press.
Cohen, Robin (1997) *Global Diasporas. An Introduction*. London: UCL Press.
Cooke, Philip (ed.) (1989) *Localities. The Changing Face of Urban Britain*. London: Unwin Hyman.
Crapanzano, Vincent (1984) "Life Histories. Review Article". *American Anthropologist* 86, pp. 953-960.
Cruise O'Brien, Rita (1975) "Lebanese Entrepreneurs in Sénégal. Economic Integration and the Politics of Protection". *Cahiers d'Études Africaines* 15/57, pp. 95-115.
Curtin, Philip (1984) *Cross-Cultural Trade in World History*. Cambridge: Cambridge University Press.
Darwish, Mahmoud (1973) "*Qatil raqam 18*" (Casualty 18), within a series of poems entitled "*Azhar al-damm*" (Blood blossoms). In Mahmoud Darwish: *al-a'mal al shi'riyya al-kamila* (Mahmoud Darwish: complete poetic works) Beirut: *al-mu'assasah al-arabiyyah lil-dirasat wal-nashr*.
Day, Graham/Murdoch, Jonathan (1993) "Locality and Community. Coming to Terms with Places". *The Sociological Review* 41/1, pp. 82-111.
De Jong, Ferdinand (1999) "The Production of Translocality. Initiation in the Sacred Grove in Southern Senegal". In Richard Fardon/Wim van Binsbergen/Rijk van Dijk (eds.) *Modernity on a Shoestring. Dimension of Globalization, Consumption and Development in Africa and Beyond*. Leiden, London: EIDOS, pp. 315-340.
Deeb, Marius (1988) "Shia Movements in Lebanon: their Formation, Ideology, Social Basis, and Links with Iran and Syria". *Third World Quaterly* 10/2, pp. 683-698.
Douglas, Mary/Isherwood, Baron [1979] (1996) *The World of Goods. Towards an Anthropology of Consumption*. London, New York: Routledge.
Duda, Herbert (1934) "Das Persische Passionsspiel". *Zeitschrift für Missionskunde und Religionswissenschaft* 49/4, pp. 97-114.
El-Bizri, Dalal (1995) *L'Ombre et son Double. Femmes islamistes, libanaises et modernes*. Beirut: Centre d'Études et de Recherches sur le Moyen-Orient Contemporain (CERMOC).
El-Cheikh, Nadia (1998-1999) "The 1998 Proposed Civil Marriage Law in Lebanon: The Reaction of the Muslim Communities". *Yearbook of Islamic and Middle Eastern Law* 5, 1998-1999, pp. 147-161.
El-Zahraa (1993) Association Libanaise Féminine de Bienfaisance. El-Zahraa. Côte d'Ivoire. Unpublished Booklet.

Elias, Norbert/John Lloyd Scotson (1965) *The Established and the Outsiders*. London: F. Cass & Co.

Elwert, Georg (1989): "Nationalismus und Ethnizität. Über die Bildung von Wir-Gruppen". *Kölner Zeitschrift für Soziologie und Sozialpsychologie* 41, pp. 440-464.

Ende, Werner (1978) "The Flagellations of Muharram and the Shi'ite Ulama". *Der Islam* 55/1, pp. 19-36.

Evers, Hans-Dieter (1990) *Trading Minorities in Southeast Asia. A Critical Summary of Research Findings*. Working Paper 139, Sociology of Development Research Centre, University of Bielefeld.

— (1994) "The Trader's Dilemma: A Theory of the Social Transformation of Markets and Society". In Hans-Dieter Evers/Heiko Schrader (eds.) *The Moral Economy of Trade: Ethnicity and Developing Markets*. London, New York: Routledge, pp. 7-14.

Evers, Hans-Dieter/Schrader, Heiko (eds.) (1994) *The Moral Economy of Trade: Ethnicity and Developing Markets*. London, New York: Routledge.

Fabian, Johannes (1983) *Time and the Other. How Anthropology makes its Object*. New York: Columbia University Press.

Falola, Toyin (1992) "The Lebanese in Colonial West-Africa". In Ade J. F. Ajayi/John D. Y. Peel (eds.) *People and Empires in African History: Essays in Memory of Michael Crowder*. New York: Longman Inc., pp. 121-41.

Featherstone, Mike (ed.) (1990) *Global Culture. Globalization, Postmodernism and Modernity*. London: Sage.

Featherstone, Mike (1991) *Consumer Culture and Postmodernism*. London: Sage.

Feld, Steven/Basso, Keith H. (eds.) (1996) *Senses of Place*. Santa Fe, New Mexico: School of American Research Press.

Filfili, Nadra (1973) *Ma vie – 50 ans au Sénégal*. Dakar: Private Publication.

Fischer, Wolfram (1978) "Struktur und Funktion erzählter Lebensgeschichten". In Martin Kohli (ed.) *Soziologie des Lebenslaufs*. Darmstadt: Luchterhand, pp. 311-336.

Fischer, Wolfram/Kohli, Martin (1987) "Biographieforschung". In Wolfgang Voges (ed.) *Methoden der Biographie- und Lebenslaufforschung*. Opladen: Leske und Budrich, pp. 25-49.

Fisk, Robert (1992) *Pity the Nation. Lebanon at War*. Oxford: Oxford University Press.

Friedman, Jonathan (1997) "Global Crises, the Struggle for Cultural Identity and Intellectual Porbarreling: Cosmopolitans versus Locals, Ethnics and Nationals in an Era of De-Hegemonisation". In Pnina Werbner/Tariq Modood (eds.) *Debating Cultural Hybridity. Multi-Cultural Identities and the Politics of Anti-Racism*. London, New Jersey: Zed Books, pp. 70-89.

Gardner, Katy (1999) "Location and Relocation: Home, 'the Field' and Anthropological Ethics (Sylhet, Bangladesh)". In C. W. Watson (ed.) *Being*

There. Fieldwork in Anthropology. London, Sterling, Virginia: Pluto Press, pp. 49-73.

Gearing, Jean (1995) "Fear and Loving in the West Indies: Research from the Heart (as well as the Head)". In Don Kulick/Margaret Willson (eds.) *Taboo. Sex, Identity and Erotic Subjectivity in Anthropological Fieldwork*. London, New York: Routledge, pp. 186-218.

Geertz, Clifford (1988) *Works and Lives*. Stanford: University Press.

Georges, Eugenia (1992) "Gender, Class, and Migration in the Dominican Republic: Women's Experiences in a Transnational Community". In Nina Glick Schiller/Linda Basch/Christina Blanc-Szanton (eds.) (1992) *Towards a Transnational Perspective on Migration: Race, Class, Ethnicity, and Nationalism Reconsidered*. New York: New York Academy of Sciences, pp. 81-99.

Gerke, Solvay (1995) *Symbolic Consumption and the Indonesian Middle Class*. Working Paper 233, Sociology of Development Research Centre, University of Bielefeld.

Gibran, Khalil (1919) *Al-Mawakib (The Procession)*, New York.

Giddens, Anthony (1990) *The Consequences of Modernity*. Cambridge: Polity Press.

Gilsenan, Michael (1977) "Against Patron-Client Relations". In Ernest Gellner/John Waterbury (eds.) *Patrons and Clients in Mediterranean Societies*. Duckworth, pp. 167-183.

Glick Schiller, Nina (1999) "Transmigrants and Nation-States: Something Old and Something New in the U.S. Immigrant Experience". In Charles Hirschman/Philip Kasinitz/Josh DeWind (eds.) *The Handbook of International Migration: The American Experience*. New York: Russell Sage Foundation, pp. 94-119.

Glick Schiller, Nina/Basch, Linda/Blanc-Szanton, Christina (eds.) (1992) *Towards a Transnational Perspective on Migration: Race, Class, Ethnicity, and Nationalism Reconsidered*. New York: New York Academy of Sciences.

Glick Schiller, Nina/Basch, Linda/Blanc-Szanton, Christina (1995) "From Immigrant to Transmigrant: Theorizing Transnational Migration". *Anthropological Quarterly* 68, pp. 48-63.

Glick Schiller, Nina/Fouron, Georges Eugene (1999) "Terrains of Blood and Nation: Haitian Transnational Social Fields". *Ethnic and Racial Studies* 22/2, pp. 340-366.

Glick Schiller, Nina/Fouron, Georges Eugene (2001a) *Georges Woke Up Laughing. Long-Distance Nationalism and the Search for Home*. Durham, London: Duke University Press.

— (2001b) "All in the Family: Gender, Transnational Migration, and the Nation-State". *Identities* 7/4, pp. 539-582.

Goldring, Luin (1996) "Blurring Borders: Constructing Transnational Community in the Process of Mexico-U.S. Migration". *Research in Community Sociology* 6, pp. 69-104.

González-Quijano, Yves (1987) "Les Interprétations d'un rite: Célébrations de la 'Achoura au Liban". *Maghreb-Machreq* 115, pp. 5-28.

Gupta, Akhil/Ferguson, James (1992) "Beyond 'Culture': Space, Identity, and the Politics of Difference". *Cultural Anthropology* 7/1, pp. 6-23.

— (1997) "Discipline and Practice: 'The Field' as Site, Method, and Location in Anthropology". In Akhil Gupta/James Ferguson (eds.) *Anthropological Locations. Boundaries and Grounds of a Field Science.* Berkeley, Los Angeles, London: University of California Press, pp. 1-46.

Haarmann, Ulrich (1998) "The Dead Ostrich. Life and Trade in Ghadames (Libya) in the Nineteenth Century". *Die Welt des Islams* 38/1, pp. 1-94.

Haeri, Shahla (1989) *Law of Desire. Temporary Marriage in Shi'i Iran.* Syracuse, New York: Syracuse University Press.

— (1993) "Temporary Marriage: An Islamic Discourse on Female Sexuality in Iran". In Mahnaz Afkhami/Erika Friedl (eds.) *In the Eye of the Storm. Women in Post-Revolutionary Iran.* Syracuse, New York: Syracuse University Press, pp. 98-114.

Halawi, Majed (1992) *A Lebanon Defied. Musa al-Sadr and the Shi'a Community.* Boulder, San Francisco, Oxford: Westview Press.

Hammer, Juliane (2001) "Homeland Palestine. Lost in the catastrophe of 1948 and recreated in memories and art". In Angelika Neuwirth/Andreas Pflitsch (eds.) *Crisis and Memory in Islamic Societies. Proceedings of the Third Summer Academy of the Working Group Modernity and Islam held at the Orient Institute of the German Oriental Society in Beirut,* Beirut: Ergon Verlag, Würzburg, in Kommission, pp. 453-481.

Hamzeh, Nizar A. (1993) "Lebanon's Hizbullah: from Islamic Revolution to Parliamentary Accommodation". *Third World Quarterly* 14/2, pp. 321-337.

Hanf, Theodor (1993) *Coexistence in Wartime Lebanon. Decline of a State and Rise of a Nation.* London: The Centre for Lebanese Studies in association with I.B. Tauris.

Hanna, Merwan (1958a) "The Lebanese in West Africa: 2. How and When They Came". *West Africa* April 26, 2141, p. 393.

— (1958b) "The Lebanese in West Africa". *Middle East Forum*, pp. 32-37.

Hannerz, Ulf (1992) *Cultural Complexity: Studies in the Social Organization of Meaning.* New York: Columbia University Press.

— (1996) *Transnational Connections. Culture, People, Places.* London, New York: Routledge.

Haraway, Donna (1988) "Situated Knowledges: The Science Question in Feminism and the Privilege of Partial Perspective". *Feminist Studies* 14/4, pp. 575-599.

Hashimoto, Kohei (1992) "Lebanese Population Movement 1920-1939: Towards a Study". In Albert Hourani/Nadim Shehadi (eds.) *The Lebanese in the World. A Century of Emigration*. London: Centre for Lebanese Studies in association with I.B. Tauris, pp. 65-108.

Häusermann Fábos, Anita (2000) "Problematizing Marriage: Minding My Manners in My Husband's Community". In Cynthia Nelson/Shahnaz Rouse (eds.) *Situating Globalization. Views from Egypt*. Bielefeld: transcript, pp. 283-299.

Herman, Judith (1997) *Trauma and Recovery. The Aftermath of Violence – From Domestic Abuse to Political Terror*. New York: Basic Books.

Hessini, Leila (1994) "Wearing the Hijab in Contemporary Morocco: Choice and Identity". In Fatma Müge Göcek/Shiva Balaghi (eds.) *Reconstructing Gender in the Middle East. Tradition, Identity and Power*. New York: Columbia University Press, pp. 40-56.

Hetherington, Kevin (1997) "Place of Geometry: The Materiality of Place". In Kevin Hetherington/Rolland Munro (eds.) *Ideas of Difference: Social Spaces and the Labour of Division*. Oxford: Blackwell, pp. 183-199.

Hirsch, Eric/O'Hanlon, Michael (eds.) (1995) *The Anthropology of Landscape: Perspectives on Space and Place*. Oxford: Clarendon Press.

Hobsbawm, Eric/Ranger, Terence (1983) *The Invention of Tradition*. Cambridge: Cambridge University Press.

Hooglund, Eric J. (ed.) (1987) *Crossing the Waters. Arab-Speaking Immigrants to the United States before 1940*. Washington D.C., London: Smithsonian Institution Press.

Hooglund, Mary (1981) "Hoseyn als Vermittler – Hoseyn als Vorbild. Anpassung und Revolution im iranischen Dorf". In Berliner Institut für Vergleichende Sozialforschung (ed.) *Religion und Politik im Iran. Mardom Nameh – Jahrbuch zur Geschichte und Gesellschaft des Mittleren Orients*. Frankfurt am Main: Syndikat, pp. 257-276.

Humphrey, Caroline (1974) "Inside a Mongolian Tent". *New Society* 31, pp. 273-275.

Humphrey, Michael (1992) "Sectarianism and the Politics of Identity: The Lebanese in Sydney". In Albert Hourani/Nadim Shehadi (eds.) *The Lebanese in the World. A Century of Emigration*. London: Centre for Lebanese Studies in association with I.B. Tauris, pp. 443-472.

Ismail, Ghena (1996) "The Story of Hala: Anatomy of an 'Honor Crime'". *Al-Raida. The Quarterly Journal of the Institute for Women's Studies in the Arab World* (Beirut) 13/72, pp. 42-43.

Issawi, Charles (1992) "The Historical Background of Lebanese Emigration: 1800-1914". In Albert Hourani/Nadim Shehadi (eds.) *The Lebanese in the World. A Century of Emigration*. London: Centre for Lebanese Studies in association with I.B. Tauris, pp. 13-32.

Jabbra, Nancy/Jabbra, Joseph (2001) *Kinship and Transnational Links in the Lebanese Diaspora*. Paper presented to the Lebanese Diaspora Conference, Lebanese American University, Beirut.

Jaber, Hala (1997) *Hezbollah. Born with a Vengeance*. New York: Columbia University Press.

Johnson, Michael (1977) "Political Bosses and their Gangs: Zu'ama and Qabadayat in the Sunni Muslim Quarters of Beirut". In Ernest Gellner/ John Waterbury (eds.) *Patrons and Clients in Mediterranean Societies*. London: Duckworth, pp. 207-224.

— (1986) *Class and Client in Beirut. The Sunni Muslim Community and the Lebanese State 1840-1985*. New York: Ithaca Press.

Jonker, Gerdien (1996) "The Knife's Edge: Muslim Burial in the Diaspora". *Mortality* 1/1, pp. 27-43.

Joseph, Suad (2000) "Civic Myths, Citizenship, and Gender in Lebanon". In Suad Joseph (ed.) *Gender and Citizenship in the Middle East*. Syracuse, New York: Syracuse University Press, pp. 107-136.

Kahn, Miriam (1996) "Your Place and Mine. Sharing Emotional Landscapes in Wamira, Papua New Guinea". In Steven Feld/Keith H. Basso (eds.) *Senses of Place*. Santa Fe, New Mexico: School of American Research Press, pp. 167-196.

Kaplan, Caren (1996) *Questions of Travel. Postmodern Discourses of Displacement*. Durham, London: Duke University Press.

Kazi, Hamida (1987) "Palestinian Women and the National Liberation Movement: A Social Perspective". In Khamsin Collective (ed.) *Women in the Middle East*, London: Zed Books, pp. 26-39.

Khalaf, Mona (1995) "Women and Education in Lebanon". *Al-Raida. The Quarterly Journal of the Institute for Women's Studies in the Arab World* (Beirut) 11/68, pp. 12-15.

Khalaf, Samir (1987a) *Lebanon's Predicament*. New York: Columbia University Press.

— (1987b) "The Background and Causes of Lebanese/Syrian Immigration to the United States before World War I". In Eric J. Hooglund (ed.) *Crossing the Waters. Arabic-Speaking Immigrants to the United States before 1940*. Washington: Smithsonian Institute Press, pp. 17-36.

— (1993) *Beirut Reclaimed. Reflections on Urban Design and the Restoration of Civility*. Beirut: Dar-an-Nahar.

— (1994) "Culture, Collective Memory and the Restoration of Civility". In Deirdre Collings (ed.) *Peace for Lebanon? From War to Reconstruction*. Boulder, London: Lynne Rienner Publishers, pp. 273-285.

Khodr, Hekmat (1988) *Le Liban en Côte d'Ivoire*. Abidjan.

Khudr, Adele (1997) "Changing Marriage Patterns in Lebanon". *Al-Raida. The Quarterly Journal of the Institute for Women's Studies in the Arab World* (Beirut) 14/36, pp. 16-17.

Khuri, Fuad (1965) "Kinship, Emigration and Trade Partnership among the Lebanese of West-Africa". *Africa* 35/4, pp. 385-395.
— (1968) "The African-Lebanese Mulattos of West Africa: A Racial Frontier". *Anthropological Quarterly* 41/2, pp. 90-101.
Kippenberg, Hans G. (1981) "Jeder Tag 'Ashura, jedes Grab Kerbala. Zur Ritualisierung der Straßenkämpfe im Iran". In Berliner Institut für Vergleichende Sozialforschung (ed.) *Religion und Politik im Iran. Mardom Nameh. Jahrbuch zur Geschichte und Gesellschaft des Mittleren Orients.* Frankfurt am Main: Syndikat, pp. 217-256.
Klaes, Ursula (1999) "'Ich habe in der Wissenschaft mein Glück gefunden' – Zur Bedeutung von Bildung bei Frauen in der libanesischen Hizb Allah". In Ruth Klein-Hessling/Sigrid Nökel/Karin Werner (eds.) *Der neue Islam der Frauen. Weibliche Lebenspraxis in der globalisierten Moderne – Fallstudien aus Afrika, Asien und Europa.* Bielefeld: transcript Verlag, pp. 200-207.
Kojok, Salma (1993) *L'Immigration Libanaise en Côte d'Ivoire avant 1945.* Mémoire de Maîtrise, Faculté des Lettres, Arts et Sciences Humaines, Département d'Histoire, Université Nationale de Côte d'Ivoire.
— (2002) *Les Libanais en Côte d'Ivoire de 1920 à 1960.* Thèse de doctorat d'histoire, Université de Nantes.
Kojok, Salma/Peleikis, Anja (2001) "Municipalité et pouvoir translocal". In Agnès Favier (ed.) *Municipalités et pouvoirs locaux au Liban*, Beirut: CERMOC (Centre d'études et de recherches sur le Moyen-Orient contemporain), pp. 339-353.
Kulick, Don (1995) "Introduction. The Sexual Life of Anthropologists: Erotic Subjectivity and Ethnographic work". In Don Kulick/Margaret Willson (eds.) (1995) *Taboo. Sex, Identity and Erotic Subjectivity in Anthropological Fieldwork.* London, New York: Routledge, pp. 1-28.
Laan, Laurens H. van der (1975) *The Lebanese Traders in Sierra Leone.* The Hague, Paris: Mouton.
— (1992) "Migration, Mobility and Settlement of the Lebanese in West Africa". In Albert Hourani/Nadim Shehadi (eds.) *The Lebanese in the World. A Century of Emigration.* London: Centre for Lebanese Studies in association with I.B. Tauris, pp. 531-547.
Labaki, Boutros (1992) "Lebanese Emigration during the War (1975-1989)". In Albert Hourani/Nadim Shehadi (eds.) *The Lebanese in the World. A Century of Lebanese Emigration.* London: The Centre for Lebanese Studies in association with I.B. Tauris, pp. 605-627.
Lachenmann, Gudrun (1992) "Frauen als gesellschaftliche Kraft im sozialen Wandel in Afrika". *Peripherie* 12/47-48, pp. 74-94.
Langness, Lewis L./Frank, Geyla (1981) *Lives. An Anthropological Approach to Biography.* Novato, California: Chandler & Sharp Publishers.
Lash, Scott/Urry, John (1994) *Economies of Signs and Space.* London: Sage.

Lavie, Smadar (1990) *The Poetics of Military Occupation. Mzeina Allegories of Bedouin Identity under Israeli and Egyptian Rule.* Berkeley, Los Angeles, Oxford: University of California Press.
— (1995) "Border Poets: Translating by Dialogues". In Ruth Behar/Deborah A. Gordon (eds.) *Women Writing Culture.* Berkeley, Los Angeles, London: University of California Press, pp. 412-428.
Lavie, Smadar/Swedenburg, Ted (1996) "Introduction: Displacement, Diaspora, and Geographies of Identity". In Smadar Lavie/Ted Swedenburg (eds.) *Displacement, Diaspora, and Geographies of Identity.* Durham, London: Duke University Press, pp.1-25.
Levitt, Peggy (2001) *The Transnational Villagers.* Berkeley, Los Angeles, London: University of California Press.
Low, Setha M./Lawrence-Zúniga, Denise (2003) "Locating Culture". In Setha M. Low/Denise Lawrence-Zúniga (eds.) *The Anthropology of Space and Place.* Oxford: Blackwell, pp. 1-47.
Luig, Ute/Oppen, Achim von (eds.) (1997a) *The Making of African Landscapes. Paideuma, Mitteilungen zur Kulturkunde 43.* Wiesbaden: Franz Steiner Verlag.
— (1997b) "Landscape in Africa: Process and Vision. An Introductory Essay". In Ute Luig/Achim von Oppen (eds.) *The Making of African Landscapes. Paideuma, Mitteilungen zur Kulturkunde 43.* Wiesbaden: Franz Steiner Verlag, pp. 7-45.
Luig, Ute (1999) "Constructing Local Worlds. Spirit Possession in the Gwembe Valley, Zambia". In Heike Behrend/Ute Luig (ed.) *Spirit Possession, Power and Modernity.* London: James Currey, pp. 124-142.
Lutz, Helma/Phoenix, Ann/Yuval-Davis, Nira (eds.) (1995) *Crossfires. Nationalism, Racism and Gender in Europe.* London: Pluto Press.
Maatouk, Frédéric (1974) *La Représentation de la Mort de l'Imam Hussein a Nabatieh (Liban-Sud).* Beirut: Institut des Sciences Sociales, Université Libanaise.
MacLeod, Arlene Elowe (1992) *Accommodating Protest. Working Women, the New Veiling, and Change in Cairo.* Cairo: The American University of Cairo Press.
Makdisi, Jean Said (1990) *Beirut Fragments. A War Memoir.* New York: Persea Books.
Makdisi, Ussama (2000) *The Culture of Sectarianism. Community, History, and Violence in Nineteenth-Century Ottoman Lebanon.* Berkeley, Los Angeles: University of California Press.
Malinowski, Bronislaw (1922) *Argonauts of the Western Pacific. An Account of Native Enterprise and Adventure in the Archipelagoes of Melanesian New Guinea.* New York.

Malkki, Liisa (1992) "National Geographic: The Rooting of Peoples and the Territorialization of National Identity among Scholars and Refugees". *Cultural Anthropology* 7/1, pp. 24-44.
Malti-Douglas, Fedwa (1995) *Men, Women, and God(s). Nawal El Saadawi and Arab Feminist Poetics.* Berkeley, Los Angeles, London: University of California Press.
Mamnoun, Parviz (1979) "Ta'ziyeh from the Viewpoint of the Western Theatre". In Peter J. Chelkowski (ed.) *Ta'ziyeh. Ritual and Drama in Iran.* New York: New York University Press, pp. 154-166.
Marston Harik, Elsa (1987) *The Lebanese in America.* Minneapolis: Lerner Publication Company.
Massey, Doreen (1994) *Space, Place, and Gender.* Minneapolis: University of Minnesota Press.
Massey, Douglas S./Arango, Joaquín/Hugo, Graeme/Kouaouci, Ali/Pellegrino, Adela/Taylor, Edward J. (1993) "Theories of International Migration: A Review and Appraisal". *Population and Development Review* 19/3, pp. 431-466.
McLuhan, Marshall (1962): *The Gutenberg Galaxy.* London: Routledge & Kegan Paul.
Melucci, Alberto (1997) "Identity and Difference in a Globalized World". In Pnina Werbner/Tariq Modood (eds.) *Debating Cultural Hybridity. Multi-Cultural Identities and the Politics of Anti-Racism.* London, New Jersey: Zed Books, pp. 58-69.
Miller, Daniel (1994) *Modernity. An Ethnographic Approach. Dualism and Mass Consumption in Trinidad.* Oxford: Berg.
Moghadam, Valentine (ed.) (1994) *Gender and National Identity. Women and Politics in Muslim Societies.* London: Zed Books.
Mohanty, Chandra Talpade (1991) "Cartographies of Struggle: Third World Women and the Politics of Feminism". In Chandra Talpade Mohanty/Ann Russo/Lourdes Torres (eds.) *Third World Women and the Politics of Feminism.* Bloomington: Indiana University Press, pp. 1-47.
Mohanty, Chandra Talpade/Russo, Ann/Torres, Lourdes (eds.) (1991) *Third World Women and the Politics of Feminism.* Bloomington: Indiana University Press.
Moors, Annelies (1995) "Crossing Boundaries, Telling Stories: Palestinian Women. Working in Israel and Poststructuralist Theory". In Inge Boer/Annelies Moors/Toine van Teeffelen (eds.) *Changing Stories. Postmodernism and the Arab-Islamic World.* Amsterdam, Atlanta: Rodopi, pp. 17-36.
Morokvasic, Mirjana (1983) "Women in Migration: Beyond the Reductionist Outlook". In Annie Phizacklea (ed.) *One Way Ticket. Migration and Female Labour.* London: Routledge and Paul Kegan, pp. 13-32.

Myntti, Cynthia L. (1978) "Changing Roles in 5 Beirut Households". In James Allman (ed.) *Women's Status and Fertility in the Muslim World*, New York: Praeger Publishers.

Nabti, Patricia (1989) *International Emigration from a Lebanese Village. Bshmizzinis on Six Continents*. Unpublished Ph.D. thesis, Department of Anthropology, University of Berkeley.

— (1992) "Emigration from a Lebanese Village: A Case Study of Bishimizzine". In Albert Hourani/Nadim Shehadi (eds.) *The Lebanese in the World. A Century of Emigration*. London: Centre for Lebanese Studies in association with I.B. Tauris, pp. 41-64.

— (1995) *Migration from a Global Village. Chain Migration and Decision-Making in the Case of Multivariant Chains*. Unpublished Manuscript, American University of Beirut.

Nagengast, Carol/Kearney, Michael (1990) "Mixtec Ethnicity: Social Identity, Political Consciousness and Political Activism". *Latin American Review* 25/2, pp. 61-91.

Nasr, Salim (1985) Roots of the Shi'i Movement. In *Merip Report*, June 1985, pp. 10-16.

Nora, Pierre (1998) *Zwischen Geschichte und Gedächtnis*. Frankfurt am Main: Fischer Taschenbuch Verlag.

Norton, Augustus Richard (1984) Harakat AMAL. In Eward Azar et al. (eds.) *The Emergence of a New Lebanon. Fantasy or Reality?* New York: Praeger Publishers, pp. 162-204.

— (1987) *Amal and the Shi'a: Struggle for the Soul of Lebanon*. Modern Middle East Series, 13. Austin, Texas: University of Texas Press.

Olmert, Joseph (1987) "The Shi'is and the Lebanese State". In Martin Kramer (ed.) *Shi'ism, Resistance, and Revolution*. Boulder, Colorado: Westview Press, pp. 189-201.

Ong Aihwa (1990) "State Versus Islam: Malay Families, Women's Bodies, and the Body Politic in Malaysia". *American Ethnologist* 17/2, pp. 258-276.

— (1995) "Women out of China: Traveling Tales and Traveling Theories in Postcolonial Feminism". In Ruth Behar/Deborah A. Gordon (eds.) *Women Writing Culture*. Berkeley, Los Angeles, London: University of California Press, pp. 350-372.

Oppen, Achim von (1999) "Die Territorialisierung des Dorfes (Nordwest-Zambia, seit ca. 1945)". Reinhart Kößler/Dieter Neubert/Achim von Oppen (eds.) *Gemeinschaften in einer entgrenzten Welt*. Studien des Zentrums Moderner Orient, 12. Berlin: Das Arabische Buch, pp. 35-54.

Ostle, Robin (1992) "The Literature of the *Mahjar*". In Albert Hourani/Nadim Shehadi (eds.) *The Lebanese in the World. A Century of Emigration*. London: The Centre for Lebanese Studies in association with I.B. Tauris, pp. 209-225.

Papanek, Hanna (1994) "The Ideal Woman and the Ideal Society: Control and Autonomy in the Construction of Identity". In Valentine Moghadam (ed.) *Identity Politics and Women. Cultural Reassertions and Feminisms in International Perspective.* Boulder: Westview Press, pp. 42-75.

Peleikis, Anja (1994) "'Ohne Kind bist Du keine Frau ...' Frausein, Ritual und Autonomie bei den Jola-Frauen in Guinea-Bissau". *Sozialanthropologische Arbeitspapiere* 59, Berlin: Das Arabische Buch.

— (1999) "'Ich bin kein Symbol, eine Frau bin ich.' Weibliche Identifikationsmuster im 'Globalisierten Dorf'. Südlibanon und Elfenbeinküste". In Ruth Klein-Hessling/Sigrid Nökel/Karin Werner (ed.) *Der neue Islam der Frauen. Weibliche Lebenspraxis in der globalisierten Moderne – Fallstudien aus Afrika, Asien und Europa.* Bielefeld: transcript, pp. 208-228.

— (2001a) "Shifting Identities, Reconstructing Boundaries. The Case of a Multi-Confessional Locality in Post-War Lebanon". *Die Welt des Islams* 41/3, pp. 400-429.

— (2001b) "Lokalität im Libanon im Spannungsfeld zwischen konfessioneller Ko-Existenz, transnationaler Migration und kriegsbedingter Vertreibung". In Günther Schlee/Alexander Horstmann (eds.) *Integration durch Verschiedenheit. Prozesse interkultureller Kommunikation, Verständigung und Abgrenzung.* Bielefeld: transcript, pp. 73-94.

— (2001c) "Locality in Lebanon. Between Home and Homepage". *ISIM (International Institute for the Study of Islam in the Modern World)* Newsletter 7, p. 26.

Pellow, Deborah (2003) "The Architecture of Female Seclusion in West Africa". In Denise Lawrence-Zúniga/Setha M. Low (eds.) *The Anthropology of Space and Place. Locating Culture.* Cambridge: Blackwell, pp. 160-183.

Peteet, Julie M. (1991) *Gender in Crisis. Women and the Palestinian Resistance Movement.* New York: Columbia University Press.

Peters, Emrys (1956) "A Muslim Passion Play. Key to a Lebanese Village". *Atlantic Monthly* October, pp. 176-180.

Picard, Elizabeth (1986) "Political Identities and Communal Identities: Shifting Mobilization among the Lebanese Shi'a through Ten Years of War, 1975-1985". In Dennis L. Thompson/Dov Ronen (eds.) *Ethnicity, Politics and Development.* Boulder, Colorado: Westview Press, pp. 159-178.

Portes, Alejandro/Guarnizo, Luis E./Landolt, Patricia (eds.) (1999) Transnational Communities. *Ethnic and Racial Studies, Special Issue,* 22/2, pp. 217-477.

Pries, Ludger (1996) "Transnationale soziale Räume. Theoretisch-empirische Skizze am Beispiel der Arbeitswanderungen Mexico – USA". *Zeitschrift für Soziologie* 25/6, pp. 456-472.

— (1999) "New Migration in Transnational Spaces". In Ludger Pries (ed.) *Migration and Transnational Social Spaces.* Aldershot: Ashgate, pp. 1-35.

— (ed.) (2001) *New Transnational Social Spaces. International migration and transnational companies in the early twenty-first century*. London, New York: Routledge.

Ranstorp, Magnus (1997) *Hizb'Allah in Lebanon. The Politics of the Western Hostage Crisis*. London: Macmillan Press.

Rees, Alwyn D. (1950) *Life in a Welsh Countryside*. Cardiff: University of Wales Press.

Reinkowski, Maurus (1997) "National Identity in Lebanon since 1990". *Orient* 38/3, pp. 493-517.

Reuter, Bärbel (1993) *'Asura-Feiern im Libanon. Zum politischen Potential eines religiösen Festes*. Münster, Hamburg: Lit Verlag.

Rich, Adrienne (1986) *Blood, Bread, and Poetry: Selected Prose, 1979-1985*. New York: Norton.

Richard, Yann (1995) *Shi'ite Islam. Polity, Ideology, and Creed*. Oxford: Blackwell.

Roberts, Bryan R./Frank, Reanne/Lozano-Ascencio, Fernando (1999) "Transnational Migrant Communities and Mexican migration to the US". *Ethnic and Racial Studies* 22/2, pp. 238-266.

Rodman, Margaret (1992) "Empowering Place: Multilocality and Multivocality". *American Anthropologist* 94/3, pp. 640-56.

Rosaldo, Michelle (1974) "Woman, Culture, and Society: A Theoretical Overview". In Michelle Rosaldo/Louise Lamphere (eds.) *Woman, Culture and Society*. Stanford: Stanford University Press, pp. 1-16.

Rosenthal, Gabriele (1995) *Erlebte und erzählte Lebensgeschichte. Gestalt und Struktur biographischer Selbstbeschreibungen*. Frankfurt/Main, New York: Campus.

Rosiny, Stephan (1996) *Islamismus bei den Schiiten im Libanon. Religion im Übergang von Tradition zur Moderne*. Berlin: Das Arabische Buch.

Said, Edward (1993) "Preface". In Samir Khalaf *Beirut Reclaimed. Reflections on Urban Design and the Restoration of Civility*. Beirut: Dar an-Nahar, pp. 9-14.

Salibi, Kamal (1991) "The Lebanese Identity". In Michael Curtis (ed.) *Religion and Politics in the Middle East*. Boulder, Colorado: Westview Press, pp. 217-225.

Salih, Ruba (2002a) "Shifting Meanings of 'Home': Consumption and Identity in Moroccan Women's Transnational Practices between Italy and Morocco". In Nadje Al-Ali/Khalid Koser (eds.) *New Approaches to Migration? Transnational Communities and the Transformation of Home*. London, New York: Routledge, pp. 51-67.

— (2002b) "Towards an Understanding of Gender and Transnationalism: Moroccan Migrant Women's Movements Across the Mediterranean". *Anthropological Journal on European Cultures, The Mediterraneans. Transborder Movements and Diasporas* 9/2, pp. 75-91.

Sayigh, Rosemary (1993) "Palestinian Women and Politics in Lebanon". In Judith E. Tucker (ed.) *Arab Women. Old Boundaries, New Frontiers*. Bloomington, Indianapolis: Indiana University Press, pp. 175-194.

Schlee, Günther/Werner, Karin (eds.) (1996) *Inklusion und Exklusion. Die Dynamik von Grenzziehungen im Spannungsfeld von Markt, Staat und Ethnizität*. Köln: Rüdiger Köppe Verlag.

Schrijvers, Joke (1993) "Motherhood Experienced and Conceptualised: Changing Images in Sri Lanka and the Netherlands". In Diane Bell/Pat Caplan/Wazir Jahan Karim (eds.) *Gendered Fields. Women, Men & Ethnography*. London, New York: Routledge, pp. 143-148.

Schubel, Vernon (1991) "The Muharram Majlis: The Role of a Ritual in the Preservation of Shi'a Identity". In Earle H. Waugh/Sharon McIrvin Abu-Laban/Regula Burckhardt Qureshi (eds.) *Muslim Families in North America*. Edmonton, Alberta: The University of Alberta Press.

Schutz, Alfred (1962) *Collected Papers, I: The Problem of Social Reality*. The Hague: Martinus Nijhoff.

Schütze, Fritz (1983) "Biographieforschung und narratives Interview". *Neue Praxis* 13/3, pp. 283-294.

Sfeir, Myriam (1996) *Hymenophobia: Virginity and Family Honour in Lebanon*. Department of Interdisciplinary Women's Studies, University of Warwick.

— (1997) "Temporary Marriage". *Al-Raida. The Quarterly Journal of the Institute for Women's Studies in the Arab World* (Beirut) 14/77, pp. 5.

Sharara, Yolla Polity (1978) "Women and Politics in Lebanon". *Khamsin. Journal of Revolutionary Socialists of the Middle East* 6, pp. 6-15.

Shore, Chris (1999) "Fictions of Fieldwork: Depicting the 'Self' in Ethnographic Writing (Italy)". In C.W. Watson (ed.) *Being There. Fieldwork in Anthropology*. London, Sterling: Pluto Press, pp. 25-48.

Simmel, Georg (1908) *Soziologie. Untersuchungen über die Formen der Vergesellschaftung*. Leipzig: Duncker und Humblodt.

Smith, Michael Peter/Guarnizo, Luis Eduardo (eds.) (1998) *Transnationalism from Below*. New Brunswick, London: Transaction Publishers.

Smith, Robert C. (1998) "Transnational Localities: Community, Technology and the Politics of Membership within the Context of Mexico and U.S. Migration". In Michael Peter Smith/Luis Eduardo Guarnizo (eds.) *Transnationalism from Below*. New Brunswick, London: Transaction Publishers, pp. 196-238.

Smith Oboler, Regina (1986) "For better or worse: Anthropologists and Husbands in the Field". In Tony Larry Whitehead/Mary Ellen Conaway (eds.) *Self, Sex, and Gender in Cross-Cultural Fieldwork*. Urbana: University of Illinois Press, pp. 28-51.

Sökefeld, Martin (1999) "Translokalität und Identität: Das Problem räumlicher Grenzen in der Ethnologie am Beispiel der Stadt Gilgit, Nordpakistan". *Zeitschrift für Ethnologie* 124, pp. 51-72.

Stacey, Margaret (1960) *Tradition and Change: A Study of Banbury.* Oxford: Oxford University Press.

Stolleis, Friederike (2002) *Leben in privaten Räumen. Eine Untersuchung am Beispiel muslimischer Frauen in Damaskus*, unpublished PhD thesis, University of Bamberg.

Taan, Dunia Fayad (1988): *Les Libanais en Côte d'Ivoire d'hier à aujourd'hui.* Beirut: Librairie de l'école, Dar al-kitab allubnani.

Taraf-Najib, Souha (1992) *Zrariye. Village Chiite du Liban-Sud. De 1900 à nos Jours*, Beirut: CERMOC (Centre d'études et de recherches sur le Moyen-Orient contemporain).

Thaiss, Gustav (1994) "Contested Meanings and the Politics of authenticity: The 'Hosay' in Trinidad". In Akbar S. Ahmed/Hastings Donnan (eds.) *Islam, Globalization and Postmodernity.* London, New York: Routledge, pp. 38-62.

Tilley, Christopher (1994) *A Phenomenology of Landscape: Places, Paths and Monuments.* Oxford: Berg.

Todaro, Michael (1969) "A Model of Labor, Migration and Urban Unemployment in Less Developed Countries". *American Economic Review* 59/1, pp. 138-148.

— (1976) *Internal Migration in Developing Countries.* Geneva: International Labor Office.

Traboulsi, Ibrahim A. (1998) "De Nicosie à Beyrouth: le mariage civil au Liban". *Travaux et Jours* 61, pp. 53-63.

Trasher, Frederic (1927) *The Gang.* Chicago: University of Chicago Press.

Urry, John (2000) *Sociology beyond Societies. Mobilities for the Twenty-First Century.* London, New York: Routledge.

Veer, Peter van der (1995) "Introduction: The Diasporic Imagination". In Peter van der Veer (ed.) *Nation and Migration. The Politics of Space in the South Asian Diaspora.* Philadelphia: University of Pennsylvania Press, pp. 1-16.

Walbridge, Linda (1995) "The Shi'a Mosques and Their Congregations in Dearborn". In Yvonne Yazbeck Haddad/Jane Idleman Smith (eds.) *Muslim Communities in North America.* Albany, N.Y.: State University of New York Press, pp. 337-357.

— (1997) *Without Forgetting the Imam. Lebanese Shi'ism in an American Community.* Detroit: Wayne State University.

Warnock Fernea, Elizabeth/Fernea, Robert A. (1997) *The Arab World: Forty Years of Change.* New York: Anchor.

Watson, C.W. (1999) "Introduction: The Quality of Being There". In C.W. Watson (ed.) *Being There. Fieldwork in Anthropology.* London, Sterling: Pluto Press, pp. 1-73.

Watson, Helen (1994) "Women and the Veil. Personal Responses to Global Process". In Akbar S. Ahmed/Hastings Donnan (eds.) *Islam, Globalization and Postmodernity*. London, New York: Routledge, pp. 141-159.

Weinrich, Ines (2002) *Die libanesische Sängerin Fayruz und die Brüder Rahbani. Arabische Musik zwischen Tradition und Wandel*. Unpublished Ph.D. thesis, University of Bamberg.

Welke, Annika Sarah (2001) *Die Debatte um die Zivilehe im Libanon. Alles nur "Schall und Rauch" – oder eine Chance für die Zukunft?* Unpublished MA thesis, University of Freiburg im Breisgau.

Wengle, John (1988) *Ethnographers in the Field: The Psychology of Research*. Tuscaloosa, Alabama: University of Alabama Press.

Werbner, Pnina (1990) *The Migration Process. Capital, Gifts and Offerings among British Pakistanis*. New York, Oxford, Munich: Berg Publishers.

— (1996) "Public Spaces, Political Voices: Gender, Feminism and Aspects of British Muslim Participation in the Public Sphere". In Wasif Shadid/ Pieter Sjoerd van Koningsveld (eds.) *Political Participation and Identities of Muslims in Non-Muslims States*. Kampen, the Netherlands: Kok Pharos Publishing House, pp. 53-70.

— (1997) "Introduction: The Dialectics of Cultural Hybridity". In Pnina Werbner/Tariq Modood (eds.) *Debating Cultural Hybridity. Multi-Cultural Identities and the Politics of Anti-Racism*. London, New Jersey: Zed Books, pp. 1-26.

Werner, Karin (1995) *Infitah und weibliche Identität in Ägypten: Auswirkungen der verstärkten Weltmarktintegration Ägyptens auf die Lebenspraxis junger Mittelklassefrauen in Kairo*. Working Paper 230, Sociology of Development Research Centre, University of Bielefeld.

— (1996) "Zwischen Islamisierung und Verwestlichung: Junge Frauen in Ägypten". *Zeitschrift für Soziologie* 25/1, pp. 4-18.

— (1997) *Between Westernization and the Veil: Contemporary Lifestyles of Women in Cairo*. Bielefeld: transcript.

Westwood, Sallie/Phizacklea, Annie (2000) *Trans-nationalism and the Politics of Belonging*. London, New York: Routledge.

Weyland, Petra (1993) *Inside the Third World Village*. London, New York: Routledge.

Willson, Margaret (1995) "Afterword. Perspectives and Difference: Sexualization, the Field, and the Ethnographer". In Don Kulick/Margaret Willson (eds.) *Taboo. Sex, Identity and Erotic Subjectivity in Anthropological Fieldwork*. London, New York: Routledge, pp. 251-275.

Winder, Bayly R. (1961) "The Lebanese in West-Africa". *Comparative Studies in Society and History* 4/3, pp. 296-333.

Wirth, Louis (1928) *The Ghetto*. Chicago: University of Chicago Press.

Yuval-Davis, Nira (1996) "Women and the Biological Reproduction of 'the nation'". *Women's Studies International Forum* 19/1-2, pp. 17-24.

— (1997) *Gender and Nation*, London: Thousand Oaks, New Dehli: Sage Publications.

Zuhur, Sherifa (1992) *Revealing Reveiling. Islamist Gender Ideology in Contemporary Egypt*. Albany: State University of New York.

Websites

3D Stickers Technoprint Lebanon, http://www.3dstickers.com/plan1.htm, visited 12.11.2002.

Achkout, Homepage, http://www.achkout.com/guest.htm, (Village Sites, Municipality, Projects and Public Utilities currently under construction), visited 03.05.2003.

Ainab, Homepage, http://www.ainabmunicipality.gov.lb/ainab/village.html, visited 03.05.2003.

Ankoun, Homepage, http://ankoun.8k.com/, visited 03.05.2003.

Beit Mery and Ain Saade, Municipalities, Homepage, http://www.mobmas.com/, visited 03.05.2003.

Chhime, Homepage, http://www.chhime.com/, visited 03.05.2003.

Cyberia, Homepage, informing about the Qana massacres, http://web.cyberia.net.lb/qana/, visited 10.10.2002.

Future TV, Homepage, informing about the Qana massacres, http://www.future.com.lb/qana/, visited 03.05.2003.

al-Mashriq, Homepage, informing about Qana massacres http://almashriq.hiof.no/lebanon/300/350/355/april-war/qana/, visited 03.05.2003.

Kalamoun, Homepage (2002), http://www.kalamoun.com/, visited 23.04.2003.

Kounine, Homepage, http://www.kounine.com/kounine1.htm, visited 03.05.2003.

Lebinfo, Homepage, http://qana.lebinfo.org, visited 04.05.2003.

Meziara, Municipality Board Council of Meziara village, Homepage (by René Georges Antoun), http://www.meziara.org/english/, visited 03.05.2003.

Joun, H&C Promotion Husni Hammoud (1999) http://joun.leb.net, visited 23.04.2003.

Qana, Homepage: informing about the massacres, http://www.qana.net/, visited 03.05.2003.

Racy, Ali Jihad (1996) "Legacy of a Star" (text on the Lebanese singer Fairuz) published at http://almashriq.hiof.no/lebanon/700/780/fairuz/legend/music.html, visited 12.11.2002.

Saida, Homepage, informing about the Qana massacres, http://www.saida.org.lb/qanasowe.htm; http://www.saida.org.lb/, visited 23.04.03.

Tannourine, Homepage, http://www.angelfire.com/on/tannourine/frames.html, visited 24.04.03.

Tyros, Homepage, informing about Qana massacres, http://tyros.leb.net/qana, visited 03.05.2003.
Vertovec, Steven, Transnational Communities (An ESRC Research Programme), Homepage, http://www.transcomm.ox.ac.uk/, visited 02.02.2003.
Yazbeck, Rabih (1999), Village of Tannourine, http://www.angelfire.com/on/tannourine/frames.html, visited 24.04.03.
Zaatari, Zeina (2001) "Fayrouz, singer of the Middle East" published on the website of the "Lebanese Women's Awakening", (www.lebwa.org), an online network on Lebanese and Lebanese American Women at http://www.lebwa.org/life/fayrouz.php, visited 23.04.2003.

Further Titles by transcript and Transaction Publishers

Urs Peter Ruf
Ending Slavery
Hierarchy, Dependency and Gender in Central Mauritania
1999, 436 pages,
pb., $ 39,95,
ISBN: 3-933127-49-1

Brigitte Holzer, Arthur Vreede, Gabriele Weigt (eds.)
Disability in Different Cultures
Reflections on Local Concepts
1999, 384 pages,
pb., $ 39,95,
ISBN: 3-933127-40-8

Margaret Rausch
Bodies, Boundaries and Spirit Possession
Maroccan Women and the Revision of Tradition
2000, 275 pages,
pb., $ 39,95,
ISBN: 3-933127-46-7

Cynthia Nelson, Shahnaz Rouse (eds.)
Situating Globalization
Views from Egypt
2000, 362 pages,
pb., $ 39,95,
ISBN: 3-933127-61-0

Sabine Maasen, Matthias Winterhager (eds.)
Science Studies
Probing the Dynamics of Scientific Knowledge
2001, 304 pages,
pb., $ 39,95,
ISBN: 3-933127-64-5

Ayhan Kaya
"Sicher in Kreuzberg"
Constructing Diasporas: Turkish Hip-Hop Youth in Berlin
2001, 236 pages,
pb., $ 39,95,
ISBN: 3-933127-71-8

Georg Stauth
Politics and Cultures of Islamization in Southeast Asia
Indonesia and Malaysia in the Nineteen-nineties
2002, 302 pages,
pb., $ 39,95,
ISBN: 3-933127-81-5

Alexander Horstmann
Class, Culture and Space
The Construction and Shaping of Communal Space in South Thailand
2002, 204 pages,
pb., $ 39,95,
ISBN: 3-933127-51-3

Please visit: www.transcript-verlag.de

Further Titles by transcript and Transaction Publishers

Anja Peleikis
Lebanese in Motion
Gender and the Making of a Translocal Village
June 2003, 210 pages,
pb., $ 39,95,
ISBN: 3-933127-45-9

Georg Stauth
On Archaeology of Sainthood and Local Spirituality in Islam
Past and present crossroads of events and ideas
Yearbook of the Sociology of Islam, Vol. 5
(ed. by Georg Stauth and Armando Salvatore),
October 2003, appr. 200 pages,
pb., $ 39,95,
ISBN: 3-89942-141-8

Markus Kaiser
Eurasia in the Making – Revival of the Silk Road
A Study on Cross-border Trade and Markets in Contemporary Uzbekistan
October 2003, appr. 250 pages,
pb., $ 39,95,
ISBN: 3-89942-142-6

Please visit: www.transcript-verlag.de